"Rick Goossen is uniquely  ook on entrepreneurship. He has 'trepreneur and corporate finan ır and university professor. In ad e also builds into the book the ex .emost entrepreneurs. While this b .ure for any aspiring entrepreneur, it is absolutely ....ential reading for students studying entrepreneurship in business schools across North America."

—Kevin G. Sawatsky, professor, and currently the Dean of the School of Business at Trinity Western University

"Rick Goossen has studied entrepreneurship by practising it in North America, and by living among some of the world's most instinctive entrepreneurs in Hong Kong. He has also thought hard about its nature, and this book reflects both those analyses and those experiences."

—Gordon Redding, Director, Euro Asian Research Centre, INSEAD, France, Professor Emeritus at the University of Hong Kong and Visiting Professor at the University of Manchester, U.K.; he is the author of *The Spirit of Chinese Capitalism*

"If you want to achieve enduring success in business and in life, and you want to do it your way, you must read this book. Rick Goossen is an entrepreneur who is constantly driven to create new business ideas. And he has an amazing track record of success, as a lawyer, journalist, author, university teacher, and corporate financier. In this book, he blends his own unique insights with the wisdom of the world's foremost experts on entrepreneurship to show others how to take the world by storm."

—Michael Alexander is the author of *How to Inherit Money*

"Rick Goossen has compiled the great thinking of entrepreneurship experts in a handy volume that should be read by every entrepreneur looking to grow and finance a company on Wall Street."

—Terry Murphy is Managing Director of Rodman & Renshaw

"Rick Goossen book should take the industry by storm, because it uniquely integrates the wisdom of seminal thinkers and practitioners of entrepreneurship. As Editor of the Journal of Business Strategy and strategic management professor, Rick has the unique experience to integrate and synthesize wisdom from the greatest entrepreneurship thinkers of all time. The need for this book has existed for years and, thus, it should be widely adopted in both entrepreneurship and strategic management courses as supportive reading material. Very likely, this book will also become popular reading for millions of entrepreneurs across the globe."

—Dr. Fred David is author of the best-selling
Strategic Management, professor of strategic management at
Francis Marion University

Entrepreneurial Excellence

Profit From the Best Ideas of the Experts

By Richard J. Goossen, Ph.D.

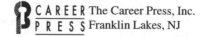
CAREER The Career Press, Inc.
PRESS Franklin Lakes, NJ

ENTREPRENEURIAL EXCELLENCE
EDITED BY JODI BRANDON
TYPESET BY MICHAEL FITZGIBBON
Cover design by Jeff Piasky
Printed in the U.S.A. by Book-mart Press

To order this title, please call toll-free 1-800-CAREER-1 (NJ and Canada: 201-848-0310) to order using VISA or MasterCard, or for further information on books from Career Press.

 CAREER
PRESS

The Career Press, Inc., 3 Tice Road, PO Box 687,
Franklin Lakes, NJ 07417
www.careerpress.com

Library of Congress Cataloging-in-Publication Data
Goossen, Richard J.
    Entrepreneurial excellence : profit from the best ideas of the experts / by Richard J. Goossen.
        p. cm.
    Includes index.
    ISBN-13: 978-1-56414-967-1
    ISBN-10: 1-56414-967-6
      1.   Entrepreneurship. 2. Success in business. I. Title.

HB615.G664 2007
658.4'21—dc22

2007025857

Dedicated to Brenda

Who can find a virtuous wife?
For her worth is far above rubies.
The heart of her husband safely trusts her;
So he will have no lack of gain.

She extends her hand to the poor,
Yes, she reaches out her hands to the needy.

Strength and honour are her clothing;
She shall rejoice in time to come.
She opens her mouth with wisdom,
And on her tongue is the law of kindness.
She watches over the ways of her household,
And does not eat the bread of idleness.
Her children rise up and call her blessed;
Her husband also, and he praises her:
"Many daughters have done well,
But you exceed them all."
Proverbs 31: 10–1; 20–1; 25–8

Acknowledgments

First and foremost, I would like to thank the entrepreneurial experts for their contributions: Larry Farrell, Irv Grousbeck, Rita McGrath, Tom Hockaday, Henry Mintzberg, Gordon Redding, Howard Stevenson, Jeff Timmons, and Karl Vesper. Although these exceptionally talented individuals are extremely busy, they were generous with their time and insights. In several instances, follow-up interviews were required and generously granted. I was amazed by their graciousness, and by their willingness to contribute to this undertaking.

The chapters were written entirely by me, and from my own perspective, but the entrepreneurship experts reviewed their contents for accuracy. That being said, any errors in the work should be attributed to my own shortcomings rather than to the insights of the experts.

I have also benefited from interviews with other insightful individuals: Peter L. Bernstein, a leading economic journalist and author; Murray Low, executive director of the Eugene M. Lang Center for Entrepreneurship at the Columbia University Business School; Joe Maciariello, professor of management at Claremont Graduate University; John Mullins, from the London Business School; Daniel Muzyka, Dean of the Sauder School of Business, University of British Columbia; and Laura Nash, formerly of Harvard Business School and now managing director of Piper Cove Fund, as well as a leading writer on values and ethics in business.

The interviews in this book were originally part of my research for the completion of a Ph.D. from the Centre for Higher Education Research, Middlesex University, in London. I would like to thank my advisor, Professor Peter Newby, Director, Centre for Higher Education Research, for his insightful comments on my thesis and research, which have helped to refine my thinking and have improved the quality of my doctoral thesis—and by extension this derivative work. The External Examination Board for my doctoral research included two highly esteemed UK educators: David Kirby, Professor of Entrepreneurship, University of Surrey, Guildford, and David Rae, Head of the Centre for Entrepreneurial Management, University of Derby. Their feedback on my doctoral thesis helped me understand my own biases and methodology and, again, improved this work as a result.

I was greatly assisted by Kirsten Dalley and Jodi Brandon, and all of the staff at Career Press in turning the original manuscript into a book; their expert insights and professional guidance were extremely helpful. My research assistant at Trinity Western Universty, Vanessa Dyck, provided invaluable help with fine-tuning the manuscript.

Finally, I would like to thank one of my former Trinity Western University students, Andrew Batey, who is now working in Los Angeles, California. Andrew, one of my most "trying" and "memorable" students, was instrumental in having this book published.

Contents

Part I

Introduction

Introduction

How Do I Start?

No matter how many books a person may have read, or how beautiful a business plan he produces, it's absolutely useless unless he has made mistakes and learned how to recalibrate in order to avoid future mistakes.

—Gordon Redding[1]

You want to pursue entrepreneurial excellence. You may be asking yourself, "How do I start?" In order to begin you need to define entrepreneurship. A related issue is to determine how a person learns about entrepreneurship.

One seasoned entrepreneur, one who has tasted both disappointment and triumph, boldly stated: "I don't think you can teach entrepreneurship. I don't think it's possible. You either have it in you or you don't. There are managers and there are leaders. Entrepreneurship is something I don't personally think you can teach."[2]

If anyone is qualified to say such a statement, this particular man is. He was born in 1928, in Saskatoon, SK, Canada, but he started working as an entrepreneur in Vancouver, BC. He recounted to me that one of the most exhilarating times in his life was in 1961, when he started his first business: a two-car showroom with a gas station.[3]

Building that business, and the others he has since accumulated, has been a challenge-laden task. He told me, "I've had the bank call my loans a couple times. Those weren't good times…. I've had a terrific amount of disappointments."[4] But his zest, determination, and undeniable entrepreneurial skills have taken him from the flatlands of Saskatchewan to the peaks of the business world.

He is now in his late 70s, and is a billionaire entrepreneur. He is the sole owner of the third-largest privately held company in Canada. He is also involved in a wide range of businesses: automotive, entertainment, export and financial, food, illuminated signs, media, packages, and periodical distribution. One of his best-known global brands is *Ripley's Believe It or Not*. Today, his company has $6.3 billion in sales, 29,000 employees, and 400 locations.[5]

How does Jim Pattison keep the entrepreneurial spirit alive in his organization? Does he truly believe you can't teach entrepreneurship?

Not really. His comment, however, focuses on some of the determinants of entrepreneurship that *are* unteachable: childhood experiences, drive, determination, the chip on one's shoulder, the need to prove one's own worth through accomplishment, and an obsession with money-making opportunities. So, to some degree, people either have it or they don't, and that is proven in the marketplace. Many entrepreneurs simply appear to be hardwired for the passionate pursuit of opportunity.

On the other hand, there are other aspects of entrepreneurship, such as understanding and pursuing innovation, that can be taught and improved upon. Jim Pattison understands this. To teach his core team of 70 or so executives about entrepreneurship, he has hired one of the experts featured in this book—Larry C. Farrell—to address key issues and teach practical tips. Farrell goes over the entrepreneurial basics as summarized in Chapter 2.

Jim Pattison's comments, then, are not contradictory—though they may seem so at first. Rather, they reveal the nuanced approach that is required to understand entrepreneurship more fully. In fact, his perspective reflects one of the key challenges of discussing entrepreneurship: finding its definition. Until we know what it is, how can we determine how to pursue it?

Many of the entrepreneurial experts in this book have wrestled with different definitions of entrepreneurship. Howard H. Stevenson, a professor at Harvard Business School, recalls that the field of entrepreneurship in the early 1980s could be compared to an intellectual onion: People peeled it back, layer by layer, and when they finally got to the center, they found nothing there—but they were crying.[6] Since that time, our understanding of the complexity of entrepreneurship has increased, but a consensus definition has remained elusive.

A brief overview of some of the entrepreneurial experts' perspectives on the definition of entrepreneurship is a fitting introduction to the complicated field. Indeed, this teaser of differing viewpoints affirms the value of this book's approach. Just as diverging paths on a mountain hike appeal differently to each explorer, so also the varying insights of these entrepreneurial experts will resonate uniquely with each individual's experiences.

Stevenson notes that there have been two traditional ways of defining entrepreneurship: either as an economic function, or as a set of individual traits.[7] The functional approach, on one hand, focuses on the role of entrepreneurship within an economy. For example, the invisible hand of the economy may result in problems that need solutions and an assortment of innovative responses arise to address the need. (Peter F. Drucker's approach to entrepreneurship, discussed later, aligns with this idea.) The other approach, focused on the personal characteristics of entrepreneurs, seeks to compile commonalities in the psychological and sociological aspects of entrepreneurship.

Stevenson finds both approaches unsatisfactory. In his opinion, the functional approach correctly highlights innovation, but leaves out the process of subsequent exploitation. Conversely, the psychological model is interesting, but inconclusive and inconsistent.

From Stevenson's perspective, entrepreneurship should be taught—and is indeed taught at Harvard Business School—as a process, not as a personality.[8] Stevenson defines entrepreneurship as an approach to management, the "pursuit of opportunity without regard to resources currently controlled."[9] His definition is broader than that of other thinkers: It includes the concept of innovation, but also transcends it. The psychological model, by comparison, may provide some backward-looking insights, but only when the individual has already pursued an opportunity.

Stevenson argues that Harvard has led the way in defining the study of entrepreneurship. He explains, "The definition of entrepreneurship we created back in the 1980s, with the focus on opportunity, was different from what others were talking about, and it formed part of the intellectual underpinnings of subsequent academic research."[10] Academics who write textbooks for business schools throughout the United States often adopt his definition of entrepreneurship.[11] Unlike common parlance, where entrepreneurship is sometimes equated with being small, and the terms *entrepreneur* and *small business operator* are used interchangeably, Stevenson's definition is a large canvas that includes most businesses.

Stevenson's definition has attracted some followers, but is not adopted by all entrepreneurship experts. Drucker, the father of modern management (who passed away in 2005), held a very specific view of entrepreneurship. In the Preface to *Innovation and Entrepreneurship,* his magnum opus on the topic, Drucker talks about what entrepreneurship is—and what it is not. At the time his book was written (1985), there was still some talk about entrepreneurship being a function of a certain personality type: either you had it, or you didn't. Drucker disagreed. The notion of an "entrepreneurial personality type" has been increasingly discounted right through to the present day.

Drucker believed that an entrepreneur can benefit from having certain traits, most of which can be acquired or developed, but that there is no such thing as an entrepreneurial personality. He talked about entrepreneurs in terms of their actions rather than their psychological make-up. Moreover, he explained that his book "presents innovation and entrepreneurship as a practice and a discipline. It does not talk of the psychology and the character traits of entrepreneurs; it talks of their actions and behavior."[12] Of course, if entrepreneurship were the outgrowth of a particular personality, then rather than studying the field in terms of practices and principles, the focus would be on psychological predispositions.

Furthermore, Drucker viewed entrepreneurship as a field that can be approached systematically—and, in this way, he saw it as similar to management. His book defines entrepreneurship as "purposeful tasks that can be organized—and are in need of being organized—as systematic work."[13] As well, his writing "treats innovation and entrepreneurship, in fact, as part of the executive's job."[14] In view of Drucker's pre-eminence as a management guru, he had the ideal foundation from which to compare and contrast the roles of the entrepreneur and the manager.

Drucker's systematic approach clashed with much conventional thought and practical experience. Entrepreneurs often relish the perverse virtue in "flying by the seat of one's pants," scurrying from one meeting to another, and emerging from chaos as an entrepreneurial triumph. Drucker asserted that success may emerge from chaos, but will more likely emerge in spite of it. He posited that innovation and entrepreneurship can—and indeed must—be pursued in a deliberate, thoughtful manner. Furthermore, successful entrepreneurs need to understand, organize, and prioritize their tasks. In this sense, tasks are better spread to executives throughout an organization, and should become part of each manager's job.

But what constitutes the core of entrepreneurship that can then be disseminated throughout an organization? Drucker opined, "Entrepreneurship is neither a science nor an art. It is a practice."[15] At one end of the spectrum, science involves experimentation— testing hypotheses to prove theories that produce predictable results—and this is not entrepreneurship. At the other end, art is an individualistic, subjective process that is impossible to quantify and replicate. Practice, however, is situated between science and art, and focuses on the realities of the marketplace. Indeed, because the knowledge of entrepreneurship is defined by what works and what does not, any discussion of entrepreneurship needs to be backed up by practical experience in the field.

A third perspective comes from Gordon Redding of INSEAD in Fontainebleau, France. He notes that the best way to understand the nature of entrepreneurship is to compare it to the world of medicine:

> How do you produce a doctor? The most critical skill in medicine is diagnosis. If you get that wrong, then you kill people. If you can't do it properly, then you're useless as a doctor. It is a very highly developed skill. It's a combination of aptitude, of interest, and also technique, but you can only learn it by practice. You have to diagnose patients in hypothetical

conditions—where other people have control of the situation—before they let you loose on real people. But once you're a good diagnostician, then you become very effective, very powerful, and you get people better.

It's exactly the same with entrepreneurship. Unless a person has developed the craft by practice, no matter how many books he may have read, or how beautiful a business plan he produces, it's absolutely useless. You must make mistakes and learn how to recalibrate in order to avoid future mistakes. The world of medicine is so far in advance of the world of management, but the principles are no different.[16]

For Redding, entrepreneurship is clearly learned in the field; there is a monumental difference between understanding theory and living in reality.

The fourth perspective is that of Henry Mintzberg, a well-known management guru. Obviously Mintzberg, as is Drucker, is known for management thinking rather than entrepreneurship. However, though both Mintzberg and Drucker's perspectives on entrepreneurship are from the context of management strategy and management education, their insights are complementary and powerful.

According to Mintzberg, management (as entrepreneurship is) "is a practice that has to blend a good deal of craft (experience) with a certain amount of art (insight) and some science (analysis)."[17] If management is a "science," then this implies that one may determine a set of laws about it; similarly, if it is a profession, then codified laws should exist. But Mintzberg believes management is, foremost, a craft, with a certain amount of art. And, because management is a craft, the learning process involves an emphasis on experience.

Mintzberg explains, "The development of such managers will require another approach to management education, likewise engaging, that encourages practicing managers to learn from their own experience. In other words, we need to build the craft and the art of managing into management education, and thereby reinforce these in the practice of managing."[18]

With that in mind, "it is time to face a fact," Mintzberg concludes:

After almost a century of trying, by any reasonable assessment, management has become neither a science nor a profession. It remains deeply embedded in the practices of everyday living. We should be celebrating that, not deprecating it. And we should be developing managers who are deeply embedded in the life of leading, not professionals removed from it.[19]

How does this apply to entrepreneurship?

Entrepreneurship, in the same way management is, is not a profession—there is no official, widely accepted base of knowledge. Unlike lawyers, who learn technical skills within the context of a carefully defined legal system and use specific legal skills within that context, entrepreneurs have no underlying code of guidance.

Entrepreneurship is also not a science. Scientists learn from experiments under carefully controlled conditions, in which they isolate various elements in order to measure the different outcomes. Their objective is to achieve similar results when conducting a series of repeat experiments. With entrepreneurship, however, the external environment is almost impossible to control. As well, history does not repeat itself; there may be similarities to past cycles, but there is no exact parallel. Thus entrepreneurship does not fit into a predictable, scientific model.

As do managers, entrepreneurs must develop skills through practice as they explore the nuances of the marketplace and develop a sense of the different dynamics at play. They must learn how to balance themselves in a rapidly fluctuating environment.

With these concepts in mind, Mintzberg does not ask managers to ignore the element of analysis. He agrees that there is a place for the technical disciplines taught at MBA schools. In addition, he does not reject the silos of information on marketing, accounting, and finance; nevertheless, he refuses to equate managerial training with the presentation of such information. That knowledge is helpful in moderation—but not in the scholastically dominant position it currently enjoys.

Mintzberg states, "You can't learn [management] in an educational institution, but you can improve it if you are given the chance to share your experience with other managers, in the light of interesting concepts."[20] He adds, "We have interesting things we can do in business schools, but we have to respect the experience of managers and what they bring to the classroom."[21]

Executive MBA programs, which only accept applicants who have experience and are presently employed, make the mistake of training people as though they are young, naive students. Mintzberg protests, "They take people with experience and try to teach them like they have no experience. We don't take advantage of their experience....I think it is a travesty when we don't."[22] In response, Mintzberg developed the "International Masters of Practicing Management" program (discussed in Chapter 6) to address these shortcomings.

These four perspectives on entrepreneurship—from Stevenson, Drucker, Redding, and Mintzberg—all vary in their emphasis. My view is similar to certain components of the perspectives previously described: I believe entrepreneurship is primarily a practice—one focused on innovation as its core activity—and, subsequently, it is a craft, a wisely developed combination of experiential lessons and skills.

What exactly is meant by the word *practice*? The *Merriam-Webster Dictionary* defines practice as a noun with two relevant denotations: first, "actual performance or application," and secondly, "a systematic exercise for proficiency."[23] On one hand, practice can mean the actual performance of the tasks. Indeed, entrepreneurship is best understood, learned, and taught as a performance grounded in the realities of application. Alternatively, practice implies the ongoing drive for perfection and persistent improvement through one's continuous focus on the process. Entrepreneurship fits this definition as well.

Why is entrepreneurship not typically viewed as a practice? There is a philosophical divide between entrepreneurs and academics. Most entrepreneurs themselves view their activities as a practice. But it is academics who are writing textbooks and doing research; they generally outnumber so-called practitioners or adjunct lecturers, or entrepreneurs in residence at business school faculties. Thus, their work, which is theory-based, prevails in most books on the subject. As both a practicing entrepreneur and an academic myself, I am convinced that "learning by doing" prioritizes practical knowledge.

Educators, whether in high school or at university, appear to simply overlook the common-sense emphasis on practice with regard to how individuals acquire and retain knowledge. Roger Schank, an educational psychologist, notes:

> We learn by doing. You learned your job on the job, not through listening to lectures or memorizing facts and figures. When you taught your child to ride a bicycle, you didn't give him a lecture about the mechanics of pedaling, or discuss ways in which he might keep his balance. Instead, you put him on the bike, held the handlebars, and let go when he seemed to have the hang of it; he needed to fall, get up, and keep practicing on his own until he became proficient. We all learn through experience, failure, and practice, a...paradigm that is largely absent from school.[24]

Although Schank directs his comments at the education of children, the same principles apply to learning about entrepreneurship. In short, entrepreneurship should be viewed foremost as a practice. This definitional compass will serve as a way of navigating through the different perspectives of the entrepreneurship experts and will serve as a common thread between many of their insights.

That said, I did not attempt to make the following chapters one synthesized, tidy opinion. Instead, each chapter highlights a different expert who shows a unique perspective on entrepreneurship, and collectively, the chapters illustrate the diversity of informed insight in the field. As demonstrated by the broad range of ideas you will read about in this book, the entrepreneurial landscape is a complex terrain. And it is no place for a dilettante.

Part II

The Entrepreneurial Experts

Chapter 1

Peter F. Drucker: The Drucker Legacy on Innovation and Entrepreneurship

Entrepreneurship is neither science nor an art. It is a practice.
—Peter F. Drucker[1]

Introduction to Peter F. Drucker

Name	Peter F. Drucker (1909–2005)
Title	Professor Emeritus
Affiliation(s)	Claremont Graduate School, Claremont, CA (1971–2005)
Education	○ Doctorate in public and international law from Frankfurt University in Frankfurt, Germany ○ Received more than a dozen honorary doctorates from universities in five countries
Experience	Advised and consulted on basic policies and long-range trends to businesses, public and private institutions, and government agencies in the United States and internationally

Notable Publications	39 books, including *The End of Economic Man* (1939), *Innovation and Entrepreneurship* (1985), *Managing For Results* (1964), and *Management: Tasks, Responsibilities and Practices* (1973), and numerous articles in academic publications and the popular press
Website(s)	*www.peter-drucker.com* *www.drucker.cgu.edu* *www.druckerarchives.net*

Biographical Highlights

⊙ His seminal work, *Innovation and Entrepreneurship*, is one of the most important books written on the topic.

⊙ His unmatchable coverage and analysis, citing events from personal experience dating back to the 1930s, has significant span and scope.

⊙ Of his 39 books, 15 deal with management, including the landmark books *The Practice of Management* and *The Effective Executive*; 16 cover society, economics, and politics; two are novels; and one is a collection of autobiographical essays. His last book, *Managing in the Next Society,* was published in fall 2002.

⊙ Drucker also served as a regular columnist for *The Wall Street Journal* from 1975 to 1995, and has contributed essays and articles to numerous publications, including the *Harvard Business Review, The Atlantic Monthly,* and *The Economist.* Throughout his 65-year career, he consulted with dozens of organizations, ranging from the world's largest corporations to entrepreneurial start-ups and various governments.

A Powerful Mind

For a man of international renown, Dr. Peter Drucker was surprisingly gracious when I contacted him via fax in April 2005. He communicated his support for my book project and invited me to interview him in his home city—Claremont, California—during the month of June.

The day before my departure, however, Dr. Drucker's wife, Doris, phoned to let me know that Dr. Drucker had fallen ill. Though Dr. Drucker indicated that he hoped to answer my questions in writing, his inability to follow through on the interview was understandable. Sadly, he passed away only a few months later, on November 11, 2005.

Jim Collins mentions in his Foreword to *The Daily Drucker* that Dr. Drucker warmly welcomed him into his home.[2] In a similar manner, I was astounded to receive a typed letter, signed by Dr. Drucker, in response to my request for an interview. This was doubly appreciated, as I had read of business journalists attempting to contact him and receiving only a standard-form letter in reply, declining their entreaties.[3] Dr. Drucker's efforts to make contact with me indicated his interest in this project and reiterated his commitment to helping others in the study of entrepreneurial excellence—right up to the time of his death. Indeed, his legacy leaves a strong presence in the field of entrepreneurship, and it must be taken into account.

Although circumstances prevented him from contributing to this chapter, I have summarized some of his central thoughts, however briefly, and received valuable feedback from Professor Joseph Maciariello, Drucker's colleague and recent collaborator on *The Daily Drucker* and *The Effective Executive in Action*.[4] Karl H. Vesper, a longtime personal acquaintance of Drucker's (featured in Chapter 10), and a man of whom Drucker spoke highly in his book *Innovation and Entrepreneurship*,[5] also provided me with some delightful anecdotes. I offer this chapter in the spirit of a "festschrift," in honor of Dr. Drucker's contribution to the field.

Entrepreneurship experts frequently cite Drucker's *Innovation and Entrepreneurship* as a leading work in the field. It offers a fresh and unique perspective, and rings true even 20 years after its original publication date. Thus, I would argue that Drucker is not only "the father of modern management," as many say, but also the father of systematic innovation and entrepreneurship.

With profound respect, Vesper reflects: "The power of [Drucker's] mind was almost unimaginable to me, and I have met some very smart people, such as the father of the H-Bomb and the inventor of the transistor."[6] Drucker's intellect was matched by a strong sense of wit. Vesper asked Drucker in spring 2005 for words of advice that Vesper could pass along to young faculty interested in entrepreneurship at the 2005 Academy of Management meeting in Honolulu. Drucker responded wryly, "If I ever had anything to say on this subject, I have already said it.... IF."[7]

Vesper also recalls Drucker's speech at the Academy of Management meetings in San Diego in 2000. Drucker was 90 years old at the time. He was up on stage using a PowerPoint presentation and addressing a large auditorium filled with management professors. When he finished his presentation, he took questions from the audience, submitted on small index cards.

Vesper recounts:

> Then there was a final question: "Professor Drucker, U.S. business schools this year will graduate 65,000 MBAs. Would you please comment?" Drucker leaned forward, squinted out at the enormous auditorium filled with management professors, and asked, "Is it possible to buy stock in this organization?" The audience enthusiastically clapped as he leaned back. When the room was quiet, he leaned forward again and said, "Well at least they are not going to be lawyers!" This time the audience stood up and cheered.[8]

Odd as it may seem, Drucker was underrated—at least, with respect to his contributions to entrepreneurship. His enormous influence in the field of management gave him wisdom about the nature of innovation and entrepreneurship. Perhaps that is why his book *Innovation and Entrepreneurship* is one of the few truly seminal works in the field. It analyzes the nature of the entrepreneurial process, and provides a philosophical understanding; comparatively, most other books are survey types, providing an overview of the mechanics of the process.

I read *Innovation and Entrepreneurship* shortly after it was published in 1985. Then I reread it in preparation for writing this chapter. The prescient nature of many of his comments is striking. To this day, I cannot think of another book that presents such valuable descriptions of the role of innovation in the process of entrepreneurship.

1.1 The Practice of Innovation

> Innovation is the specific instrument of entrepreneurship, the act that endows resources with a new capacity to create wealth. There are seven key sources of innovative opportunity: four within the business, and three due to changes outside the business.

Drucker's definition of entrepreneurship has a specific focus: innovation. Thus, he distinguishes between entrepreneurial businesses, which involve innovation, and other small businesses, which do not. For example, a person who develops and markets a new product is an entrepreneur, whereas the typical corner grocer is not. Likewise, a restaurant franchisee may not be an entrepreneur, whereas an independent restaurant owner may be.

In other words, entrepreneurs focus on innovation, and innovation is rooted in creating change and endowing existing resources with new wealth. Entrepreneurs view change as the source of opportunity in the marketplace: They embrace change, rather than avoid it. In addition, such thinking is the norm for entrepreneurs; for others, it is an aberration. Drucker writes that an entrepreneur continually "searches for change, responds to it, and exploits it as an opportunity."[9] This means doing something different, which is the realm of innovation, rather than simply excelling at something that is already being done. The latter may be profitable, but falls into the realm of increased productivity through operational improvements.

Furthermore, according to Drucker, entrepreneurs learn to practice systematic innovation through identifying and pursuing opportunities; this is the process of entrepreneurship. Change creates an opportunity for the entrepreneur to generate personal wealth and, indirectly, provide value to the overall economy. Drucker remarks, "Innovation is the specific instrument of entrepreneurship. It is the act that endows resources with a new capacity to create wealth. Innovation, indeed, creates a resource."[10] The created resource—as this is not a zero-sum game—provides value in the marketplace by deploying unproductive resources for more productive purposes.

Drucker affirms that, because entrepreneurship is not a mere personality trait, individuals can learn the innovation process. Obviously, increasing one's ability to innovate does not guarantee financial success, but it will provide more opportunities for consideration. Drucker posits, "Systematic innovation therefore consists in the purposeful and organized search for changes, and in the systematic analysis of the opportunities such changes might offer for economic and social innovation."[11] Rather than presenting a broad definition that defies meaningful analysis,

Drucker's explanation demystifies the process of entrepreneurship. As well, his specific focus provides a clear starting point for developing one's own entrepreneurship practice. Drucker identifies seven sources of innovative opportunity. Four sources lie within a business, and the other three are due to changes outside the enterprise or industry. The first source is the "unexpected" occurrence: the unexpected success, the unexpected failure, or the unexpected outside event. Drucker recounts the well-known tale of Ray Kroc—not the founder of McDonald's Restaurants, but the person who built the company into the colossus that it is today, with its globally-recognizable Golden Arches and its famous cast of cartoon characters. Ray Kroc was selling milkshake machines to small-scale restaurants when he noticed that one of his customers, the McDonald Brothers Restaurant, bought an unusually large number of the appliances. This unexpected event led him to discover that the restaurant had an overwhelming amount of customers due to its streamlined menu, low prices, and fast service. In response, he eventually bought out the brothers and built his burger empire.

According to Drucker, a second source of innovative opportunity may be an "incongruity" between reality as it *actually is* and reality as it is *assumed to be*, or *should be*.[12] In the mid-1980s, when Drucker wrote *Innovation and Entrepreneurship,* O. M. Scott & Co. was the leader among U.S. producers of lawn-care products (grass seed, fertilizer and pesticides). It then became a subsidiary of a larger corporation called ITT.[13] Basically, the company became a leader in the industry because of a simple mechanical gadget called a "spreader," a small, lightweight wheelbarrow with holes that allowed the proper quantities of Scott's products to pass through in an even flow. Prior to the Scott Spreader, no supplier of lawn-care products gave the customer a tool to control the process.[14] Yet without such a tool, there was a total incongruity in the logic of the process; there was no way to control the amount of fertilizer dispensed.[15]

A third source of innovation within the enterprise is innovation based on a process need, a restatement of the cliché that "necessity is the mother of invention." As an example, Drucker cites the development of photography. In the 1870s, photographic processes required heavy and fragile glass plates, which had to be lugged around and treated with great care. The plates themselves required an equally heavy camera, and a long preparation time before one could take a picture.[16] In the 1880s, George Eastman, the founder of Kodak, replaced the heavy glass plates with cellulose film of negligible weight, and designed a lightweight camera around the film. Within 10 years, Kodak was the world leader in photography.[17] Interestingly, at the turn of this century, the postlude of continuing technological developments in photography—namely, the invention and popularity of digital photography—has created serious challenges for film companies such as Kodak. No less than in the late 1800s, the companies that recognized change, and thus capitalized on opportunity, now claim leadership in the field today.

Drucker's fourth, and final, source of innovative opportunity within the enterprise is changes in industry structure or market structure that catch most people unaware.[18] Drucker mentions differentiation within the car industry, where brand names for vehicles strategically carve out niches in the market. A vehicle has long ceased to be merely a means of transportation; now it is a status symbol, and a reflection of one's personality. The phrase "you are what you drive," despite its facileness, is the mantra for many consumers. For example, a Rolls Royce automobile, the world's most expensive car, is fit for royalty—and others who can afford to spend royally. A BMW sports car is attractive to the up-and-coming executives, and the Mercedes-Benz sedan is respectable and reliable luxury on wheels.

As the market changes, due to fluctuating preferences and buying power, new niches arise. One can look back to the mass arrival of Japanese cars in America in the 1980s, when consumers turned their back on poorly built, fuel-inefficient American cars, and emptied their wallets for reliable, well-built Japanese models. This shift in the market caught most of Detroit unaware, as did the more recent shift to hybrid vehicles (which happened first in the United States when Toyota introduced the Prius).

In addition to these four sources of innovative opportunity within a business, Drucker makes note of three changes outside the enterprise that create sources of innovative opportunity. The first is shifting demographic trends—including changes in population size, composition, employment, educational status, and income. Popular age-defining terms are _Baby Boomers, Baby Busters,_ and _Generation X,_ designations that connote various opportunities as these groups move through their life cycles. Drucker explains that the success of Club Med in the travel and resort business stems from their capitalization on "demographic changes," specifically the growing number of wealthy and well-educated young people with working-class family backgrounds.[19] Club Med tapped into this opportunity, recognizing that the individuals in their demographic focus are "ready-made customers for a new and 'exotic' version of the old teenage hangout."[20] Club Med continues to exploit demographic trends, having recently diversified locations for singles, couples, and families.

Another source of innovation opportunity is a change in perception, mood, and meaning. Drucker recounts how people previously ate based on income and class; thus, ordinary people "ate" and the rich "dined."[21] Today's trend has been towards "feeding," however, which is simply a matter of getting edible food in the fastest and simplest manner possible. Customer satisfaction depends on speed of delivery rather than quality of product. How many people will patiently wait in a McDonald's line for more than a minute? Very few, indeed. Successful food service companies have been those who understood and exploited this attitude.

The third source of innovation opportunity outside the enterprise is the "superstar" of entrepreneurship: new knowledge, both scientific and non-scientific.[22] Drucker describes the features of this source: First, it has the longest lead time of all innovations. Specifically, scientific discoveries, such as those in biotechnology and pharmaceuticals, require regulatory approvals that involve a tedious completion process. Secondly, new knowledge is usually based on several pieces of prior knowledge converging, not all of which are technological or scientific. As well, not all of the knowledge necessary for innovation is available. Therefore, one must conduct a careful analysis of all the factors required to perfect the product. Following that process, a company must develop this new knowledge for commercialization, and that company must identify its strategic position in relation to its competitors. Finally, in order to successfully execute the commercialization, the company must aim for dominance—because the innovation based on new knowledge will probably have plenty of competition. The innovator must get it right the first time.

To summarize, Drucker highlights seven sources of innovative opportunity: four within the enterprise, and the remaining three outside the enterprise. His discussion of these opportunities reflects a systematic and purposeful approach to identifying, understanding, and applying the heart of entrepreneurship, which is innovation.

1.2 The Principles of Innovation

Five do's and three don'ts act as principles for the successful pursuit of innovation.

The subheading of *Innovation and Entrepreneurship* is "Practice and Principles." We have reviewed the practices, and now we will examine the principles—namely, we will determine how to follow through with being an innovative enterprise. Drucker reviews the dos, the don'ts, and three conditions.

Drucker identifies five "do's." First, he tells people to analyze the seven sources of innovative opportunities discussed in the prior section.[23] Second, he points out that innovation involves both concepts and perceptions.[24] In other words, look at numbers and talk to people. Get consumer feedback; test out an idea in practice. Third, he believes successful innovations are "simple" and "focused."[25] A wedge into a marketplace cannot be too complex.

Fourth, one must start small. Drucker remarks that innovation "may be as elementary as putting the same number of matches into a matchbox"—which, for the Swedish innovators who did so, opened the door to filling matchboxes automatically; this simple idea gave its Swedish inventors dominance in the match-making industry for almost 50 years.[26] Lastly, a successful innovator aims for leadership, in order to establish a niche in the marketplace. Put together, these five do's provide one dimension of the principles of innovation.

The other dimension of the principles of innovation is the don'ts. Drucker lists three. First, don't try to be clever. In other words, the innovation should not test the extent of a person's unbridled ingenuity, but should rather tailor something to the needs of the market. Drucker's succinct comment: "Innovations have to be handled by ordinary human beings." Moreover, Drucker asserts that, if the innovations become popular, they will be handled "by morons and near-morons."[27] (One need only think of many technological gadgets, from cell phones to "handy-cam" video recorders: ironically, most consumers fail to use up to 90 percent of these devices' functions.)

Next, don't diffuse efforts by trying to do too many things at once. One successful innovation is a good start; don't burden yourself at the outset. Lastly, don't innovate for the future. Innovate for the here-and-now, what people need at this moment. Drucker offers Edison's story as a great historical example. While other entrepreneurs were working on "the light bulb of the future," Edison set his attention on making a "light bulb of the present." He understood where and how the technology was available, and he practically exploited resources to meet the demands of the time.[28]

In addition to the five do's and the three don'ts, Drucker highlights some conditions for the principles of innovation. To begin with, he acknowledges that innovation is laborious, and that retrospective explanations of an individual's successful innovation will often minimize the degree of effort involved. Indeed, there is still no known substitute for hard work. Also, innovators need to build on their strengths—otherwise a successful breakthrough will be difficult. There is very little innovation among dilettantes. And finally, because innovation creates a change in the way people think, act, and accomplish tasks, challenges will surface along the way. Others may prefer to be spectators rather than participants, but entrepreneurs must embrace change easily.

1.3 Entrepreneurial Management

> Entrepreneurial management is not natural, creative, or spontaneous, but instead is based on a systematic, thoughtful approach of supportive policies and practices.

Drucker believes there has been a shift from a "managerial" to an "entrepreneurial" economy in the United States, evidenced by job creation among small businesses and by the increasing popularity of self-employment. (From the time of Drucker's writing to the present date, the number of jobs created by small businesses in the United States has continued to expand.) What these small enterprises have in common is transferable entrepreneurial skills.

Drucker refers to entrepreneurial management as a "new technology."[29] Moreover, he believes this technology of management fosters a significant social shift in "attitudes, values, and above all, behavior"—and thus creates the "entrepreneurial economy" environment in North America.[30] In essence, Drucker seeks to provide a systematic approach to entrepreneurship, rooted in practice. As a result, the starting point for successfully launching a new venture is the development of the principles, practice, and discipline of entrepreneurial skills.

Drucker proposes a set of principles that apply in a variety of circumstances. He also writes that a specific guide to the practice of entrepreneurship should be developed for different types of organizations: namely the existing business, the public-service organization, and the new venture. Drucker again stresses the potential for a systematic, thoughtful approach in the context of this discussion—despite the fact that entrepreneurship is typically viewed as spontaneous, fluid, and even chaotic. He states, "Where the conventional wisdom goes wrong is in its assumption that entrepreneurship and innovation are natural, creative, or spontaneous."[31] Of course, Drucker begs to differ with this "conventional wisdom": In his view, entrepreneurship is not merely "natural" or "creative." Rather, he believes it is "work."[32] He likely offers this perspective as an antidote to the perception that people who concoct bright, innovative ideas are gifted with unusual creative genius—a popular idea that is simply not the case.

Effective entrepreneurial management requires strategic development in four major areas. First, an organization must strive to create an entrepreneurial climate. The organization must become receptive to innovation, willing to perceive change as an opportunity and not a threat. Such openness does not happen by itself; rather, the entrepreneurial manager must implement policies and practices to foster this climate. Present examples are 3M of Minnesota and Procter & Gamble of Ohio, two companies famous for their innovative policies and for procedures that spawned an unprecedented stream of new products.

Second, an entrepreneur must systematically measure, or at least appraise, a company's performance. Unless he or she uses some form of evaluation based on measurable criteria, success is indeterminate, and strategic planning is undermined. Third, he or she must carry out specific practices pertaining to organizational structure, staffing and managing, and compensation and rewards.

The entrepreneurial climate must flourish in tangible ways throughout the organization. Lastly, entrepreneurial management involves certain "don'ts," as we will discuss shortly.

An entrepreneurial culture will be promoted through policies rooted in the pursuit of opportunity. As an entrepreneur, one must make innovation attractive to managers, whether through financial or other incentives. Without the committed effort of managers, an entrepreneur's drive for innovation will not get past the planning session.

To get management on board, Drucker believes businesses must instill an attitude that they are "greedy for new things."[33] In other words, change must be a desirable norm; a company must embrace "the pursuit of new things" as its operating mantra. As well, the company must suggest criteria for innovative endeavors: how much innovation? In what areas? Within what time frame?

Businesses could also incorporate a policy of systematic abandonment: If something isn't working, encourage your company to allocate resources elsewhere. Keep in mind that unless you clarify the goals of innovation, the company will likely not achieve them. Merely hoping for a spontaneous bout of creative change is futile and fanciful. Instead, the company needs to have a clear plan, with objectives and time lines, to facilitate effective planning.

Entrepreneurial practices complement these policies. Managerial vision must be focused on opportunity; the managers must spend sufficient time strategizing about company prospects. Furthermore, the same entrepreneurial spirit must exist throughout the ranks of the company. One may achieve this by organizing company planning sessions, during which members throughout the organization communicate innovative ideas. Another policy is for top management in an organization to meet with junior management in different departments and solicit ideas for improvement. Still another is to provide incentives by offering large rewards to successful innovators.

Drucker also lists some don'ts with respect to entrepreneurial practices. Namely, don't mix managerial units with entrepreneurial ones.[34] This would be a culture clash between those who are gathering resources to pursue new and untested ideas and those who are charged with managing existing resources. As well, don't try to be innovative by taking an existing business out of its own field.[35] Uprooting a business dilutes expertise and business know-how, and makes the business likely to falter. Finally, don't try to make your business entrepreneurial by buying a small entrepreneurial venture.[36] Mergers and acquisitions often don't work well, due mostly to the resulting conflicts between company subcultures. Moreover, the larger, organizational culture would simply subsume the acquired entrepreneurial venture. In addition, the leaders of the entrepreneurial venture would be prone to leave the stifling environment of a large, stagnant company.

1.4 Entrepreneurial Strategies

> There are four key entrepreneurial strategies. Three intend to introduce an innovation—"fustest with the mostest," "hit them where they ain't," and "ecological niches"—and the fourth is innovation itself.

In *Innovation and Entrepreneurship* Drucker highlights four entrepreneurial strategies. For the first strategy, he cites a Confederate cavalry general during the American Civil War who explained that he was able to consistently win his battles by taking initiative with concentrated force and energy—being "fustest with the mostest." Drucker then mentions a similar strategy for entrepreneurs, who must seek "leadership, if not dominance, of a new market."[37] This high-risk and high-return strategy usually fails, because a firm allocates so many resources to the undertaking.

Drucker explains that the weakness of this strategy is its demand on time, energy, and resources. Other strategies are often better to employ, because in a majority of cases, "the opportunity is not great enough to justify the cost, the effort, and the investment of resources required for the 'Fustest with the Mostest' strategy."[38]

As a successful example of the strategy, however, Drucker describes the origins of the Mayo Clinic. Two surgeons in Rochester, Minnesota, the Mayo brothers, decided to establish a medical center based on totally new concepts of medical practice, especially on building teams of outstanding specialists who would work together under the guidance of a co-coordinating team leader. Because they were innovators in the field of medicine, focused on building a leading clinic, they were able to assemble outstanding practitioners in every branch of medicine. They were also able to attract patients who could pay significant fees.[39] In their case, "fustest with the mostest" was a worthwhile approach.

Drucker calls the second entrepreneurial strategy "hit them where they ain't," a phrase also derived from the advice of a Confederate general. This expression embodies two different lines of attack: creative imitation and entrepreneurial Judo. Drucker describes creative imitation as a process of refining someone else's new innovation. Although one company may have invented a product or technology, that company may not be using the invention to its full potential.[40] For example, Drucker cites the early battle between Apple and IBM in the field of personal computers. The idea for a personal computer belonged to Apple; IBM believed that a small, freestanding computer was a mistake— uneconomical and expensive. When Apple succeeded, however, IBM began designing a similar (and slightly improved) machine. The result was the PC, a model that took leadership from Apple and became the fastest-selling brand within two years.[41] This strategy carries less risk than "fustest with the mostest, because someone else has already identified the market and established the demand. But, with less risk comes potentially fewer benefits, as the current leader may be difficult to dislodge."

The other tactic involved in "hit them where they ain't" is "entrepreneurial Judo." Judo, as with most Asian martial arts, focuses on turning an opponent's energy and momentum against him or her. Drucker uses the reference to Judo in particular because it is Japanese in origin, and the Japanese, from the 1940s on, have achieved success by attacking the strengths of their American competitors. Japanese companies, such as Sony, have been able to dominate the electronics market in the United States with products such as transistor radios, television sets, and digital watches. Also, Japanese auto manufacturers Toyota and Honda challenged the monopoly of the "Big Three" auto manufacturers (GM, Ford, and Chrysler) in 2005 and following: For the first time in history, the Big Three claimed less than 50 percent of the domestic market share for new vehicles sold in the United States. Toyota, for example, exercised entrepreneurial Judo by excelling at an area the Big Three had not yet considered: the production of hybrid cars. Entrepreneurial Judo, as Toyota's example demonstrates, is a relatively low-risk strategy with a high success rate.

Overconfident companies have five bad habits that allow competitor firms to use entrepreneurial Judo. One bad habit is the "not invented here" arrogance,[42] most common among companies within a country. Large high-tech firms are sometimes skeptical of innovations arising from small companies, believing that, with their vastly superior resources, a minor competitor's invention cannot pose a serious threat. The large company may assume, "If it were that good, we would have thought of it."

A second bad habit is the tendency to cream a market and stick with a high-profit segment. Other areas of the market are probably still profitable, but the company turns a blind eye to them. For example, a large brewery may focus on developing a nationwide market for its beer as a ubiquitous part of every sporting event. This may be a profitable business, but, in the meantime, micro-breweries have sprung up, offering a local, customized beer for a niche market. International breweries have now recognized the niche by setting up their own micro-breweries to "tap" this market.

Third, a company may mistakenly focus on quality—based on the effort and expense of creating the product—rather than considering the consumer's perception of a product's value, which often emphasizes special "features."[43] Another bad habit for a company is the "premium price" delusion, an open door for competitors to offer better prices for the same product. And yet another bad habit is when companies attempt to maximize rather than optimize: As the market grows, they try to satisfy every segment instead of focusing on their most profitable niches.[44] In short, these weaknesses are a perfect invitation for entrepreneurial Judo; what companies see as their strengths actually become their weaknesses, simply because they are playing into the hand of their opponents.

The third entrepreneurial strategy is a search for "ecological niches," aiming at obtaining a practical monopoly in a small area.[45] According to Drucker, there are three distinct "niche" tactics: the toll gate strategy, the specialty skill strategy, and the specialty market strategy. With respect to the toll gate strategy, Drucker provides the example of the Alcon Company, which developed an enzyme to eliminate an illogical feature of the standard surgical operation for senile cataracts.[46] Once the company had developed and patented this enzyme, it had a toll gate on the process. All surgeons, of course, would now need to use a teaspoonful of the enzyme for each cataract operation. As well, the enzyme's cost was insignificant in relation to the cost of the total operation. Furthermore, because the total worldwide market for the product was a projected $50 million, it was not large enough to attract attention from competitors. Alcon successfully found an untapped place in the market. Although the technology has changed since Drucker's discussion of Alcon, the example shows the potential of securing a practical monopoly.

A second ecological niche is the specialty skill strategy. A common example is the automobile industry, where brand names such as Ford, Mercedes, and BMW, are well known, but parts suppliers are not. Drucker refers to the company A.O. Smith of Milwaukee, which for decades has been making every single frame used in an American passenger car. Another firm, Bendix, used to make every single set of automotive brakes for the American car industry.

The third ecological niche is the specialty market strategy. Though the specialty skill strategy is built around a specific product or service, the specialty market strategy emphasizes expert knowledge of a particular market. For example, Drucker lists two medium-sized European companies that supply the great majority of automated baking ovens for cookies and crackers. The strength of these two companies is their knowledge of a very specialized market: They know every single baker, and every single baker knows them.

Whereas the first three entrepreneurial strategies introduce an innovation, the fourth strategy is innovation itself. Innovation can transform a long-established product or service into something new. There are four dimensions to this approach. The primary dimension, customer utility, is reflected in the origins of the postal service. People generally credit Rowland Hill of England with having invented the postal service in 1836. He didn't; after all, the Romans had a postal service centuries earlier. However, Hill did create "mail" by devising the system whereby postal carriers could transport letters and packages for a fixed, prepaid fee (indicated by a stamp). His innovation allowed an impractical and disorganized service to vastly expand and improve its modes of operation.

Second, there is innovation with respect to pricing. King Gillette did not invent the razor, but, because of his shrewd pricing strategy, he dominated the market by the late 1800s. Gillette practically gave away the razor, selling it at 1/5 of its manufacturing cost—but his design could only be used with its patented blades, which he sold at five times their manufacturing cost.

A third strategy is adaptation to the customer's social and economic reality. General Electric established world leadership in the sale of large steam turbines: When GE discovered that its clients, electrical companies, did not have the skill to install and maintain the turbines, GE set up a massive consulting organization. The company also generated profits by selling high-priced replacement blades to customers. By carefully analyzing the customers' needs, GE was able to amplify the scope of its services.

The last innovative strategy is to deliver value to the customer. Herman Miller, for example, moved from manufacturing furniture to designing whole offices, and then he went on to establish a Facilities Management Institute, which advises companies on layout and design ideas that increase worker productivity. Herman Miller's pursuit of innovation was determined by his customers' needs.

Drucker's Key Points

1.1. Innovation is the specific instrument of entrepreneurship, the act that endows resources with a new capacity to create wealth. There are seven key sources of innovative opportunity: four within the business, and three due to changes outside the business.

1.2. Five do's and three don'ts act as principles for the successful pursuit of innovation.

1.3. Entrepreneurial management is not natural, creative, or spontaneous, but instead is based on a systematic, thoughtful approach of supportive policies and practices.

1.4. There are four key entrepreneurial strategies. Three intend to introduce an innovation—"fustest with the mostest," "hit them where they ain't," and "ecological niches"—and the fourth is innovation itself.

Chapter 2

Larry C. Farrell:
The Spirit of Enterprise

Entrepreneurship, in my philosophy, is one of the most generic things in the world. The actual practice of entrepreneurship is almost culture-free. Different cultures have different rates of entrepreneurship, because there are some differences in terms of how people perceive it as a career, but once you get into it, entrepreneurs in Hong Kong and entrepreneurs in Sao Paulo, Brazil, basically have to do the same thing to succeed. It's not like there is a big difference. In that sense it is a bit like a worldwide technology.

—Larry C. Farrell[1]

Introduction to Larry C. Farrell

Name	Larry C. Farrell
Title	Chairman and Founder, The Farrell Company
Affiliation(s)	The Farrell Company, Staunton, Virginia
Education	B.S. (Arizona) AMP (Harvard)

Experience	o Vice President, American Express, New York
	o President, Kepner-Tregoe, Princeton, New Jersey
	o Board Member, The Economic Development Society (United States) and *The Journal Of Strategic Change* (London)
Notable Publications	o *Searching for the Spirit Of Enterprise* (1994)
	o *The Entrepreneurial Age* (2000)
	o *Getting Entrepreneurial!* (2003)
	o "Entrepreneuring" (column), *Across The Board* (2004–present)

Biographical Highlights

⊙ During the past two decades, Larry Farrell has personally taught entrepreneurship to more individuals, organizations, and governments than any person in the world.

⊙ Today, with 22 affiliates in Asia, Europe, Latin America, and Africa, nearly one million participants in 40 countries, across seven languages, have attended The Farrell Company's programs.

⊙ He has written three highly acclaimed practice-oriented books on entrepreneurship.

⊙ His column, "Entrepreneuring," appears regularly in *Across the Board,* the magazine of the Conference Board, New York City.

⊙ His expertise has been validated throughout the world by a range of Fortune 1000 clients and government organizations.

⊙ He lectures widely at universities, and his entrepreneurial program has formed the basis for university entrepreneurship centers, such as that at Oklahoma City University.

2.1 The Entrepreneurial Life Cycle

The life cycle of all organizations involves a progression from "entrepreneurial practices" to "managerial practices": start-up, high growth, decline, and survival. Maintaining entrepreneurial practices sustains growth and counteracts decline.

How does a company grow? According to Larry Farrell, the key to understanding how companies grow is to understand their life cycle. Entrepreneurs can learn growth-related lessons from most companies, but only when looking at the right point in their life cycle: When were they at their peaks, and the envy of their industries?

Today's dinosaurs were yesterday's innovators. Even though Wal-Mart displaced Sears, at some point in its life cycle Sears was an innovative company that seized market shares from its rivals and dominated the industry. IBM, likewise, set the pace in its industry for decades—prior to the 1980s, when it squandered opportunities to its nimble upstarts, Microsoft and Apple. The list goes on.

Farrell stresses his revolutionary insight that entrepreneurial learning comes from studying companies at the point in their life cycle when they are young, growing rapidly, and innovative. This perspective enhances one's understanding of how entrepreneurs can sustain growth in their own companies.

Farrell's message resonates with conference attendees throughout the world. He states:

We claim that there are four stages to a company's life cycle: start-up, high growth, decline, and survival. This life cycle usually takes about fifty years. On the left hand side of this life cycle chart [see Figure 2.1] is the start-up and high growth phase, which may take ten to thirty years. This is where entrepreneurial practices are most dominant. As the company gets bigger and older, the original entrepreneurial team may retire. Entrepreneurs rarely replace themselves with entrepreneurs— they replace themselves with professional managers. So, for example, you may have a thirty-year-old company with five thousand employees that is run by MBA-educated professional managers with their modern management theories. This produces a growing bureaucracy, and the company begins to move into the "decline" phase of the company life cycle. At this point, expensive MBA-trained management consultants are called, which typically makes things worse![2]

Farrell notes that when he gives his seminars, a light bulb goes off in the heads of company executives. They start seeing their company in the context of the life cycle, and recognize that they are on the down side.

Figure 2.1. The Life Cycle of All Organizations[3]

The fundamental point for company managers to understand in order to sustain growth is the difference between "the entrepreneurial practices way" and "the managerial practices way." One of the hurdles for MBA-trained managers is that, as Farrell elucidates, "most of the management rules they have learned in business schools come from studying big companies,"[4] which is, ironically, when those companies were past the entrepreneurial, high growth part of their life cycles. Thus, from Farrell's standpoint, business schools are teaching about companies that are operating in a state of decline.

Sustained company growth does not result from being at either extreme of the life cycle spectrum, but from recognizing the dynamic tension and striking a balance between entrepreneurial and managerial practices. Farrell explains:

I am careful to say to my audience that you need to have both entrepreneurial and managerial skills in the twenty-first century. I would be the first to admit that you cannot run a company with only "crazy" entrepreneurial passion. You also need the discipline of managerial competencies: accountants and production and quality control. But we can't forget the basic principles for creating high growth. As Steve Jobs says, managing is the easy part; growing is the hard part!

With respect to life cycle, a key issue is to maintain a balance in the company between entrepreneurial practices and managerial practices. My contention is that most large companies are about ninety-five-percent managerial and five-percent entrepreneurial. One of my favorite entrepreneurs in Hong Kong is Victor Fong, of Lee & Fong Company. Victor was a Harvard business school professor earlier on in his career who decided to give up academia and go back to Hong Kong and run the family business. He's an expert in both entrepreneurial and managerial principles. In Victor's opinion that ratio should be eighty-percent entrepreneurial and twenty-percent managerial. My conclusion is, and we tell all our clients, that companies should at least aim for a fifty-fifty balance between entrepreneurial, high-growth practices and management practices.[5]

Farrell on Peter Drucker[6]

"The great thing about Peter Drucker is that even though he is 'the father of modern management,' he is smart enough and clever enough to understand that, as he told me in private before we both spoke at a Business Week _magazine conference in Taiwan, 'You're absolutely right!' [regarding the difficulties large companies face when trying to create real growth]. Drucker lamented, 'I won't even do consulting for large companies anymore. 'Bigger is better' is one of the great myths of the twentieth century. In most industries the mid-sized companies are superior to the giant companies.' Drucker is an individual who doesn't have anything to lose by speaking his mind. He's big enough, so he can say we have to re-instill entrepreneurship, since big businesses have become bureaucracies."_

(For more information about Peter Drucker, see Chapter 1.)

Farrell's first key principle is rooted in an understanding of entrepreneurial and managerial practices and their relationship to the life cycle of organizations. In _Getting Entrepreneurial!_, Farrell points out:

> The most fundamental thing we have learned in eighteen years of researching and teaching entrepreneurship is that growing a business and managing a business are separate universes. Entrepreneurs are great at growing businesses. Managers are great at managing businesses. Managing is actually the easy part. Creating and growing a business demand that you do more than manage.[7]

Companies go through a life span, just as individuals do. But, whereas an individual cannot cheat death, a company can. By maintaining entrepreneurial practices and staving off managerial inertia, a company can continue its growth.

How Tom Peters Led Larry Farrell From "In Search of Excellence" to "In Search of Growth"[8]

"After Tom Peters published In Search of Excellence *in 1982, he called me up. He was aware that I knew a lot about the international training and consulting market. He gave me the marketing rights to his 'Excellence' seminars everywhere except the [United States] and Canada. I started in July 1983 by setting up offices in London and Singapore. I used my own money. I put a huge second mortgage on my home and invested everything in this business. I felt that I could not miss, since the seminars were based on the best-selling business book in history.*

"Then, after eighteen months of being on my own and marketing the seminars, on November 5, 1984, the cover of Business Week magazine ran an expose on the fallacies of the book! They had done their homework. Of Peters' 43 best-run companies in America, they found that one-third of those companies, only two years after the book came out, were in financial free-fall!

"I learned this in Tokyo while I was trying to convince Texas Instruments to sign up for the 'Excellence' Seminar. The Japanese Human Resources manager pulled out that week's issue of Business Week [November 5, 1984] and said, 'Mr. Farrell, have you seen this?'

After a painful reading of the cover article, I figured one of two things. One, I better get a new product, as this thing may go downhill in a hurry. Second, and probably a lot more importantly, if the best-selling business book in history wasn't reliable 18 months after it was published, 'Where are we going to find the truth on what it takes to grow businesses?'

"From that thought, and supported by the fact that I now had experience as a small-time entrepreneur, I began to think that maybe people like Peters and all the other gurus are asking the right questions, but they're looking at companies in the wrong era. Instead of looking at IBM in the 1980s, which we now know was already going downhill, maybe you should look at what it did in the 1920s, 30s, and 40s, when it became so great. Instead of looking at the Disney Company today, maybe we should look at the Disney Company in the 1930s, 40s, and 50s, when Walt Disney made it the world's greatest entertainment company. So I pursued this angle, that it's not the mature Fortune-500-type of company we should be studying for secrets to

success, but rather the 'entrepreneurial phase' of these companies— the first 10., 20, 30 years—and the great entrepreneurs that created them. That's what got me started."

2.2 The Entrepreneurial Basics

"The entrepreneurial basics" provide a framework for successful entrepreneurial pursuits: sense of mission, customer/product vision, high-speed innovation, and self-inspired behavior.

Larry Farrell has distilled the wisdom he gained from 20 years of researching the actual practices of the world's leading entrepreneurs into four common characteristics of successful start-ups. Any entrepreneur can use this basic framework to achieve initial success. And any corporate management team can use the framework to instill growth in the business. Farrell's teaching track record indicates that clients the world over find his analysis compelling.

First, the entrepreneur must have a clear sense of mission, which he says includes both **what** the mission is and **how** he or she is going to achieve it. This begins with tailoring the company's product to a particular market, which Farrell calls having a product/ market strategy. Next is "how" a person can achieve that strategy: "Entrepreneurs have to get this right. Concentrating your energies on becoming the best in the world at one or two key things will give you powerful, competitive advantages."[9]

He further states, "When your values directly support your product/market strategy, hang on! It's the most powerful way ever invented to energize a group of individuals to achieve a common purpose. That's why having a powerful sense of mission is the first entrepreneurial practice."[10] The history of IBM shows that a strong sense of mission can fuel company growth, and that a loss of mission can derail a company later in its life cycle.

Farrell explains how IBM, "Big Blue," was founded in 1914 by Thomas Watson. Watson infused staff with his mission through a pithy set of values: customer service, respect for the individual, and superior effort in all tasks. He saw IBM's competitive advantage as outstanding customer service, whatever the product. For years, its corporate advertising simply declared that "IBM Means Service." As well, IBM crowed that, because of this service emphasis, 95 percent of all product ideas came from its customers.[11] Interestingly enough, these values were so pervasive that they were not written down until 1963, when Thomas Watson, Jr., recorded them—50 years after his father founded the company. The founder's leadership and personal embodiment of core principles had kept these values alive.

IBM was a great organization for a long time. Today, it still ranks highly in sales and profits on the Fortune 500 list, but, Farrell notes, "It's fair to say they're past their peak, some 20 years into the down side of their life cycle."[12] IBM's original mission and resulting entrepreneurial zeal evaporated in the 1980s, when IBM nearly collapsed. In the 1990s, despite some revival, IBM still was a lumbering, slow-moving behemoth in an area that was overtaken by innovative high-growth competitors. Company growth is propelled by a strong sense of mission, such as IBM had in the early stage of its life cycle.

Second, the entrepreneur needs to have a definite "customer/product vision." In practical terms, this means the entrepreneur must be very clear about who is going to buy the product and why. Farrell writes, "The single most crucial vision all entrepreneurs must have is a clear picture of a specific set of customers who need, and will pay for, a specific set of products and services. Nothing could be more basic to the entrepreneur."[13]

Farrell's research also indicates that a successful entrepreneur is almost always both a "product person" and a "customer person." He or she is a make-and-sell craftsman with the classic customer/product vision. Farrell recounts the story of Walt Disney, the "greatest product creator in the history of the entertainment business".[14] Disney produced the first talking cartoon in 1928 ("Steamboat Willie"), the first feature-length animated cartoon in 1937 (*Snow White*), the first stereophonic movie in 1940 (*Fantasia*), and the world's first 360-degree projection at Disneyland in 1955. In television, Disney also created *The Wonderful World of Disney*, the longest-running prime-time series ever (1954–83). He opened Disneyland in 1955, and, before he died in 1966, he laid the groundwork for Disney World in Florida. What was his magic?

According to Farrell, the real "magic" of Walt Disney is simple: "He was a product expert and a customer expert at the same time. A scientist and a salesman. An unbeatable combination."[15] Farrell explains, "The trick, then, is to become passionately expert on your own products and customers. After all, they are the two most important ideas in business."[16]

Third, an entrepreneur needs to deploy "high-speed innovation." Farrell states, "There are two golden rules for high-speed innovation: first, you and your people must see innovation as an absolute necessity in the business, and, second, there must be a high sense of urgency to take action and implement new ideas. We call it the necessity to invent and the freedom to act."[17] He notes, "The evidence is indisputable that young, entrepreneurial companies can, and regularly do, simply beat the socks off their larger, more mature competitors. And almost always, their number-one competitive advantage is that they move faster and they're more creative than their larger rivals."[18] Further, "I have never known an entrepreneur who operated without pretty high levels of emotion and without a strong sense of urgency."[19] The entrepreneur needs to act swiftly before the competitive landscape changes and the windows of opportunity close.

Farrell tells the tale of Larry Hillblom and the founding of DHL. Hillblom was a young law student in northern California who did freelance courier work on weekends, carrying packages across the Pacific on 20-hour flights. He scratched out an idea for an international courier company with two of his law school friends who were also freelance couriers. They formed DHL (Dalsey, Hillblom, and Lynn) and began to offer overnight delivery, but they needed an international network of offices immediately.

The result: "They opened an amazing 120 country offices in the first [10] years of DHL's existence (1972 to 1982), which is still the fastest international expansion of any company in history."[20] Hillblom's company now generates approximately $15 billion in revenue. Of course, subsequent international courier companies have been created, such as FedEx, but the rise of DHL was rooted in almost-unbelievable high-speed innovation. Moreover, high-speed innovation is a necessary part of the infrastructure for DHL's services. Entrepreneurial success requires acting immediately and decisively in response to an opportunity in the marketplace.

Fourth, an entrepreneur must have "self-inspired behavior"— to spur himself and his employees. The entrepreneur is the engine, and his company is the vehicle. Farrell clarifies: "To start your own business, *you* have to be self-inspired. Then, to grow your enterprise, you have to learn to inspire others. That is why mastering the final entrepreneurial practice, *self-inspired behavior,* is the underpinning of all entrepreneurial success."[21] He goes on, "To successfully grow beyond the proverbial one-man shop, some enterprising, self-inspired behavior needs to be instilled in the employees. Inspiring yourself is laudable—that's where it has to —but inspiring 10, or a hundred, or even thousands of workers is the real trick."[22]

Farrell cites the example of Soichiro Honda, founder of the Honda Motor Company, whom he calls "hands down, the most interesting Japanese entrepreneur of the twentieth century."[23] The son of a blacksmith, with only a third-grade education, Honda built a company famous for its attention to customers and its efficient system, through which workers (whether in Japan or in the United States) created highly competitive cars. His death in 1991 produced a wide outpouring of grief among employees worldwide. Honda was not only a highly self-motivated individual, but he also inspired his entire organization.

2.3 An International Perspective

An international perspective opens up opportunities. Do not be a prisoner of your own national culture.

Our world is interconnected through the ease and low cost of travel, the speed of Internet communications, and the instantaneous diffusion of information. Therefore, opportunities in one's own backyard are impacted by global expansion. In the field of entrepreneurship, an individual's prospects will be magnified through an international outlook that values the insights of other cultures and seeks to understand and work with those of other backgrounds. Farrell states:

Entrepreneurship, in my philosophy, is one of the most generic things in the world. The actual practice of entrepreneurship is almost culture-free. Different cultures have different rates of entrepreneurship, because there are some differences in terms of how people perceive it as a career, but once you get into it, entrepreneurs in Hong Kong and entrepreneurs in Sao Paulo, Brazil, basically have to do the same thing to succeed. It's not like there is a big difference. In that sense it is a bit like a worldwide technology.[24]

The international perspective Farrell injects into his books is far greater than that possessed by the average American.

How did Farrell develop this international outlook?

When I was just out of undergraduate school I went into the American Peace Corps. They sent me to the Middle East…a good two-year experience. That opened my eyes to the world. My early jobs had an international dimension. At American Express I was the Marketing VP of an international subsidiary. Then I worked with Kepner-Tregoe, which had offices in about twenty different countries, eventually becoming the President and Chief Operating Officer. The value of this international perspective was reinforced when I became involved in marketing the Tom Peters Excellence seminars around the world. All of Peters' examples were U.S. companies. That in itself was a tough sell in Japan and in Germany. They would say, "How does the culture here work with that?"[25]

The lack of an international perspective limits an entrepreneur's range of opportunity. For example, despite Peters's enormous success and guru status, Farrell notes that he is "a prisoner of American culture. He truly did not understand much outside of the United States. When I was working with him, I brought him to London to give a big speech, and he was practically booed off the stage!"[26]

Farrell, on the other hand, has intentionally adopted an international perspective:

For this reason, I have attempted to make my message international in scope, application, and presentation. I decided that in addition to studying the earlier history of companies, I would also make sure that my examples were roughly one-third European, one-third American, and one-third Asian, with a smattering of South American examples thrown in.[27]

This is important for a U.S. audience. Farrell remarks, "People in North America, particularly in the Unites States, know very little of what is outside the United States It really drives me nuts!"[28]

Jannie Tay: The Chinese "Mamacita"[29]

Jannie Tay founded The Hour Glass Company, a watch and jewelry retailer in Singapore. More than 20 years, the company has grown to three hundred employees, three hundred million dollars in annual revenue, and 15 outlets throughout Southeast Asia and Australia. The company is known for high-quality products and excellent service. According to Farrell, the company's growth has been "driven by Jannie Tay's greatest personal asset: her amazing instincts for

> *inspiring her people." Tay deflects this praise by stressing that the top asset of her company is her employees. She calls herself a "Chinese Mamacita." She elaborates: "The key to everything we do is treating ourselves like a family. They [the employees] become your family, and you have unconditional love for each other—you forgive and forget, and you share the good and the bad."*

Has an international perspective benefited Farrell's own consulting activities? He responds:

> We have done more than 50 percent of our business outside of the United States. We currently have 20 international affiliates, and we have recently begun new relationships in India and China. We have enjoyed a long-standing presence in other markets. We have been in South Africa for twelve years now, Brazil for f14 years, and Singapore and the UK for 20 years.[30]

However, not all entrepreneurs envisage international opportunities. People from one corner of the globe may be superficially familiar with another group of people and yet remain entirely ignorant of the other culture and, in fact, may display disdain for it. As Farrell points out: "Those people who are prisoners of the American culture had better wake up, because between India and China you have 40 percent of the world's population. So for the 21st century, if you are just thinking about American examples and American products for American consumers, then this will be the road to oblivion."[31]

2.4 Practice Makes Perfect

As befits a leading world practitioner and advisor, Farrell emphasizes being a participant rather than a spectator. An armchair quarterback never threw a game-winning touchdown pass on the last play of the game! Farrell encourages people to move into action, or as he often puts it, "get entrepreneurial!"

His conference attendees often ask, "What's really required to get started?"[32]

Farrell pares the answer down to three bare essentials. First, create an entrepreneur-friendly culture in and around your company. The exemplary characteristics of this culture are easy to remember: specifically, "keep it small"—smaller operating units within a large company foster accountability, job satisfaction, and familiarity among employees. Then, "keep it personal"—constantly confirm the importance of each individual's contribution to the company's mission, which will raise overall performance and commitment. "keep it honest"—maintain integrity, and follow through on your word to customers and employees. If you don't, they'll never trust you again. Clearly convey to employees and managers the objectives and strategies of the company so they identify with the firm's goals. Also, "keep it simple"—focus on the nuts and bolts of the business. In other words, get the basics right, and make sure everyone understands them. Finally, "start over with the basics"—ensure that all employees, regardless of their function, focus on delivering great products to satisfied customers—which is, after all, the reason for the company's existence.

Secondly, "a bit of money" is required to start up any business.[33] Although Farrell's conference attendees rarely, if ever, challenge his overall formula for entrepreneurial success, he notes, that "The most common rejoinder I get, which you could call a bit of a critique, is that people ask, 'What about money?'"[34]

Farrell's response:

First, the way we teach it, money is a result. You don't go to work every day and 'do money.' You go to work every day and create and sell a product and manage your people in an inspiring way....Second, while some amount of capital is usually required at start up, it is not a large amount for most entrepreneurs. Our research shows that the average cost of starting a business in the United States today is only about $14,000.[35]

As Farrell notes, according to *Inc. Magazine,* start-up funding comes mainly from personal savings, credit cards, and loans from friends and relatives.[36] One important implication of these points is that the money does not come from banks and venture capitalists. But regardless of the amount, and where it comes from, the key component all successful start-ups share is a product or service that customers are willing to pay for.

Third, entrepreneurs need "a bit of knowledge."[37] Farrell points out: "The number-one reason for business failure is not a lack of money. It's more basic than that. It is, simply, you haven't come up with a product or service that anyone wants to buy."[38] If you have that, the cash flow—which is the lifeblood of any company—will follow. Thus, the essential knowledge for an entrepreneur is the ability to make something or provide a service that the world needs and will pay for.

In short, going from inertia and complacency to launching your own entrepreneurial ventures involves a simple three-step action plan: Create an entrepreneurial culture, get a bit of money, and acquire the knowledge to create a service or product that people will pay for. As Farrell concludes, this is what you need to do to "get entrepreneurial!"[39]

Moreover, Farrell is adamant that "management knowledge" is not a fundamental requirement for becoming an entrepreneur.[40] The shortcoming of many managers is simply that they do not have the necessary product knowledge. As Steve Jobs, the founder of Apple Computers, once said of his own company, "The managers knew how to manage, but they didn't know how to *do* anything."[41] The examples of the entrepreneurs described in all of Farrell's writings can be summarized as follows:

The one mighty thing they do have in common when it comes to knowledge, is that they became very good at *something*. They understood that what's required to create a high-growth enterprise is not becoming great at managing but becoming great at making and doing something that a lot of people in the world need and will pay good money for.[42]

Thus, the goal of an entrepreneur is to find a key product or service, and establish the resources to back it up. Then, once he or she has created a business, he or she must keep the company alive by fostering an entrepreneurial culture within it.

Farrell's Key Points

2.1. The life cycle of all organizations involves a progression from "entrepreneurial practices" to "managerial practices": start up, high growth, decline, and survival. Maintaining entrepreneurial practices sustains growth and counteracts decline.

2.2. "The entrepreneurial basics" provide a framework for successful entrepreneurial pursuits: a sense of mission, a customer/product vision, high-speed innovation, and self-inspired behavior.

2.3. An international perspective opens up opportunities. Do not be a prisoner of your own national culture.

2.4. Launching your own entrepreneurial venture involves a simple three-step action plan: Create an entrepreneurial culture, get a bit of money, and acquire the knowledge to create a service or product for which people will pay.

Chapter 3

H. Irving Grousbeck: Demystifying Entrepreneurship

I feel deeply about taking the high road, doing the right thing, and treating people fairly. This is extraordinarily important to me. In many business schools today, there is too much focus on the content and teaching of entrepreneurship and not enough emphasis on thinking about living your life.

—Irving Grousbeck[1]

Introduction to H. Irving Grousbeck

Name	H. Irving Grousbeck
Title	MBA Class of 1980 Consulting Professor of Management; Codirector of the Center for Entrepreneurial Studies
Affiliation(s)	Stanford University Graduate, School of Business
Education	AB, Amherst College (1956)MBA, Harvard University (1960) Doctor of Humane Letters (Hon.), Amherst College (2000)

Experience	○ Cofounder, Continental Cablevision, Inc., 1964; President, 1964–80; Chairman, 1980–85 ○ Currently on the Board of Directors of Alta Colleges, Inc., and Asurion Corporation
Notable Publications	○ *New Business Ventures and the Entrepreneur, 5th Ed.* (Irwin, 1999) ○ Numerous Stanford teaching cases
Website(s)	*gsbapps.stanford.edu/facultybios/bio.asp?ID=53*

Biographical Highlights

⊙ Grousbeck was a cofounder of Continental Cablevision, Inc., which became the third-largest cable company in the United States. He served as president of the company from 1964 to 1980, and as chairman of the board of directors from 1980 to 1985. The company sold to US WEST Media Group in November 1996, for more than $11 billion.

⊙ He has been a director of Asurion (the largest provider of wireless roadside assistance services in North America) since its inception in 1995. The company, which now has 6,000 employees and has a projected $1.3 billion in revenue for 2007, was founded by two of Grousbeck's former students.

⊙ He is the codirector of the Center for Entrepreneurial Studies (founded in 1996) at Stanford Business School.

⊙ Grousbeck teaches one of the most popular courses at Stanford Business School, "Managing Growing Enterprises," in which featured entrepreneurs participate in classroom discussion.

⊙ He is one of four comanaging partners and 19 limited partners who purchased the Boston Celtics basketball team for $360 million in 2002.

Silicon Valley, Stanford, and Grousbeck

For many people, the term *Silicon Valley* conjures up images of leading high-tech companies in hardware development, software creation, or Internet-related advances. The name is so well known, in fact, that it has become a figure of speech: In Canada, Vancouver claims to be "the Silicon Valley of the North," and on the East Coast of the United States, New York refers to its high-tech hub as "Silicon Alley."

But, the epicenter of the original Silicon Valley has an even more monumental claim to fame: It is the location of Stanford University, an elite school that pulses with the life-giving blood of the world's high-tech revolution. Numerous high-tech stars have received training and made key connections in this cauldron of creativity. Stanford's campus has birthed companies such as Hewlett-Packard, Sun Microsystems, Silicon Graphics, Cisco Systems, Yahoo, eBay, and Google. Would there be a Silicon Valley without Stanford University? Perhaps, but it definitely wouldn't look the same.

In 1996, the Graduate School of Business at Stanford established the Center for Entrepreneurial Studies (CES), not only to teach students, but also to "provide resources for students and alumni embarking on entrepreneurial ventures" and "establish relationships with the local entrepreneurial community."[2] The CES is not merely an instructional resource; it is a proactive force in the Silicon Valley community. According to *Fortune Small Business,* "Stanford feeds the new [high-tech & internet] economy a steady stream of engineers, lawyers, bankers, and moguls-in-training," and the magazine goes on to say, "At the heart of the academic machine is H. Irving Grousbeck."[3]

Grousbeck, the codirector of the CES, has helped lead many high-tech businesses to success. With strong ethical convictions, and a passion for teaching, he seeks to take business education to an entirely new level. Moreover, he appreciates Silicon Valley's unique concentration of expertise to launch high-tech endeavors.

Grousbeck explains, "[In Silicon Valley,] there is undoubtedly a symbiosis that occurs between all of the elements that contribute to entrepreneurial formation: the banking system, the subordinated debt market, the angel capital market, and the abundance of entrepreneurs—who are, in effect, pathfinders for others who say, 'If they can do it, so can I.'"[4] He points out that Silicon Valley features an abundance of human resources available for advice and guidance, economic resources for high-tech financing, and an overwhelming amount of talented technology employees. He notes, "There are so many successful high-tech entrepreneurs available—as opposed to any other area in the U.S.—that the experience of learning first-hand is invaluable."[5]

Stanford itself plays a role in the life of Silicon Valley. Grousbeck teaches "Managing Growing Enterprises," a popular course at the business school that prepares graduates for real-world situations. Grousbeck also believes strongly in the role of the Center for Entrepreneurial Studies (CES) of catalyst and matchmaker: its extensive database of entrepreneurs and service providers introduces students to critical connections. Yet, in keeping with Grousbeck's customary modesty, he adds, "There are many companies formed in Silicon Valley that have nothing to do with Stanford, so I don't want to overstate our role."[6]

Is there anything unique about the CES at Stanford that sets it apart from other entrepreneurial programs? Grousbeck recognizes that what Stanford does likely exists in whole or in part elsewhere.[7] However, one of the CES's distinctive facets is its emphasis on having students rethink their understanding of business risk. According to Grousbeck, one societal misconception of entrepreneurs, often reflected by the freshman class at his business school, is that entrepreneurs are inveterate risk-takers.[8] Grousbeck's antidote is to present entrepreneurs as, in fact, risk-adverse. He explains, "We encourage people to be very thoughtful and cautious, and to shrink risk out of a situation as much as possible by assembling the best team, getting the best backing, and leaving themselves as much of a cushion as they can."[9] The objective, in Grousbeck's words, is to develop "cautious entrepreneurs." He admits this "may sound paradoxical and even dysfunctional, in the sense that entrepreneurs are supposed to be bold."[10] However, "we don't want to take the boldness out of the picture, but we want them to be risk-sensitive. We want them to say to themselves, 'What risks am I taking here that I don't need to take?'"[11] The goal is for future entrepreneurs to significantly reduce manageable risks, not for them to fear the risks they have no control over.

In short, Grousbeck believes an informed view of risk is essential for an aspiring entrepreneur.

3.1 Demystifying Entrepreneurship

> One can illumine the process of entrepreneurship by modeling the five core attitudes of successful entrepreneurs and understanding fundamental business issues.

Many entrepreneurs are in search of one "holy grail": the secret to becoming rich, self-sufficient, and personally fulfilled. They read about others achieving their goals, attaining considerable renown, and acquiring indescribable wealth, and they ask themselves how they, too, can scale those same heights of success. Unfortunately, there is no simple formula—what worked for one entrepreneur, at one place and point in time, is not easily replicated. Some entrepreneurs attempt to model previous successes, but changing market conditions dump them on the trash heap of the economic landscape.

Thus, entrepreneurship remains shrouded in mystery. Akin to an archaeologist digging through centuries of rubble, a curious entrepreneur can piece together parts of the process; however, even after a lifetime of excavation, the complete picture is still unintelligible. That being said, the following pieces of advice are comparable to artifacts, each offering clues about a much larger reality. Interestingly, you will notice these insights surfacing in other chapters as well.

One component of demystifying entrepreneurship is to identify commonalities among successful entrepreneurs. Grousbeck identifies five attitudes that, as he has observed, often accompany success:

1. First, accomplished entrepreneurs demonstrate "an unending dissatisfaction with the status quo."[12] The entrepreneur thinks he or she can do something better than the way it is being done at present; in other words, he or she pursues opportunity through change.

2. Second, an entrepreneur must have "a healthy self-confidence."[13] Grousbeck explains that an entrepreneur must be "willing to be lonely, to make tough

decisions, to stand on a level of the organization chart with no peers, and to have the buck stop with him/her."[14]

3. Third, an entrepreneur must be good at what he or she does; Grousbeck calls this "reasonable competence."[15] Without skill or talent, an entrepreneur will have difficulty assembling a team and launching a venture.

4. A fourth beneficial attitude is "concern for detail."[16] Although some entrepreneurs are big thinkers and visionaries, they always have someone looking after the details.

5. Fifth, an adept entrepreneur must have a "tolerance for ambiguity";[17] in other words, he or she must be willing to accept an uncertain future. After all, not every venture succeeds, and rarely does one evolve according to plan. Grousbeck clarifies, however, that being comfortable with ambiguity is not the same as accepting unnecessary risk.[18]

Grousbeck not only teaches these attitudes; he lives them. Amherst College, when awarding Grousbeck an honorary Doctorate of Humane Letters, told Grousbeck that the five attitudes were "a self-description as well, one that has led you [Grousbeck] to the heights of both business and education."[19] As his life shows, these five attitudes are a starting point for success in the entrepreneurial process.

Another component of demystifying entrepreneurship is to understand the fundamental issues of money and timing. First, with respect to money, Grousbeck teaches that the functions of the entrepreneur and the capital provider are very different.[20] According to Grousbeck, don't bring your own money to your new venture. He and his cofounder each provided $3,500 to found Continental Cablevision in 1964; these personal resources were then supplemented by $650,000 in bank and investor financing. (See Section 3.2.) Grousbeck states that an entrepreneur who relies on his own money for launching a venture typically puts a ceiling on ambition, because "one tends to define the scope of one's venture by the size of one's pocketbook."[21]

With respect to timing, Grousbeck warns, "An entrepreneur may need to live for six months to two years without any income while his or her idea is being market-tested and perfected."[22] In other words, an entrepreneur must figure out how to buy some time—and shouldn't plan on instant success. Furthermore, Grousbeck notes that careful analysis is part of the equation: "Analysis is not something to be left at the doorstep; rather, it is a critical element in optimizing the odds of entrepreneurial success."[23]

3.2 High-Tech vs. Low-Tech Approaches to Entrepreneurship

The five core attitudes of successful entrepreneurs apply equally to high-tech and low-tech (or no-tech) sectors of business.

The five core attitudes of successful entrepreneurs described in Section 3.1 apply generally to the entrepreneurial process, rather than to a particular sector. As a result, whether a business is high-tech or low-tech, the pathway to nurturing a high growth company is similar. Interestingly enough, although Grousbeck lives in Silicon Valley, his particular focus is not high technology. Instead, he is much more interested in service companies and low-tech or no-tech companies.

His cable company is a prime example. Cofounded with classmate Amos Hostetter, the company began as "little more than an antenna service to boost local TV signals that lost strength outside cities," according to the *Harvard Business School Bulletin.*[24] Customers originally received a meager 10 channels. But the company's growth shocked even its founders, expanding to service 117,000 customers by 1974.[25] As mentioned earlier, it became the third-largest cable company in the United States. Yet Grousbeck notes that the cable business is "not really a high-tech business. The technology was and is very simple."[26] He recounts that the five attitudes he teaches his high-tech students applied to his profitable low-tech venture as well.

Of the many thriving high-tech companies in Silicon Valley, Grousbeck chose to mention eBay as an example of entrepreneurial success. Self-described as "The World's Online Marketplace,"[27] the company has more than 100 million registered users. In addition, eBay currently has approximately $4 billion in revenue and a market capitalization of $54 billion, and its five-year growth has averaged 59.5 percent.[28]

The cofounders of eBay are Pierre Omidyar and Jeff Skoll. Skoll had previously founded his own systems consulting firm and a personal computer rental company, but he sold both businesses and enrolled at Stanford Business School in 1993. After graduation he joined Knight-Ridder, but became frustrated when the company failed to grasp the potential of his internet-related initiatives.[29]

Meanwhile, Pierre Omidyar had founded Auction Web as a sole proprietorship while employed elsewhere. Skoll and Omidyar, who had known each other since 1995, resigned from their jobs in the summer of 2006 to develop Auction Web together. The Stanford Case Study on eBay explains their division of labor: "Omidyar focused all his efforts on developing the technology and systems infrastructure. Skoll focused on the business plan, strategy, and recruiting personnel."[30]

In January 1997, Auction Web recorded monthly transactions valued at $2.5 million and revenues of $165,000 (up 80 percent from the prior month). The budding opportunity required capital and in June 1997, Omidyar and Skoll concluded a deal whereby Benchmark Capital invested $5 million in exchange for 20 percent of the company. This funding allowed Omidyar and Skoll to fortify their management team: In February 1998, they hired Meg Whitman as president and CEO, a position she retains to this day.

Skoll continued to focus on building the strategy team, eventually hiring former Stanford classmate Reed Maltzman as a key contributor. Another milestone for Skoll and Omidyar was August 18, 1998, when the company (which, obviously, changed its name from Auction Web to eBay) completed its Initial Public Offering and raised $63 million by selling 9 percent of its stock. The IPO was priced at $18 per share, and by December 1999, the stock was trading at $63 per share. The total market capitalization within only three years of starting eBay was approximately $8 billion. Of course, the dotcom crash of March 2000 was just around the corner. The company lost 80 percent of its market value during 2000, despite being consistently profitable since inception. Nonetheless, eBay has long since bounced back.

Skoll is one of Grousbeck's former students, and they have remained in contact through the years.[31] Does Skoll have the presence of a high tech dynamo? Well...not really.

Grousbeck muses, "He is a very interesting personality. If you put him on stage without an introduction, and asked him to say a few words, and then asked the audience what his profession was, they would likely say librarian or accountant. He is very studious-looking—with glasses, slightly bent over, very unassuming and understated."[32] But that is only what one sees on the outside. Grouse continues, "He has a drive and a vision that have become palpable."[33]

Skoll clearly demonstrates the attitudes of a successful entrepreneur: dissatisfaction with the status quo (leaving a company that underrated his Internet initiatives), competence (prior experience), confidence (willing to go out on his own), and contentment with ambiguity (working through the challenges of setting up a business on the rapidly evolving Web).

In short, Grousbeck teaches that entrepreneurs with the right perspective can succeed in both low-tech and high-tech businesses. One's application of proper attitudes is more important than his or her degree of technological sophistication.

Investment Group Buys Boston Celtics[34]

As noted earlier, Grousbeck is one of four managing partners and 19 limited partners who acquired the Boston Celtics for $360 million on December 31, 2002. The Celtics have won 16 NBA championships and are one of the most storied franchises in professional sports. One of the other managing partners is Grousbeck's son, Wycliffe.

According to Wycliffe, he and his father "had wanted to buy a sports team starting in the 1980s, but couldn't find an opportunity in which they would have a chance to field a winning team and not lose their shirts. The Celtics earn above-average revenues year after year, because the team has been good and the fans are fanatical."

From a financial standpoint, Wycliffe claims that, even in a losing year, the revenues more than cover interest payments on a $180 million loan. Grousbeck estimates that investors will earn 10–12 percent annually over the long term; while the payoff may not be substantial, most investors bought in because of their interest in the sport.

3.3 The Entrepreneurial High Road

Individuals should pursue entrepreneurship by taking the "high road": acting in an ethical fashion and taking a long-term view by asking how they want to be remembered at the end of their lives.

If "ethics" is simply another course in a business curriculum, or one more item on an executive's to-do list, it is a futile undertaking. Just as planting a seed in rocky soil is a futile endeavor, so also ethical behavior won't take root in people who are content to follow the easiest course. Thus, the process of teaching ethicality in business involves cultivating and encouraging students' character, motivating them to make sacrifices for the sake of maintaining integrity.

In recognition of this challenge, Grousbeck's book, *New Business Ventures and the Entrepreneur,* does not have one specific chapter on ethics, as other leading books do.[35] Instead, he has found that "ethics is more effectively taught when it is interwoven into what appears to be a for-profit discussion."[36] Rather than segregating ethics from the rest of business practice, and confining it to one lesson or class, Grousbeck tries to incorporate it throughout his teaching. Thus, in the middle of describing a typical business situation to his class, he will "introduce and integrate an element of what is fair, what is right, and what is reasonable."[37] He stresses, "The importance of ethics is woven into every class of mine."[38] In his opinion, the alternative—"Let's put on our white hats and come to the ethical solution"[39]—is much less effective.

"I am a strong preacher in my class," Grousbeck avers. "One of my faults is that I get up on the soapbox."[40] He addresses the matter of ethics in entrepreneurship from a broader perspective: "I feel deeply about taking the high road, doing the right thing, and treating people fairly. This is extraordinarily important to me. In many business schools today, there is too much focus on the content and teaching of entrepreneurship and not enough emphasis on thinking about living your life."[41]

An entrepreneur faces a unique ethical challenge, in contrast to the typical manager, because he or she is an owner or significant shareholder of the company. Grousbeck contrasts a manager/ administrator, who may be focused on a salary and bonus, with an entrepreneur, who can earn a large return on the overall growth of a company.[42] The entrepreneur's potential for reward is much greater—and thus the temptation to cut corners ethically is also more of an issue. Of course, recent financial scandals indicate that many top executives (with huge pay packages) seek primarily to earn a large return, regardless of the method through which that occurs.

The entrepreneur also sets the culture for the organization, including its approach to ethical issues. If "a fish stinks from the head down," as the popular saying goes, then the lead entrepreneur's ethical shortcomings (or ethical virtues) will emanate to the rest of the company. In Grousbeck's opinion, "It has to do with span of control and influence. The founder who is still running a company has the ability to exert far more influence than one of the members of the executive team. When it's your company, you are building the team—you're setting the tone, deciding who gets hired—and the infusion of culture initially stems from you."[43]

He recommends clarifying to employees that "in this company there is only one way we do business, and that is from the top of the deck. If you are not sure whether something is right or wrong, it's probably wrong."[44] He would also advise employees to rely on the common measuring stick: "Imagine how you would feel if your actions appeared as a headline in tomorrow's newspaper."[45] Moreover, a company should have clear guidelines that reinforce the importance of ethical behavior: "We will fire you the minute we find that you are doing something unethical, regardless of whether or not it is immediately profitable."[46]

In Grousbeck's view, ethics interlock with a balanced life. "I try not to be too preachy," he remarks, "but I attempt to introduce issues of life balance and what's fair to all parties in a particular situation. Have you thought about the people with whom you are negotiating? Have you considered not only what's fair to you, but also what is fair to them? Trying to introduce some principles of ethics is necessary for me. I just have to do that."[47] As his questions suggest, an ethical person instinctively pursues fairness, which shows in personal relationships; thus, an ethical person seeks to succeed in business, but not at the expense of others.

But how does an ethical, balanced approach relate to the success of an entrepreneur? Grousbeck concedes that, though there may be many entrepreneurship educators who teach students to simply stay within the bounds of the law, "that does not do it for me."[48]

The recent "spirituality at work" or "God in the workplace" trend—the idea that the "whole person" comes to work, where he or she spends the bulk of his or her time, and thus that a search for spiritual meaning and fulfillment should occur in the workplace—is an idea Grousbeck regards with justifiable skepticism. In his opinion, an entrepreneur or employee should "set aside his or her own set of beliefs" and establish or maintain the company policy of acting in a fair and equitable manner.[49] Grousbeck definitely supports a balanced, ethical approach, but he notes, "I am not going to substantiate my position by referring to the tenets of the Koran, the Bible, or some other text."[50]

Yet his business practices are by no means devoid of personal reflection. He tells his students to look at their businesses in the context of what their lives are about. They need to think deeply from a long-term perspective. "You're now 28 years old," he challenges. "Are you going to be happy as a partner at McKinsey & Co. or Goldman Sachs? Or do you need something else to be fulfilled in your work? Because if you are just punching the time clock and you can't wait to get home, it's going to reverberate through all facets of your life.... You should figure out what will give you satisfaction."[51]

According to Grousbeck, the type of business career a person wishes to pursue "does not have anything to do with spirituality—but it has a lot to do with entrepreneurship. In other words," he states, "it has a lot to do with entrepreneurship being related to meaning in life, but not religious meaning in life."[52] In other words, a person's motivation for seeking meaning in life, whether from a particular religious belief or not, does not directly impact the entrepreneurial process itself. Grousbeck explains that an entrepreneur should be involved in a business that he or she finds meaningful and that is significant to him or her, above and beyond simply earning a living.

As an example, Grousbeck mentions one of the most inspiring entrepreneurs he has come to know personally: a woman named Rosemary Jordano, who runs a backup daycare company called ChildrenFirst (*www.childrenfirst.com*; based in Boston, Massachusetts). If a professional, such as a lawyer, has a child who is sick and cannot attend school on a certain day, the lawyer can take his or her child to this daycare facility—which is conveniently located in the lawyer's workplace—and ensure that the child receives proper care and attention. The lawyer can then check on his or her child throughout the day, without leaving work.

Grousbeck observes, "Rosemary, an MBA 89, is a woman of great commitment to children. She wanted to start a for-profit business around taking care of children, so she developed this concept. The company is not making a big splash—yet—but it is located in several cities in the United States. Rosemary has been very successful at it; her combination of successful business practice and positive social contribution is very inspiring."[53] He goes on, "It's not Google, but it is not designed to be Google."[54] In other words, taking the high road may mean starting a business that may not be the most profitable option available, but makes a positive impact on society. At the same time, as Jordano's company proves, the venture can still be growth-oriented and financially successful.

Another inspiring entrepreneur Grousbeck mentions is Jeff Skoll (see Section 3.2), who inspired eBay to take an active role in philanthropy in 1998 by establishing the eBay Foundation through the allocation of pre-IPO shares. In 1999, he created the Skoll Foundation, which "takes an entrepreneurial approach to philanthropy, seeking out and empowering the world's most promising social entrepreneurs in order to effect lasting, positive social change worldwide."[55] Skoll has devoted a considerable amount of his time to charitable causes.

Using Jordano and Skoll's examples, Grousbeck asks his students, "When you are 60 years old and looking back on your life, what are you going to remember? If you treated people with the back of your hand, that is going to be hard to live down, unless you are completely insensitive."[56] He tries to appeal to students by saying, "[Behaving ethically] is the right thing to do," and if that doesn't impact an individual, then he urges him/her, "[Act ethically] on the basis that you will regret it at the end of your life [if you don't]."[57] Grousbeck's most important piece of wisdom for an aspiring entrepreneur is, "Associate with good people, and maintain a high-quality team and high ethical standards."[58]

ChildrenFirst: The Leader in Corporate-Sponsored Backup Childcare

ChildrenFirst was founded by Rosemary Jordano in 1992. The company's mission is a result of her academic research at Wellesley College and Oxford University, for which she visited children in a variety of settings and witnessed an opportunity to advance the quality of care children received. ChildrenFirst was founded to address these needs and deliver quality for working parents, children, and employers.

Jordano's company manages the largest and highest-quality network of dedicated backup childcare centers. A form of business interruption insurance, ChildrenFirst reduces absenteeism, offers back-to-work assistance, protects employee productivity, enhances retention and recruiting, promotes the advancement of women, and assists with the company goal to "Make Your Firm an Employer of Choice."

ChildrenFirst serves the employees of more than 260 leading companies, and working parents have utilized its dedicated centers more than 500,000 times since its opening in 1992.

Jordano founded the nation's first and largest network of backup childcare centers, one that also has a reputation for the highest quality care available. She pioneered the concept and offers memberships to a consortium of businesses—regardless of employee size. Through her dedication to hiring quality professionals and designing state-of-the-art center environments, she has set new industry standards of excellence in the care and early education of children.

Grousbeck's Key Points

3.1. One can illumine the process of entrepreneurship by modeling the five core attitudes of successful entrepreneurs and understanding fundamental business issues.

3.2. The five core attitudes of successful entrepreneurs apply equally to high-tech and low-tech (or no-tech) sectors of business.

3.3. Individuals should pursue entrepreneurship by taking the "high road": acting in an ethical fashion and taking a long-term view by asking how they want to be remembered at the end of their lives.

Chapter 4

Tom Hockaday: From Idea to Opportunity

You don't make money out of technology—you make money out of a business that successfully commercializes technology.

—Tom Hockaday[1]

Author's Note: I have included Tom Hockaday in this book because of his practical expertise in technology transfer. Though he has not published extensive academic writings on entrepreneurship, his position, qualifications, and experience speak for themselves. This chapter is based not only on my interviews with Hockaday, but also on several supplementary sources. I provide a general introduction on ideas and opportunities within an entrepreneurial context. I have also incorporated comments from published interviews with Tim Cook, deputy chairman of Isis, and Kevin Matthews, CEO of Oxonica (an Isis spin-off company featured in the chapter). Throughout the chapter, I attempt to clearly delineate Hockaday's comments from those of myself and others.

Introduction to Tom Hockaday

Name	Tom Hockaday
Title	Managing Director
Affiliation(s)	Isis Innovation Ltd., University of Oxford
Education	B.A. (Hons.), King's College (London)
Experience	o University College, London (1989–93) o Managing Director, Bristol Innovations Ltd., Bristol University (1993–2000) o Director of Special Projects, Isis Innovation Ltd. (2000–06) o Managing Director, Isis (2006–present) o Chairman, UNICO, the United Kingdom's university technology transfer association (2003)
Website(s)	*www.isis-innovation.com*

Biographical Highlights

- Since 1989, Hockaday has focused on the "twilight zone" (as he describes it) between university research and business.

- Hockaday on job satisfaction: "Taking early stage technology and trying to get that technology applied and used in a positive way is quite satisfying."[2]

- Tim Cook, Deputy Chairman of Isis, on Tom Hockaday: "Tom built up Tech Transfer in Bristol over seven years from 'nothing' to 'quite good'... As Mr. Technology Transfer in Bristol, he had a high reputation in the national professional network of technology transfer."[3]

- Since 1997 (Hockaday has been involved since 2000), Isis has launched 57 spin-out companies and only three have gone bankrupt—an impressive 95-percent success rate for launching start-up ventures.

Introduction: The University of Oxford Model of Technology Transfer

How can researchers, toiling away in a laboratory in the ivory towers of the academic world, successfully convert discoveries to marketable products? This question is also relevant in a broader context: How do nascent entrepreneurs prudently determine whether or not markets exist for their ideas? The researcher and the nascent entrepreneur both face the same challenge. A valuable research-based invention—whether a product, medication, or service—may be a necessary starting point, but it won't guarantee the successful launch of a new venture.

Often researchers and prospective entrepreneurs do not understand the vital distinction between an idea and an opportunity. They come up with a brilliant cure, or a new product, and they assume people will respond with overwhelming interest. This is the so-called "mouse trap fallacy": believing that, as Ralph Waldo Emerson once said, "If you...build a better mouse trap, the world will beat a path to your door."[4] Such thinking has falsely enticed many individuals into bold new ventures, only to leave them bankrupt and confused. Then they realize that success requires much more than a good idea.

One would expect that the University of Oxford's researchers, compared to those at other educational institutions in the world, would be among the most well-situated to prosper in the marketplace. (I subsequently refer to the University of Oxford as either "Oxford" or the "University.") Oxford's prestigious international reputation alone would provide an invention with a patina of initial credibility. Yet even a good idea, supplemented by institutional credibility, must have market interest to move from a laboratory to a store shelf. This process is more complicated than inventors—whether at Oxford or elsewhere—may anticipate.

In order to understand the transition from idea to business opportunity at Oxford, a historical overview of the University and its technology transfer program provides important contextual information.

Oxford was founded in 1167. The first example of transferring research knowledge from the University and bringing it in a practical way to the marketplace—the process of "commercialization"—involved printing technology: Oxford published its first book, the Bible, in 1478.[5] Since then, printing has become a critical component of the University's identity. Oxford University Press is a flag-bearer of the institution's brand name, and, with a presence in more than 50 countries, is the largest university press in the world.[6] In fact, Oxford University Press owns the trademark for the word *Oxford*.[7] Consequently, any new venture that wishes to use the word *Oxford* in its name (and is launched by an Oxford researcher) requires permission from the Oxford University Press.

Despite the long history of commercialization at Oxford, however, the University was not able to exploit its academic base of world-leading research expertise until the Margaret Thatcher era of 1979 to 1990, when the British government began to privatize many state-owned industries.[8] Thus, in 1988, the University established a wholly owned technology transfer company under the name Isis Innovation Ltd. (referred to as "Isis" in these pages).

Tom Hockaday, a native of the town of Oxford, joined Isis in 2000 as director of special projects, and he has been managing director since 2006. Hockaday lives in an 18th-century farmhouse with a large garden 20 miles north of Oxford. The views are fantastic and it provides a respite from the daily stresses of work and life. The entire Isis team consists of about 40 individuals; Hockaday has seven members reporting directly to him. He enjoys the camaraderie of the team and believes that "good people do good things; better people do them even better."[9] Hockaday notes that Isis has had an "absolutely enormous" positive impact on Oxford so far.[10] One of the benefits of his position is that he on speaking engagements from Europe, North America, and Asia talking about technology transfer.

The role of Isis is to manage "the University's intellectual property portfolio, working with University researchers on identifying, protecting, and marketing technologies."[11] These tasks are significant, as the research foundation of the University encompasses 4,200 researchers and 6,700 doctoral students in life sciences, physical sciences, social sciences, and humanities.[12] Isis provides these accomplished individuals with "commercial advice" and "funds patent applications and legal costs, negotiates exploitation and spin-out[13] company agreements, and identifies and manages consultancy opportunities."[14] In other words, Isis effectively acts as a new-venture incubator for its researchers.

After valuable research is identified, Isis will then decide which of three different means of commercialization is most suitable: licensing, launching a spin-out, or a material sales agreement. First, Isis may license a technology to companies who will invest in developing and selling that technology. This is a straightforward route to the marketplace when a company that can effectively use the technology already exists. Isis selects companies as license partners based on their resources and intentions for technology development in the market, as well as their commitment to developing products or technologies in a timely and ethical manner. For example, with respect to ethics in the healthcare sector, Isis licensees must ensure that final products are accessible and affordable in developing countries.

Second, Isis may create a spin-out company. When there are no available license partners, as the research may be in a field with few established firms (or the existing firms may have different strategic priorities), then Isis determines if the value of the research warrants the establishment of a spin-out. Because this process, as opposed to other forms of research advancement, requires Isis to commit resources, it presents the potential for greater upside— and risk—for both the researcher and the University.

Thirdly, Isis may simply engage in "material sales." In such an instance, licensing or starting a spin-out may not be practical options. Instead, Isis may simply negotiate a straightforward sales agreement for materials developed within the University (such as biological and physical science materials). This is the lowest-risk proposition for Isis, as it merely involves the sale of a researcher's product for a specified price. Isis has previously entered into materials sales related to discoveries of antibodies and protein complexes.

In terms of deciding which of the three commercialization routes to pursue, Hockaday describes it "as the art of the possible"—the market will determine what can be achieved.[15] Isis reviews approximately 150 "new invention disclosures" per year,[16] and overall sis has deftly used the three forms of commercialization to produce impressive results. Since 1997, Isis has been responsible for more than 200 licensing agreements, the creation of 57 spin-out companies (including Oxonica plc, highlighted in Section 4.3), and several materials agreements. There have been two phases in the short history of Isis. The first phase began in 1987, when the British government transferred the rights to university research away from an organization called National Research and Development Corp. (now called the British Technology Group) and into the hands of the universities themselves (as mentioned earlier). Hockaday notes that "the Conservative government [led by Margaret Thatcher] was very keen to create a climate to stimulate venture capital," and this government impetus coalesced with universities' increasing interest in commercializing the fruits of their labor.[17]

Despite this favorable climate, Isis received minimal University support from 1987 to 1997. Isis had three employees during this time, and essentially covered its costs based on revenues of £300,000 per year from the Oxford Innovation Society (roughly $608,000). The Oxford Innovation Society, founded in 1990 to enable industrial companies to have a window on scientific developments, was able to generate revenue as a matchmaking service between industry and the University.

The second phase of Isis runs from 1997 to the present. During the course of these years, Oxford has seized the opportunity of commercializing research in a prudent manner by gradually increasing its funding of Isis. With respect to profitability, Tim Cook, Deputy Chairman of Isis, comments, "I think the University got back [during the past 10 years] about ten times what [it] invested. Funding Isis is a good thing for the University to do."[18]

Hockaday explained in a U.S. Library of Congress presentation that the main objective of Isis "is to transfer technology out of the university into industry, and…in light of our base of research at Oxford, [to] make money while doing so."[19] The results are strikingly apparent: In 2006 alone, Isis filed 57 new priority patent applications, adding to a portfolio of more than 400 "patent families" (the international patents that derive from the first priority filing). Isis also concluded seven material agreements in 2006, and launched six spin-outs.

Today, other universities across England have followed Oxford's example by starting similar technology transfer offices[20] to commercialize their research. These offices, similar to Isis, endeavor to ensure an equitable outcome for the researchers, the university, and outside investors.

4.1 Ideas and Opportunities

> The starting point to consider converting an "idea" into an "opportunity" is when a researcher—and, indeed, any entrepreneur—has a patentable and unique discovery that meets a need in society. This process, known as commercialization, will be successful when supported by an "entrepreneurial culture," an effective technology transfer mechanism, and endorsement from professional and financial advisors.

Every new venture starts with a kernel: an idea. The idea may involve a new way of delivering a service or manufacturing goods, or it may advance the field of medicine. Though this chapter focuses on ideas generated by Oxford researchers, the processes discussed—which separate the wheat from the chaff and prepare start-ups to wrestle with the challenges of a fast-moving marketplace—apply to the entrepreneurial process generally.

In the Oxford context, researchers explore unique aspects of the life sciences, physical sciences, social sciences, and humanities. All research output in these various fields of inquiry must undergo a careful and painstaking analysis to determine if it has any possible commercial benefit. Examiners ask a basic question: Can any of this research be converted to a product that consumers will pay for?

Entrepreneurial writings are rife with discussions that highlight the need to distinguish between ideas and opportunities.[21] An *idea* is a discovery or invention with unknown potential, whereas an *opportunity* is something that, upon due diligence, demonstrates a reasonable likelihood of undergoing successful commercialization. As noted earlier, not every bit of great research is an opportunity: A novel and very interesting discovery may be of no value in the marketplace.

With that in mind, the first step in an idea's successful exploitation—whether through licensing, a spin-out, or material sales—is to patent the idea. This method of legally protecting an invention is the basis for a competitive advantage in the marketplace (though it does not guarantee success). The key concept underlying patent law in both the United Kingdom and the United States is that legal protection is granted for a novel way of doing something.[22] According to the U.S. Patent and Trademark Office, Utility patents (which would apply to the present discussion) "may be granted to anyone who invents or discovers any new and useful process, machine, article of manufacture, or composition of matter, or any new and useful improvement thereof."[23] Thus, determining whether or not an idea is patentable provides a starting point for deciding if the researcher's product is unique and fills a need in the marketplace. Another litmus test is to estimate an idea's commercial value based on its exclusivity: is it one of the only ways to accomplish a certain task?

Based on such considerations, technology transfer offices will decide which ideas to develop further. Along those lines, Larry Farrell (featured in Chapter 2) stresses that an entrepreneur's foremost concern should be his venture's consumer appeal: Who will buy the product, and why? In other words, patentability reflects potential success by highlighting the strength (or weakness) of the link between the product and the consumer.

Isis works closely with the Research Services Department of the University, and all grants and contracts go through that office. From there, Hockaday and his multidisciplinary team at Isis work with researchers to decide if the researchers' advancements are capable of commercialization. In fact, Hockaday's main goal is to identify discoveries or inventions that will have market appeal. However, based out of a university context, Isis's policy is also to bring a wide range of research successfully to the market—not just the research that will presumably generate the greatest return (which, in any event, would be difficult to determine at an early juncture).

So, in view of the challenges outlined, how does Isis create an infrastructure among stakeholders that can support the process of commercializing University research output? Isis has developed three structural elements that assist researchers involved with its program.[24] First, Isis strives to maintain a "university entrepreneur culture," challenging the entire Oxford community to see the practical value of research for the marketplace. Isis encourages researchers to not only pursue research, but also to make it available to a much broader community. The University entrepreneurial culture manifests itself through Isis's economic incentives, which are given for expended effort in fields of research with clear commercial applications.

Secondly, Isis seeks to provide Oxford's researchers with an effective technology transfer mechanism. Just as Isis must have confidence in the quality of Oxford's researchers, so also must the researchers believe that Isis can give their ideas the best possible chance of commercialization. Therefore, a critical and final component of infrastructure for successful commercialization is the endorsement of external parties. To that end, Isis attempts to connect researchers with the business community; unless external financiers are prepared to invest in the research, the commercialization effort is for naught. All three aspects of the identified infrastructure are necessary for successfully taking an idea and turning it into an opportunity.

4.2 Guidelines for Successfully Starting a New Venture (Spin-Out)

> The successful commercialization of research by way of a spin-out requires committed and sustained effort by the researcher, and demands a range of services from Isis. Moreover, the researcher must work cooperatively with Isis and other stakeholders in order to overcome inevitable challenges.

Cigarette packs have a prominent label indicating that the product inside may cause cancer and have other ill effects. Similarly, Isis's guideline booklet called "Starting a Spin-out Company" (which I refer to in shorthand as "Spin-out Guide" in this chapter) offers a "health warning" for those interested in tackling the process of commercialization: "Setting up a spin-out is a stressful activity and will distract you from your research. You will need to work with business managers and investors whose objectives may be very different from your own."[25]

Isis devotes considerable resources to each particular opportunity it assesses and therefore does not wish to proceed down the arduous path to commercialization if the researcher is not fully committed. This is comparable to any entrepreneurial venture:

If the founder does not truly believe in the start-up's potential, then there is limited scope for success. Thus, in light of the pivotal role of the researcher, Isis not only requires upfront commitment, but also facilitates ongoing motivation by ensuring that the researcher has appropriate expectations.

Furthermore, because the process of commercialization involves a range of Isis team members, researchers must be able to work well with other people. Hockaday understands that researchers and market-driven advisors have very different mindsets, and notes that researchers must be willing to adapt accordingly.

Hockaday describes many of the academic people he works with as extremely focused: "They are brilliant researchers, because they set out on a path to do really good research in a university context."[26] These individuals likely decided early in their careers that the university was their "preferred working environment," and they found success by following the conventional path within that environment.[27] Hockaday explains, "People succeed in [the university context] by doing good research, publishing good research, being thorough, and being meticulous. They generally climb up the university promotions ladder through very high quality publications and [strong] teaching."[28]

These personal habits and skills cultivate excellent ideas, but often bog down the process of commercialization. Hockaday sums up the essential dilemma, stating, "The challenge is that you have technologies and research outputs developed by brilliant researchers on the one hand, and you have the business world on the other hand. You then have to integrate people from each environment with one another."[29] This is a quintessential entrepreneurial dilemma when bringing new technologies to market: Researchers and inventors are rarely able to successfully commercialize their own products. Thus, both the researchers and the facilitators of commercialization must embrace the challenge of working together. Unfortunately, because of the striking differences between entrepreneurial and academic mindsets, researchers may be frustrated that (as Hockaday said in his warning) they are working with "business managers and investors whose objectives may be very different from [their] own."[30]

Tim Cook (mentioned earlier in the chapter) provides another perspective on working with researchers. He notes, "Commercialization will only work if academics want to do it."[31] According to his observations, Isis deems a project attractive only if it is "a function of the strength of the science" and the academic is cooperative in the commercialization process.[32] This may seem odd, but anyone with entrepreneurial experience knows that the negative disposition of a key inventor or researcher can undermine even the most promising products.

As markers for whether or not Isis should enter into time-intensive, complex, and stressful undertakings with specific researchers, Cook asks some basic questions about the researchers' personalities: "Do they turn up on time for meetings? Do they have any embarrassing personal characteristics that will alienate licensees [or investors]? Do they want to work with us?"[33] These questions reveal critical character strengths or flaws in the researcher.

Clearly, Isis cannot be in the position of a motivator; that would be a counterproductive undertaking. Instead, the researcher must be powerfully self-motivated to see the product in the market. So how does Cook assess determination? He states, "We work with the ones who choose to come to Isis, finding their own tortuous way in. Our method gives us a self-selecting sample of the kind of people we want to work with."[34] Though Isis makes "noise all the time" in the University community, Cook emphasizes, "We generate a lot of interest, but only deal with those researchers who come to us."[35]

Hockaday echoes this approach when he discusses pathways of commercialization with researchers. He paints a very realistic picture of the challenges of the process and secures the researchers' full, informed commitment before embarking. Obviously, this is not a matter of Hockaday trying to convince or cajole researchers into becoming involved in the commercialization process. On the contrary, Hockaday sometimes confronts researchers with the harsh reality that they are entering an entirely different sphere than the research environment.

Once Isis decides to commercialize a particular piece of research, and a spin-out is determined to be the preferred route, it contributes in three practical ways. First, Isis assists with preparing a business plan, which is the primary reference point for investors who are deciding whether or not to fund a new venture. When crafting the business plan, Isis works toward a consensus with the researcher on core issues such as the method of financing, corporate strategies, and securing key personnel. Therefore the business plan reflects the joint position of Isis and the researcher, and it forms the foundation of the spin-out.

Although some leading entrepreneurship writers believe principals should write their own business plans and minimize external help,[36] Isis works as a collaborator in birthing the strategy of the spin-out and demonstrating the potential of the product, so its direct involvement in the business plan is logical. Moreover, because an industry rule of thumb is that only 1–3 percent of all business plans successfully lead to an investment, the assistance of an experienced consultant/advisor can improve the odds for a fledgling spin-out company. Isis has a highly impressive track record of success, as only three of 57 spin-outs over a 10-year period have filed for bankruptcy.

The Spin-out Guide describes the practical nuances of preparing a business plan for Oxford researchers, and these insights apply equally to most new ventures. One of the first considerations is whether or not meaningful financial projections can be prepared. Although investors want to determine the possible return, a business may be at such an early stage that worthwhile calculations are not feasible. As the Spin-out Guide notes, "In these cases the investment decision will be made on the basis of confidence in the researchers, proposed spin-out managers, and the technology."[37]

The Spin-out Guide further states that the business plan will evolve as new facts and ideas emerge; moreover, various stakeholders may have sensible input in fine-tuning strategy, and this will result in revised financial projections. Thus, from a practical standpoint, any initial contact with investors may focus primarily on an executive summary—as short as one page in length—to initiate discussion, with the common understanding that a working relationship will result in a review of the company's strategic plan.

In addition to assisting the researcher with a business plan, Isis helps develop the organizational structure and strategy of the spin-out. The researcher and his product are at the core of this procedure. The Spin-out Guide states, "It is important that the team has a leader."[38] Though this comment may seem simplistic, it stems from experience: Many researchers are clever inventors, yet not effective company leaders. And, though other parties may become involved, they will not take on primary leadership because they are not inventors of the product. Thus, Isis must ensure that the researcher is a team-oriented leader, and also that this individual is surrounded by a group with complementary skill sets.

Then, Isis helps the researcher raise funds for the new venture. Before approaching financing sources, Isis must properly set and manage the expectations of researchers. Isis educates researchers that, regardless of how promising a new idea seems, investors view a spin-out as a high risk venture requiring a commensurate return.

Isis scours a wide range of financing sources: bank loans, angels (wealthy individuals who invest in high-potential, usually early-stage, ventures), venture capitalists, seed capitalists, institutional capitalists, and corporate venturing capitalists. Venture capitalists, a common source of financing, provide insight into the challenges of securing financing for a spin-out (which, by definition, has no revenue and no corporate track record). Venture capitalists look at hundreds of plans, but invest in few companies. And, despite all their experience and exhaustive due diligence, even when they do invest, the majority of new ventures fail.

Venture capitalists desire any single venture to show a return of 10 to 20 times the initial investment, to balance losses on their other ventures. Consequently, to increase the potential for success, a venture capitalist will often take on some level of active involvement in the spin-out. In that case, the researcher must recognize the venture capitalist's contribution to the spin-out and work cooperatively. Stated simply, securing a financial investment from a venture capitalist is a daunting task; moreover, the funds are always accompanied by conditions that give the venture capitalist input into the strategic direction of the company. As a result, Hockaday's advice to spin-out companies is to secure the initial seed rounds of investment from business angels (wealthy private investors, typically with their own entrepreneurial experience) rather than venture capitalists. Hockaday has discovered that venture capitalists find the initial round too risky to satisfy their investment criteria (they are managing a pool of funds under strict investment criteria), whereas business angels (who are investing their own funds) view the risk differently.[39]

Another basic issue when starting a spin-out—or any new venture, for that matter—is to determine how to divvy the ownership of the company. How should the pie be divided between the researcher, Isis, and investors (such as venture capitalists)? The Spin-out Guide provides a guideline in the form of a "Share Dilution Chart."

The researcher's contribution is fundamental; however, as we have seen, it is merely a starting point. The challenge when dealing with researchers (or inventors) is that they are likely to overemphasize the value of their own contributions. However, Isis explains to them that, based on risk and investment, an equal division of equity between the researcher and Oxford is a fair proposition. Isis's objective is to make the project a success—and that means Oxford has to benefit along with the researcher in order to make its contributions sustainable and financially worthwhile for the University.

The Spin-out Guide clarifies the rationale behind Isis's expectation that Oxford should be an equal shareholder with the founder researchers: "There are a number of factors to be taken into account: for example, the roles of the individual researchers, the amount of capital required, the involvement of the University in reaching the stage where a spin-out is possible, and the importance of the association with the University."[40]

The Spin-out Guide further states that "the division of spin-out equity between all those involved and the management and employees is a key issue and must be addressed early in the procedure."[41] Again, Isis must be proactive in setting reasonable expectations before it devotes resources to the pursuit of commercialization.

Once the University and the researcher agree on the conditions of respective ownership, they can then determine what percentage of the company to sell to investors. As the Share Dilution Chart shown here indicates, an investor may dilute the respective ownership of the researcher and Isis from 50 to 33 percent each. The investor, however, is providing critical funds to drive the process forward. Of course, an investor with a lot of leverage (perhaps the spin-out is desperately short of cash) may require the University or the researcher, or both, to reduce shareholder percentages less than 33 percent.

Also, as the Share Dilution Chart (pg. 85) demonstrates, when a company raises more funds (such as in "Stage 3"), it issues more shares and reduces the percentage ownership of the original shareholders even further. Needless to say, the longer it takes for a spin-out to become financially self-sustaining—and thus the more outside financing is necessary—the more ongoing dilution to the shareholding of Isis and the researcher will occur.

SHARE DILUTION CHART[42]						
	Stage 1		Stage 2		Stage 3	
	shares	%	shares	%	shares	%
Founders	50	50	50	33.3	50	29.4
University	50	50	50	33.3	50	29.4
Investors			50	33.3	50	29.4
Management					20	11.8
Shares	100		150		170	
%		100		100		100

In many ways, the process Isis proposes for researchers who want to launch a new venture is similar to the entrepreneurial journey for inventors with little or no business experience. These researchers or inventors may have created something of value, but they cannot successfully set up a company without help. For Oxford researchers, Isis provides all the necessary start-up services through one vehicle; for most entrepreneurs, however, these services must be gleaned from a variety of sources. In such a case, the lessons from Isis's methods of operation provide important information for any inventor who wishes to commercialize an invention.

The Spin-out Guide emphasizes four realities for researchers, which also have value for inexperienced entrepreneurs. First, a researcher must devote considerable time to the venture, and this may be time that the researcher would prefer to spend on research. Second, external skill and resources must be secured. Third, the researcher must engage in much "mundane work" (meetings, presentations, correspondence, and phone calls). Finally, a "measure of luck" is required—as Hockaday explains, "You can do everything perfectly and still fail."[43]

Unknown competitors may arise, or market demand may shift. The synergy of a talented team may fall into dissension; investors may have a personality clash with the researcher-founder. Hockaday jests that "an interplanetary alignment"[44] is needed to facilitate success. The following section illustrates the actual challenges faced by an Isis spin-out.

4.3 Growing and Financing a New Venture: Oxonica plc[45, 46]

> The successful development of a start-up venture requires careful and flexible strategic planning, bootstrapping skills, determination and persistence, the support and resources of financiers, committed leadership, and a focus on long-term value creation.

The chapter thus far has emphasized the challenges of moving from an idea to successful commercialization. As well, Section 4.2 highlighted some of the significant issues related to starting a spin-out, including the crucial step of securing financial support. To understand these fundamental guidelines in greater detail, I will focus on one spin-out company launched by Isis: Oxonica plc (referred to here as "Oxonica"). Oxonica owns patented properties in an important industry, has achieved significant milestones over its first nine years of operation and is a well-regarded company in its field. And yet the path to its present level of success was fraught with peril and near-death experiences.

Nanox Limited, which has since become Oxonica plc, was founded in 1998. The company began with Professor Peter Dobson and Dr. Gareth Wakefield, both engineering researchers in the field of nanotechnology. (The Foresight Nanotech Institute of Palo Alto, California, states that "the definition [of nanotechnology] most frequently used by government and industry involves structures, devices, and systems having novel properties and functions due to the arrangement of their atoms on the 1-to-100-nanometer scale."[47]) Professor Dobson, who is internationally recognized in the field of nanotechnology and is the Academic Director of the Begbroke Science Park (which includes the University of Oxford's Institute of Advanced Materials), advised the Oxonica Group (as it was then known) under a consultancy agreement, in connection with the development of nanoparticles.

Dr. Wakefield, who led the group's research activities, began working on novel nanomaterial systems at Oxford in 1994, which led to the development of some of the core intellectual property of Oxonica (as it is now known). Since then, Dr. Wakefield has published extensively in the area of nanotechnology. Oxonica has maintained a close relationship with Oxford, which provides access to specialized equipment, highly qualified technical personnel, potential customers, and partners. Moreover, the head office of Oxonica remains in Oxford.

Oxonica's original aim was to develop and market phosphor technology for field emission displays; in fact, the company raised about £750,000 (about $1,500,000) for that purpose.[48]After 12 months, however, commercial realities revealed that the phosphor market was largely controlled in the Far East, and that the displays market had too many competing technologies. As a result, Oxonica changed direction and stopped marketing field emission systems. Unfortunately, however, most of the company's £750,000 had been spent by that time. After only three years in existence, Oxonica was in serious trouble: It needed to expand its technological base, clarify its strategic direction, and refocus its management team.

In the year 2000, Oxonica secured £100,000 (about $203,000) through an angel finance round. A year later (April 2001), the company hired Dr. Kevin Matthews as its full-time CEO. In light of the failed foray into the phosphor market, Matthews had to assess the situation quickly. He remembers:

> My challenges as CEO were to refocus a large operational board into a strategic body focused on ensuring that the company remained funded, kept a clear direction, and had the appropriate policies and reporting in place; and, also, to convert a business with low morale and no real product focus—lots of research but no real commercial focus—into a dynamic successful team.[49]

And all of this with no money. Matthews recalls, "The biggest risk for me was that when I joined Oxonica, it had only eight weeks' cash left."[50] Of course, as with any entrepreneurial venture, cash flow is oxygen—and it is vitally important when the company is not yet in a profit-making position. The issue is always whether or not there is enough cash to get to the break-even point, when the product can finally get to the market and be accepted at a reasonable price. Thankfully, in Matthews's case, some pre-work had been done prior to his arrival. He marketed the company to investors as soon as he was hired as CEO and was able to complete a third angel round that raised £540,000 (roughly $1,100,000).

Matthews came to three immediate conclusions. First, he realized, "Oxonica had to focus on some commercial opportunities very quickly. We could not continue burning money as a research house [that] still had a 'university' approach."[51] One of his challenges was to get the researchers not to focus on the process but rather on the commercial viability of the output (this issue was mentioned in Section 4.2). A second revolutionary change was to alter the focus of the board—away from the previously-adopted initiatives, and toward the new direction he believed was vital to Oxonica's survival.

Third, Matthews felt the ever-present concern of any company that is burning cash—the desperate need for survival. During that time, Matthews understood, "We must soon raise a substantial amount of cash, to allow us to develop a real business. Since people are in business to make money, anything else is pretending—as a prelude to hoped-for profitability."[52] One particular hurdle was that in the field of material sciences, as opposed to the field of software development, a substantial amount of cash is necessary. The board realized that £540,000 (about $1,100,000) would only last through 2001.

At this early juncture, Matthews was already trying to position the company for an eventual listing of its shares on a public stock exchange. A keen eye to positioning the company in the mind of venture capitalists and investment houses was critical in terms of present and future value creation, because a company will be valued differently depending upon its marketplace categorization.

Knowing this fact, Matthews decided to focus on fuel-saving technology and sunscreen technology; he believed these fields could be labeled under "specialty chemicals" and given an appropriate price-earnings ratio. He also wanted to keep the company's bio-diagnostic activity alive in order to balance the company's portfolio and provide upside.

Oxonica launched a new venture capital financing only two days before the September 11, 2001, terrorist attacks The devastation reverberated in financial markets worldwide. Matthews' response was to persist, and to throw the net as wide as possible: "In the event, about 90 venture capital groups reviewed our business plan. I met with some 55 of them, 36 twice, and all that activity coalesced to a single term sheet. Despite all the interest from venture capital groups, only one wanted to lead our financing."[53]

How did the company survive in the meantime? The answer, in blunt terms: with very little cash in hand. Oxonica finished 2001 with £40,000 (about $81,000). Matthews describes: "Our burn rate was still £80,000 [about $162,000] a month, but we'd already taken action to generate cash, and we were able to continue until June 2002 without further capital-raising."[54] As with any entrepreneurial venture, this one required bootstrapping at its best in order to make ends meet. Oxonica obtained cash from taking a small loan, doing contract work, and using a government research and development tax credit. Thus, Oxonica was able to survive just long enough to close the venture capital round along with BASF, a large, multinational corporation that was interested in the material sciences space.

Matthews summarizes the end result: "The lead was taken by VCF Partners, a UK fund representing two Venture Capital Trusts (VCTs),[55] Trivest, and Foresight. Northern Venture Managers came in, as did Generics Asset Management, [both] solid groups of investors with capacity to [finance further rounds]."[56] The June 2002 financing raised £4.2 million (roughly $8,520,000), taking the company through its most significant financial challenge. Thereafter, in early 2004, the company raised a further £4 million (about $8,113,000) through a rights offering (an offering of shares to existing shareholders).

In July 2005, Oxonica was floated (that is, listed) on the Alternate Investment Market (AIM) of the London Stock Exchange (trading symbol OXN), raising £7.1 million net at 95.8p (pence) per share (roughly $14,400,000 at $2.54 per share). Up to the time of the listing, Oxonica had raised a total of £12.5 million (about $25,350,000), including the founding investments and angel rounds.

The challenge for every entrepreneurial venture is not only to get financing, but also to obtain those funds from the most suitable partners. As Section 4.2 points out, a spin-out company must cooperate with a number of stakeholders, including investors who will often become involved in the strategic direction of the company.

Oxonica was able to attract large, credible venture capitalists with a great track record who also had the capacity to do ongoing rounds of financing. In addition, these types of venture capitalists can garner specialized expertise and connections in the particular industry. Oxonica illustrates that *smart money* does not just fall into a company's lap: Entrepreneurs have to work hard for it.

AIM Listing Information	
Placing Price per Ordinary Share	95.8 pence
Number of existing Ordinary Shares prior to Admission	25,104,244
Number of Ordinary Shares in issue following the placing	36,805,329
Market Capitalization at the Placing Price	£35.3 million
Number of Ordinary Shares being placed by the Company	8,658,796
Percentage of enlarged issued share capital subject to the Placing	23.5%
Net proceeds of the Placing to be received by the Company	£7.1 million
Admission and commencement of dealings in Ordinary Shares on AIM	July 20, 2005

Once Oxonica was able to achieve financial stability, it had the means to begin building its business and capitalizing on its patented research. In 2005, Oxonica had gross revenue of £1.2 million. Then in July 2006, Oxonica signed an initial supply agreement with Petrol Ofisi A.S., Turkey's leading national oil company, for Oxonica's Envirox fuel-borne catalyst. The agreement resulted in £7.6 million (roughly $15,400,000) of additional revenues for the year. Another positive development in 2006 was the signing of a license and collaboration agreement with Beckton Dickinson & Co. (a leading global medical technology company) for Oxonica's proprietary Nanoplex technology in the in-vitro clinical diagnostics market. As part of the agreement, Beckton Dickinson invested $2 million in ordinary shares of Oxonica. Together, these agreements increased Oxonica's 2006 gross revenue to £10.2 million (about $20,700,000).

As noted, Oxonica has overcome a number of obstacles throughout its 10-year history, illustrating the many challenges faced by start-up companies. However, it is now a relatively stable company with 60 employees and three locations: Oxford (31 employees), focused on energy and materials; Mountain View, California (27 employees), concentrated on healthcare and security; and Singapore (2 employees), working on energy.[57] Oxonica has a significant base of revenue and has entered into contracts that affirm its current strategic direction. While Oxonica will no doubt face additional hurdles as it strives for continued growth, the Company has already achieved many entrepreneurial milestones.

Oxonica Financing Summary		
Founder Investment		(undisclosed)
First Round (Angel Financing)		£750,000
Second Round (Angel Financing)	2000	£100,000
Third Round (Angel Financing)		£540,000
Government R & D Tax Credit, Contract Work, and a Small Loan		£380,000
New Venture Capital Financing (June 2002) (VCF Partners, Northern Venture Managers & Generics Asset Management	2002	£4.2 million
Rights Offering (early 2004)	2004	£4 million
Total finance (Pre-AIM Listing)	1997–2004	£12.5 million
Net Proceeds from AIM Listing at 125p/share (July 2005)	2005	£7 million
Beckton Dickinson(US$2 million)	2006	£1 million
Total finance (Pre & Post AIM Listing)	1997–present	£20.5 million

4.4 The Lessons of Technology Transfer

There are three main lessons with respect to the commercialization process:
1. Set and maintain the proper focus.
2. Confront the challenge of raising money.
3. Do not underestimate the obstacles you will face along the way.

This chapter has detailed the process of taking an idea from its initial stage to its successful commercialization. We have discussed the Oxford environment and the distinction between an idea and an opportunity, and we have examined a spin-out called Oxonica to highlight potential difficulties barring entrepreneurial success. In conclusion, I would like to highlight three lessons Hockaday offers with respect to technology transfer.

First, launching a successful new venture requires a clear strategy for breaking into intended markets. Hockaday notes that "a characteristic of early stage companies is often the breadth of the offering."[58] There may be many potential applications for a new, patented technology, but which one can yield the greatest chance for commercial success? The company must determine the application that has the greatest potential for success, and then pursue it with a keen focus.

So, which opportunity should be focused on? Hockaday challenges the company's leadership: "You have to do a lot of market analysis of a technology that will only be ready in a few years, to a marketplace that will only be there for a few years."[59] Such a prediction seems almost as abstract as the prophecies of a soothsayer; yet, increased wisdom comes with experience. In order to be successful, a company must focus on a specific and carefully selected market.

Then, a company must raise funds. Hockaday forces researchers to answer the following question: "You're asking other people to spend their money on your ideas—why should they?"[60] All entrepreneurs looking for money need to ask themselves that same question. Whereas researchers and entrepreneurs may envision sugar plums and vast riches, financiers are more practical.

Hockaday notes that when financiers consider making an investment, they have to make an opportunity decision (choosing one technology over another), and then they have to invest in the concept's long-term development to bring it to market.

Thus, researchers and entrepreneurs need to have a well-constructed and diligently researched response to Hockaday's question. They must move beyond a simple it-might-make-money-and-make-the-world-a-better-place pitch to financiers, and instead present a compelling value proposition for a unique product.[61] A great idea will generate some interest (this is the "sizzle"), but only the underlying research and due diligence (the "steak") can secure an investment.

Once interest is established, Isis works with the investors and researcher(s) to negotiate the terms and conditions of the investment. In Hockaday's experience, investors often require "warranties and guarantees, and they want the whole deal sewn up so that, if it fails, they get their money back, roughly speaking."[62] Hockaday appreciates the motivation behind these high expectations, but, on behalf of Isis and the researchers, he tells investors, "It doesn't work like that."[63] Ironically, Hockaday not only educates the inventors of a product; he also has to set the expectations of financiers. He explains, "It is not realistic to expect a university researcher to get involved in making promises and guarantees about whether a very early stage technology company is going to succeed in the marketplace."[64]

Another main lesson for a start-up company is that the challenges of the commercialization process cannot be underestimated. Oxonica is a case in point. Kevin Matthews of Oxonica reflects, "When you are trying to introduce a new product technology, the number of hurdles you must jump is high. So you have to motivate the team and keep them driving forward in the face of the odds."[65] Section 4.2 highlighted the range of challenging issues to be addressed while on the path toward successful commercialization.

Hockaday blames "the sheer gulf between the outputs of university research and what is needed in the business world" for the intensity of this issue.[66] As part-educator, commercialization tutor, and mentor, preparing researchers for the road ahead, Hockaday and his team are quite familiar with entrepreneurial obstacles. In most instances, he will be the first one to explain the commercialization process. And, for the inexperienced, he repeats one of his most common sayings: "You don't make money out of technology—you make money out of a business that successfully commercializes technology."[67]

For Hockaday, working with world-class researchers is a rewarding process; getting paid to do so is a bonus. As he ponders the results of the efforts of the entire Isis team, he can spot a collection of champagne corks neatly placed on a small rack in the bookshelf at his Isis office. Hockaday explains:

> When we launch a new spin-out company we organize a "completion" meeting where all the documents are signed off and the investors sign their cheques to finance the business. The University becomes a shareholder [and not Isis directly], so all we are left with is the cork from the champagne everyone drinks—and the satisfaction of launching a strong new technology business.[68]

Hockaday is looking forward to collecting many more corks in the future.

Hockaday's Key Points

4.1. The starting point to consider converting an "idea" into an "opportunity" is when a researcher—and, indeed, any entrepreneur—has a patentable and unique discovery that meets a need in society. This process, known as commercialization, will be successful when supported by an "entrepreneurial culture," an effective technology transfer mechanism, and endorsement from professional and financial advisors.

4.2. The successful commercialization of research by way of a spin-out requires committed and sustained effort by the researcher, and demands a range of services from Isis. Moreover, the researcher must work cooperatively with Isis and other stakeholders in order to overcome inevitable challenges.

4.3. The successful development of a start-up venture requires careful and flexible strategic planning, bootstrapping skills, determination and persistence, the support and resources of financiers, committed leadership, and a focus on long-term value creation.

4.4. There are three main lessons with respect to the commercialization process:

1. Set and maintain the proper focus.
2. Confront the challenge of raising money.
3. Do not underestimate the obstacles you will face along the way.

Chapter 5

Rita Gunther McGrath: The Entrepreneurial Mindset and Discovery-Driven Planning

A mindset can be developed, enhanced, and improved. A mind, on the other hand, implies that you are either born with it or you are not....[Y]ou may not become the next Jeff Bezos [founder of *Amazon.com*], but you can always improve.

—Rita Gunther McGrath[1]

Introduction to Rita Gunther McGrath

Name	Rita Gunther McGrath
Title	Associate Professor
Affiliation(s)	Columbia University (New York, New York)
Education	B.A., Barnard (1981) M.P.A., Columbia (1982) Ph.D., Univ. of Pennsylvania (1993)

Experience	o Teaches MBA and Executive MBA courses in strategy and the innovation process at Columbia o Teaches regularly in Columbia's top-rated executive education programs o Faculty Director for Leading Strategic Growth & Change, Creating Breakthrough Strategy, and Executing Breakthrough Strategy o Active consultant and instructor for corporate executive education programs o Has been a corporate IT director, and has founded two start-ups
Notable Publications	o *The Entrepreneurial Mindset* (1999) o *Market Busters* (2005)
Website(s)	*www.marketbusting.com* *www0.gsb.columbia.edu/index.html*

Biographical Highlights

- McGrath is the coauthor of *The Entrepreneurial Mindset,* a leading text on entrepreneurship that is used widely by businesses.

- She is Director of the Strategic Management Society, the premier professional organization for strategists.

- She has won numerous writing awards: McKinsey Best Paper Award; Strategic Management Society Award (2001); Maurice Holland Award; Best Paper Published in Research Technology Management (2000); Industrial Research Institute Award; Best Paper, Academy of Management Review (1999); Entrepreneurship Theory and Practice Award for Best Conceptual Paper (1992 and 1996); and Best Paper, European Foundation for Entrepreneurship Research (1995).

- She has worked with companies such as 3M, Nokia, DuPont, Deutsche Telekom, the Japan Bank for International Cooperation, and Swiss Reinsurance, Inc.

5.1 Developing an Entrepreneurial Mindset

> Individuals and corporations need to adopt ways of thinking about business that capture the benefits of uncertainty. Such is the entrepreneurial mindset of "habitual entrepreneurs."

Through the intertwined concepts of an entrepreneurial mindset (discussed in this section) and discovery-driven planning (covered in the following section), Rita McGrath offers a practical method of thriving on uncertainty in entrepreneurship. Her two coauthored books, *The Entrepreneurial Mindset* and *MarketBusters,*[2] offer examples of individual entrepreneurs and managers who pursue a clear plan of action through intrapreneurship (entrepreneurship within an existing, often large and hierarchical, organization) in corporations. Many entrepreneurial writers highlight the dynamics of the entrepreneurial environment, but McGrath offers a roadmap out of the maze.

McGrath defines an "entrepreneurial mindset" as "a way of thinking about your business that captures the benefits of uncertainty."[3] The entrepreneurial mindset is part of the constitution of "habitual entrepreneurs," those individuals who are able to carefully assess and benefit from opportunities in the midst of fluctuating circumstances.[4]

Why use the term *mindset* instead of *mind*? McGrath argues that a "mind" implies intelligence you either are or are not born with; a "mindset," on the other hand, can be developed, enhanced and improved.[5] McGrath wants to "make clear that a person may not have what it takes to be a Jeff Bezos [the founder of *www.amazon.com*], but he or she can always improve."[6] In her courses at Columbia Business School, McGrath stresses that the word *mindset* implies "the notion that, as a company, it's an attitude or perspective: It says we're always looking for opportunities, we're always out there trying to look at what the next big thing is—we're not just going to exploit today's business."[7]

McGrath mentions five defining characteristics of the entrepreneurial mindset:

1. First, habitual entrepreneurs "passionately seek opportunities";[8] they look for the constantly

developing niches and needs that result from a fluid environment.

2. Second, habitual entrepreneurs "pursue opportunities with enormous discipline."[9] Discipline involves maintaining a register of opportunities, assessing them, and determining which are worthy of pursuit.

3. Third, habitual entrepreneurs "pursue only the very best opportunities and avoid exhausting themselves and their organizations by chasing after every option."[10] They generally stick with their area of expertise, which allows them to accurately assess the nature of an opportunity and reduce the risk to themselves.

4. Fourth, they "focus on execution—specifically, adaptive execution."[11] Habitual entrepreneurs know how to get the job done, but they also know how to adapt along the way. They sort out the details for a process *after* it is underway, avoiding the fruitless inertia of too much pre-production analysis.

5. Fifth, habitual entrepreneurs "engage the energies of everyone in their domain."[12] They are not solo operators; instead, they bring in various team members or organizations to fully exploit an opportunity.

With these five characteristics of an entrepreneurial mindset, the next step is to determine which opportunity should be pursued. For this process, McGrath uses the concept of "the entrepreneurial frame," which is "a specific, measurable challenge to enhance the value of your piece of the business."[13] There are two components of the entrepreneurial frame: attaining the minimum amount of additional profits needed to make it worthwhile, and achieving the required return on assets.[14] One must analyze the value of his or her existing business: If a new venture is not as profitable, then there is no point in proceeding. If, however, the venture still looks promising, the entrepreneur must then format an "opportunity register" to organize and assess his or her ideas.

In classic entrepreneurship theory, uncertainty is an essential component of economic ebb and flow, allowing new entities to displace old ones that do not respond to the new environment. Various sources of uncertainty include deregulation, globalization, and technological change. As well, the necessary skills for high-growth entrepreneurs, who routinely thrive in the midst of unpredictable circumstances, dovetail with the skills of managers in larger companies who must adapt to today's ever-changing world. In the year 2000, McGrath proposed that it was the right time "for a new integration of entrepreneurship and strategic management."[15] The result: future strategists in larger companies who act with an entrepreneurial mindset will be able to thrive in uncertain conditions.

In our 2005 interview, McGrath affirmed that this trend has continued, although the terminology now promotes "growth strategy" and "strategies for organizational development."[16] McGrath noted, "More than ever, we are seeing huge companies highly concerned with 'where the next act is coming from.'"[17] In other words, what upcoming innovation will take the company forward? McGrath mentioned a key example: "At General Electric right now they are constantly talking about innovation, swinging for the bleachers and big bets."[18] Capitalizing on such opportunities demands an entrepreneurial mindset.

5.2 Discovery-Driven Planning

A person with an entrepreneurial mindset pursues an opportunity through "discovery-driven planning," which involves framing, competitive market reality specification, specification of deliverables, assumptions testing, managing to milestones, and parsimony.

Let's assume an individual has an entrepreneurial mindset, and has established an opportunity register. The next step is asking what McGrath calls "the central question" of the entrepreneurial mindset: "How do you plan and manage an initiative whose direction and outcomes are not yet known?"[19] In response, McGrath developed the term discovery-driven planning, because one cannot determine the strategy in advance (and an attempt to do so may actually be counterproductive). The discovery-driven planning approach reflects the habitual entrepreneur's propensity to action, and his or her subsequent readjustment through careful attention to a strategy's evolution. This approach is much different from conventional planning, which focuses on trying to envisage the end result and securing corporate allocation of resources to achieve those goals. McGrath teaches that, in the context of uncertainty, conventional planning is suspect at best and dangerous at worst.

McGrath establishes six disciplines of discovery-driven planning. Whereas conventional planning is rooted in past experience and precedent, discovery-driven planning focuses on entirely new patterns. With that in mind, the six disciplines of the discovery-driven planning framework balance traditional attention to costs and cash flow with the cutting-edge input of creativity and new ideas. McGrath's intended outcome, then, is "real options reasoning in a highly disciplined planning and control process."[20] She defines "real options reasoning" as "starting in such a way that investments and launch costs are minimized until the upside potential is demonstrated."[21]

The six disciplines are as follows:

1. **Framing:** According to McGrath, any new initiative must have "the prospect of a substantial, quantifiable impact"—otherwise, why bother?[22] The goal of framing is to clearly specify the "unit of business," which McGrath defines as "the product or service that actually triggers a revenue-generating event."[23] This unit of business, which varies from a billable hour for lawyers to a policy for life-insurance agents, defines the business model.

2. **Competitive Market Reality Specification:** One must conduct the planning process within the bounds of a realistic appraisal of the particular market. A company should bear in mind the range of competitive challenges, namely the effect of new companies, or the threat of existing companies that will reallocate resources. Though in-depth knowledge is not necessary at this stage, the entrepreneur has to grasp "what the benchmark parameters of the project must be for the venture to succeed competitively and what the scope of the market must be to make it worthwhile at all."[24] This discipline may quickly eliminate unrealistic ideas.

3. **Specification of Deliverables:** An entrepreneur must translate his or her broad strategy into daily operating activities in order for the idea to become a reality. Deliverables are defined in relation to the frame of the business model in the context of a discovery-driven plan. McGrath points out four reasons why deliverables should be specified. First, the process converts a lofty strategy to the specific production goals and abilities of team members. Second, the specific deliverables provide a focus for competence creation. (For example, collecting a certain percentage of funding from delinquent customers may require telephone skills, a certain number of calls per staff, and a minimum number of staff.) Third, this step exposes any of the planners' fallacious assumptions by confronting their ideas with operational reality: Is the venture truly feasible? Specifically, the salespeople can quickly judge if customers are likely to buy the new product, and at what price, regardless of what management expects to happen. Fourth, the more closely deliverables are intertwined with the actual needs of customers, the more difficult it will be for a competitor to break that bond.[25]

4. **Assumptions Testing:** In a conventional plan, people test the end result; in discovery-driven planning, however, testing assumptions is a continual process. A list of assumptions accompanies each deliverable and its operating requirements. As the execution procedure progresses, owners test these assumptions against reality, with the objective of "converting the maximum number of assumptions to knowledge at minimum costs."[26]

5. **Managing to Milestones:** McGrath defines milestones as "critical, identifiable points in time at which key assumptions are tested."[27] This discipline is, of course, related to testing assumptions at frequent junctures in the discovery-driven process. The core concept is that an individual plans as far ahead as current information will sensibly allow; then he or

she stops and reassesses the assumptions, after which he or she manages to the next milestone.[28] Throughout the process, the individual maps and re-charts the major milestones that are likely to occur. For a manufacturing procedure, such milestones typically include concept test, model development, focus group test, prototype, market test, pilot plant, and full-scale plant initial run.[29] One challenge in this process is to stage a sequence of events that "will minimize cash burn and corporate expectations while you are engaged in learning."[30] The advantage of the discovery-driven approach is that company directors are changing strategies to conform to continual feedback, as opposed to ascribing to expectations established prior to the start of the program, when knowledge was merely speculative.

6. **Parsimony:** The last discipline proposed by McGrath is "parsimony"—creatively finding ways to minimize the costs of the planning process. Faulty assumptions, whether in regard to production costs or acceptable consumer price levels, can be very expensive. Again, McGrath encourages companies to commit minimal resources until assumptions have been tested. She advises, "Challenge people to spend their imagination before spending your money, including incurring small losses in order to avoid big losses."[31]

5.3 Entrepreneurial Leadership

Entrepreneurial leaders, whether individuals or organizations, create an entrepreneurial culture by developing climate-setting practices, orchestrating the entrepreneurial process, and championing new initiatives.

An entrepreneurial leader succeeds when the discovery-driven process occurs routinely, as part of an organization's culture, rather than as a deliberate act of the leader. McGrath presents three broad categories of leadership practices that will create this entrepreneurial culture.

The starting point is for the entrepreneurial leader to model climate-setting practices. The CEO needs to underscore the value of finding new opportunities; growth must become everyone's responsibility, and entrepreneurial initiatives must be integral to the identity of the company. The company should allocate substantial attention, resources, and talent to entrepreneurial initiatives.

Second, the entrepreneurial leader must orchestrate the process. The leader has to "demarcate the acceptable arena for entrepreneurial development by setting the parameters that define which business initiatives are acceptable."[32] This concept ties in with "real options reasoning" in which you make investments with a limited downside to learn whether further investment is warranted.[33]

As well, the entrepreneurial leader must actively champion initiatives. Along those lines, there are four distinct activities he or she can engage in: identify insights, convert each insight into an actionable business description, build pervasive organizational resolve, and discharge entrepreneurial leadership. The last initiative is comprised of obligations of framing, absorbing uncertainty, evaluating limiting conditions, clearing a path, and underwriting the highest-potential opportunity.

5.4 Strategic Growth Through Marketbusters

> Forty strategic moves, grouped under five central strategies, can drive growth for the purpose of creating "marketbusters" (significant changes in revenue position).

McGrath's approach to strategic growth belongs in the context of this topic's development during the past several decades. Strategic thinking changed in 1980, when Michael Porter published the landmark book _Competitive Strategy: Techniques for Analyzing Industries and Competitors_. Porter proposed that industry competition is a composite of five forces: rivalry among competing firms, the potential entry of new competitors, the possible development of substitute products, the bargaining power of suppliers, and the bargaining power of consumers.

According to McGrath, Porter's ideas had two negative byproducts. First, strategic thinking began to focus on industry first, and only later on the individual company.[34] Second, because of Porter's emphasis on stable industry forces, which he himself acknowledges in the preface of his book, McGrath notes that many companies developed "a tendency to think strategically in more static terms than we would today."[35]

Porter's book spawned certain trends in strategic management thinking, but McGrath also mentions three other significant shifts in perception.[36] To begin with, she states, "[S]trategy today places more emphasis on dynamism, fast reaction, with current business bestsellers using terms such as 'hardball competition,' 'hyper competition,' and 'radical innovation.'"[37] These terms were not in the strategy lexicon 25 years ago. Moreover, although few mid-level managers from past decades faced the brutality of free market competition, recent factors such as globalization, information technology development, and shifting communication patterns have forced companies to deal with such issues on an operating level. Finally, as competition boundaries have weakened, cycles of stable competitive forces are getting shorter and rivalries have intensified. Companies now seek to develop dynamic, fast-moving strategies.

In light of this competitive environment, an entrepreneurial mindset and entrepreneurial leadership are the foundations upon which a company can frame an opportunity, use the discovery-driven process, and turn its objective into reality.

McGrath and coauthor Ian MacMillan wrote a book called *MarketBusters: 40 Strategic Moves That Drive Exceptional Business Growth,* which maps out promising ways to pursue an opportunity. (Though I discuss the five core strategies here, I do not list the 40 moves, which can be found in *MarketBusters.*) The focus of their work is on strategic growth through "marketbusting" tactics—moves that identify and track opportunities for growth.

Their motivation for writing this follow-up book to *The Entrepreneurial Mindset* (2000) grew from two recent changes in the entrepreneurial field. First, the Internet is playing an ever-increasing role in creating opportunities. *MarketBusters* addresses this trend with a number of Internet-related examples.

Second, the job of the manager—the person attempting to adopt an entrepreneurial mindset—has become more difficult. McGrath notes, "CEOs are in office for shorter and shorter periods of time."[38] Further, "middle managers' jobs are expanding beyond any reasonable hope of personal feasibility, and companies are coming under much more pressure around growth than they were in 2000."[39] Although the ideas in her first book remain valid, she discerns, "There is a different sensibility today."[40]

MarketBusters distills McGrath and MacMillan's three years of research into a set of 40 moves, clustered around five core strategies. Each of these actions is designed to create a "marketbuster," which McGrath and MacMillan define as a 2-percent gain or loss in market share (as a result of its moves or those of another player); annual growth of 10 percent or more in sales, during at least two years, due to a new entry by an innovator; or, annual sales or shipment growth that is 5-percent greater than an incumbent's growth in the underlying market.[41]

McGrath and MacMillan use a three-part system to explain the five core strategies: the first part is the lens, the starting point of the analysis; second is the strategy itself; and last is the tool used to execute the strategy.

The first of the five core strategies is to examine your customers' total experience and, ultimately, transform it. The first two parts of the analysis—the customer and the customer's experience—are self-explanatory. But how does the "consumption chain analysis" work?

The consumption chain represents the set of activities customers engage in to meet their needs. This varies significantly, depending if the product is a hamburger or an automobile. Restaurants can transform their customers' experience by installing a drive-through window; on a different scale, car manufacturers can transform their customers' experience by selling vehicles online instead of at a car lot.

You can also transform your products and services by identifying chances to add or eliminate features, or by breaking apart offerings to target more specific customer categories. To determine a company's product positioning in relation to that of its competitors, McGrath proposes an "attribute map"—a tool that attempts to predict the consequences of marketbusting moves. In other words, do the moves please or displease key customer segments, and why?

Whereas the first two strategies focus on the customer, the third strategy focuses on investors. The approach: Redefine metrics that drive products by radically changing important variables that reflect the standards of competition in your industry. McGrath states,

"The goal is to create advantages in your markets, but also to have a positive effect on your firm's stock market capitalization."[42]

This concept requires the use of "key metrics," which is "a measure that captures something about how many units of business you are likely to sell and how much money you will make selling them."[43] (As explained in Section 5.2, a unit of business can be anything from an insurance policy to a meal; in essence, it is the type of service or product your company provides.) Analyzing key metrics with an entrepreneurial mindset allows you to redefine the main drivers of profit.

McGrath and MacMillan's fourth strategy is to place the lens on "industry" and adopt a method of exploiting shifts. They present an "industry shifts framework" based on four patterns of industry change: industry swings through cycles of surplus and scarcity; a shift in an industry constraint or barrier that changes power relations; natural industry evolution; and shifts in patterns of costs or bottlenecks that cause value chain reordering.[44] A company will need to recognize these shifts or changes in the competitive environment and then adjust its strategy accordingly.

The four previous strategies dealt with existing industry dynamics. The fifth core strategy, however, focuses the lens on emerging opportunities and adopts the strategy of entering new markets. The affiliated tool is "the tectonic triggers table," named based on its similarity to shifting tectonic plates on the Earth's surface.[45]

McGrath identifies a list of tectonic triggers: an invention that changes what is technologically feasible or affordable (for example, an airplane or elevator); a shift in social norms that alters behavior (such as the ban on smoking in restaurants); a change in some aspect of nature (for example, diseases such as AIDS or SARS, or environmental conditions such as global warming); institutional and regulatory change (such as deregulation of the airline industry); and demographic changes (Baby Boomer bulge, for example).[46]

Implementing the five "marketbuster" strategies requires a combination of rigorous analysis and creative planning. McGrath and MacMillan map out strategic moves for high growth and provide a framework for developing an entrepreneurial mindset, but their advice is only the beginning. McGrath reflects that, for most entrepreneurs and managers, success depends on continually using decent tools, developing sound analytical techniques, and demonstrating a healthy degree of discipline.

She posits, "The bulk of formulating strategies is really hard work—thinking through implementation, assessing obstacles, ensuring alignment of goals, and putting work streams in place."[47] In other words, although a framework for planning is important, there is much more. To complete the process, one must make room for a creative spark to emerge.

What are the tea leaves telling us? McGrath explains, "The art of...developing insights, seeing deeper patterns, and getting that 'aha' moment is part of the strategy process."[48] In short, balancing analysis with creativity is critical for executing strategic moves.

> **McGrath's Key Points**
>
> 5.1. Individuals and corporations need to adopt ways of thinking about business that capture the benefits of uncertainty. Such is the entrepreneurial mindset of "habitual entrepreneurs."
>
> 5.2. A person with an entrepreneurial mindset pursues an opportunity through "discovery-driven planning," which involves framing, competitive market reality specification, specification of deliverables, assumptions testing, managing to milestones, and parsimony.
>
> 5.3. Entrepreneurial leaders, whether individuals or organizations, create an entrepreneurial culture by developing climate-setting practices, orchestrating the entrepreneurial process, and championing new initiatives.
>
> 5.4. Forty strategic moves, grouped under five central strategies, can drive growth for the purpose of creating "marketbusters" (significant changes in revenue position).

Chapter 6

Henry Mintzberg: Entrepreneurship and Organizations

True entrepreneurs often have an artistic bent—they are visionaries with frequent insights. As such...many ignore MBA programs. These are individualists intent on breaking away from the crowd, while MBAs more commonly want to be in the middle of it.
—Henry Mintzberg[1]
Managers, Not MBAs, 131

Introduction to Henry Mintzberg

Name	Henry Mintzberg
Title	Cleghorn Professor of Management Studies
Affiliation(s)	McGill University (Montreal, Quebec)
Education	B.Sc. Eng., McGill M.Sc. Eng., Ph.D. MIT

Experience	o Named Distinguished Scholar of the Year (2000) by the Academy of Management, and won its George R. Terry Award for the best book of 1995 (*The Rise and Fall of Strategic Planning*) o An elected Fellow of the Royal Society of Canada (the first from a management faculty) o An officer of the Order of Canada
Notable Publications	o Author of 13 books, including *Mintzberg on Management* (1989), *The Rise and Fall of Strategic Planning* (1995), and *Managers, Not MBAs* (2004) o McKinsey prize-winner for two of his articles in *Harvard Business Review*

Biographical Highlights

⊙ In many rankings, Mintzberg is one of the top management gurus in the world, based on his influential, persuasive, and unconventional ideas.

⊙ Mintzberg is an articulate and high-profile challenger of the value and nature of MBA education, which is the primary delivery mechanism for the teaching of entrepreneurship.

⊙ He is an academic innovator through the creation of the "International Masters of Practicing Management" program, which emphasizes learning by doing, and learning from experienced managers.

⊙ His writings on strategic management clarify the unique nature of innovative and entrepreneurial organizations in relation to other organizations.

⊙ His insightful critique of education in business schools, though focused on managerial training, also applies to entrepreneurship.

6.1. Entrepreneurial and Intrapreneurial Organizations

The entrepreneurial organization and the innovative (intrapreneurial) organization have fundamentally different structures, and they flourish in different contexts.

Leaders around the world respect Henry Mintzberg for his insights into organizations and organizational policies. His unique nomenclature sets him apart from other entrepreneurship analysts, and his managerial wisdom gives him a distinctive approach. As well, his numerous books, honors, and awards reflect the profound magnitude of his contributions to the study and practice of entrepreneurship.

As part of Mintzberg's organizational analysis, he examines two types of organizations: *entrepreneurial* and *innovative.* Those he designates "entrepreneurial" are similar to small businesses, engaging in "simple" innovations.[2] By comparison, those he calls "innovative" are generally larger organizations that engage in "intrapreneurship" (as noted previously, innovation within an existing organization). Mintzberg believes that by understanding the structure of each organization and the context in which that structure thrives, people can determine how a particular organization functions.

As Mintzberg sees it, an entrepreneurial organization is a step on a journey to somewhere else: "Most organizations in business, government, and not-for-profit areas pass through the entrepreneurial configuration in their formative years, during startup."[3] In the entrepreneurial organization, the focus of attention is on the leader. Mintzberg notes, "The organization is malleable, and responsive to that person's initiatives."[4]

He examines several questions with respect to the entrepreneurial organization:

1. **First of all, how does it organize itself (or resist doing so)?** The entrepreneurial organization has a simple structure: few staff, a loose division of labor, and a small managerial hierarchy. Little of its activity is formalized, and it utilizes only minimal planning procedures or training routines.[5] The power in an entrepreneurial organization belongs to its chief executive, who exercises his personal will. Formal controls on an entrepreneur's activities by way of an effective board or collaborative management structures are either not instituted or not followed.

2. **How, then, does the entrepreneurial organization function?** Decision-making is flexible, and a highly

centralized power system allows for rapid response. With that in mind, Mintzberg adds, "It is not surprising, therefore, that the resulting strategy tends to reflect the chief executive's implicit version of the world, often an extrapolation of his or her own personality."[6]

3. **What conditions are likely to foster an entrepreneurial organization's development?** The entrepreneurial configuration grows in an external context that is both simple and dynamic. It must be simple for one person at the top to retain dominant influence. (In the classic case, the leader is the owner.) Yet, at the same time, the small firm's flexible structure allows it to outmaneuver bureaucracies. Often the entrepreneur who owns such a firm loathes the bureaucratic system, so he or she keeps his or her organization lean and flexible. Mintzberg explains, "Entrepreneurs often found their own firm to escape the procedures where they previously worked."[7] These organizations are typically young and aggressive, but avoid complex markets. Thus, Mintzberg concludes, "[M]ost organizations in business, government, and not-for-profit areas pass through the entrepreneurial configuration in their formative years, during start-up."[8]

4. **What problems does an entrepreneurial organization encounter?** Mintzberg's response is concise: When power belongs to a single individual, company growth suffers.

5. **What is the structure and context of the innovative organization?** Mintzberg refers to the innovative organization as an "adhocracy," based on the Latin term *ad hoc* ("because of this"). This organization's basic orientation is "intrapreneurship": Mintzberg describes, "[W]hereas the entrepreneurial configuration innovates from a central individual at the top, this one depends on a variety of people for its strategic initiatives."[9] The adhocracy provides sophisticated innovation—and possibly a good deal of disruption, chaos, and wasted resources. The antithesis of a machine organization with relatively stable,

well-organized systems of operation, the adhocracy features an absence of structure so extreme that it may even resemble chaos. But, strangely enough, this unruly approach is a type of structure in itself; moreover, in its proper context of complex and unpredictable environments, it is a very logical and reasonable approach. Sophisticated innovation is able to fuse experts from different disciplines into smoothly-functioning ad hoc project teams.[10] Innovative organizations tend to display little formalization of behavior, though there are specialized jobs based on expert training, and there is a tendency to group specialists. However, because innovation involves breaking away from established patterns, an innovative organization cannot rely on standardization for coordination. Although the entrepreneurial organization also retains a flexible, organic structure, and so can innovate, it is restricted to simple situations that a single leader can comprehend. Thus, sophisticated innovation demands a more complex—and seemingly crazy—structure.

	Entrepreneurial Organization[11]	Intrapreneurial Organization
Structure	o Simple, informal, flexible, with little staff or middle-line hierarchy o Activities revolve around the chief executive, who controls the company personally, through direct supervision	o Fluid, organic, selectively decentralized, "adhocracy" o Functional experts deployed in multidisciplinary teams of staff, operators, and managers to carry out innovative projects o Coordination by mutual adjustment is encouraged by liaison personnel, integrating managers, and matrix structure

Context	o Simple, dynamic environment o Strong leadership, sometimes charismatic, often autocratic o Company is a startup, or in a crisis, or in the middle of a turnaround phase o Small organizations, "local producers"	o Complex and dynamic environment, including high technology, frequent product change (due to severe competition), and temporary and mammoth projects o Organization becomes more bureaucratic the longer it is in existence o Common in young industries o Two basic types: operating adhocracy for contract project work, or administrative adhocracy for own project work—the latter often applies when operating core is truncated or automated

6.2. Entrepreneurial and Intrapreneurial Strategies

An entrepreneurial organization has a "visionary model" for strategy formation: strategy is bold, and wrapped up in the founder's vision, with a precise execution method. By contrast, the innovative (intrapreneurial) organization has a "grassroots model": Unconventional strategies respond continuously to a complex, unpredictable environment.

Entrepreneurial and innovative (or intrapreneurial) organizations have different structures that flourish in different contexts. How does this affect their strategies? Though many definitions of strategy exist, Mintzberg provides a complementary definition rooted in five different dimensions.[12]

As a *plan*, strategy deals with how leaders try to establish direction for their organizations, to set them on predetermined courses of action. As a *ploy*, strategy takes us into the realm of direct competition, where companies use threats, feints, and various other maneuvers to gain advantage. As a *pattern*, strategy focuses on action, reminding us that the concept is an empty one if it does not take behavior into account. As a *position*, strategy encourages us to look at organizations in their competitive environments. Lastly, as a *perspective*, strategy raises intriguing questions about an organization's intention in a collective context.

Just as Mintzberg uses the term *craft* with respect to doing management, he uses the "craft" framework with respect to developing strategy. He explains, "My thesis is simple: The crafting image better captures the process by which effective strategies come to be. The planning image, long popular in...literature, distorts those processes and thereby misguides organizations that embrace it unreservedly."[13]

Furthermore, when discussing strategy as a "plan," the entrepreneurial organization is generally disinterested.[14] According to Mintzberg, "Planning, plans, and planners are likely to meet considerable resistance in the entrepreneurial form of organization.... [E]verything revolves around the chief executive; that person controls activities personally, through direct supervision."[15] In fact, "Serious planning may get in the leader's way, impeding free movement..."[16] He goes on:

I have always maintained that good entrepreneurs are very plugged into their business, and very hands-on. Formulation and implementation tends to be a closed loop—they go back and forth, and what they are doing on the ground feeds back to what they are thinking about. So, their strategies evolve.

These are people who are usually very dedicated to their industry. They do adapt, unless the change is very fundamental— then they may be stuck in their thinking.[17]

Mintzberg further explains, "I don't think entrepreneurs look at risk at all. They are so dedicated that they just drive forward and don't think of failure. They don't worry, 'There is a risk; I will fail!' They are totally dedicated."[18]

In addition, as mentioned earlier, entrepreneurial organizations pursue bold ideas with precise execution.[19] The leader's intimate, detailed knowledge of the business, or of analogous business practices, is critical in these situations. As a result, "clear, imaginative, integrated strategic vision depends on an involvement with detail, an intimate knowledge of specifics."[20] By closely controlling implementation, the leader is able to reformulate en route. The strategy is a personal vision: "[D]ecisions concerning both strategy and operations tend to be centralized in the office of the chief executive," Mintzberg observes. "This centralization has the important advantage of rooting strategic response in deep knowledge of the operations."[21] He concludes: "[E]ntrepreneurship is very much tied up with the creation of strategic vision, often with the attainment of a new concept."[22]

But how does planning occur in an innovative organization? In Mintzberg's view, it entails "...a very loose form of strategic programming, which outlines broad targets and a set of milestones while leaving considerable flexibility to adapt to the dead ends and creative discoveries along what must remain a largely uncharted route."[23] In other words, strategy formation in an innovative organization is unconventional: It responds continuously to a complex, unpredictable environment. It cannot rely on deliberate game plans.[24]

Mintzberg refers to a "grassroots" model of strategy formation for innovative organizations, comprised of six points. First, "Strategies grow initially like weeds in a garden; they are not cultivated like plants in a hothouse."[25] Plainly, let the strategy emerge: don't over-manage it. Second, "Strategies can take root in all kinds of places, virtually anywhere people have the capacity to learn and the resources to support that capacity."[26] At the outset, no one knows which strategy will succeed in the marketplace.

Third, "such strategies become organizational when they become collective—that is, when the patterns proliferate to pervade the behavior of the organization at large."[27] In this manner, an emergent strategy may replace an existing one. Fourth, "the processes of proliferation may be conscious, but they need not be; likewise, they may be managed, but they need not be."[28] The response of the environment—the market—can determine a strategy's adoption into the company.

Fifth, "new strategies, which may be emerging continuously, tend to pervade the organization during periods of change, which punctuate periods of more integrated continuity."[29] Basically, there is a seasonal fluctuation: a time to sow, a time to reap. Lastly, "to manage this process is not to preconceive strategies, but to recognize their emergence and intervene when appropriate."[30] Just as gardeners do, companies must prune their branches when necessary. In essence, Mintzberg's "grassroots" strategy grows from the base of an organization, rooted in the earth of its operations rather than in managerial imposition.

Strategy Formation in an Entrepreneurial Organization[31]

Steinberg's was a Canadian retail chain that began in 1917 with a tiny food store in Montreal. During its almost-60-year reign in the industry, it grew to boast sales in the billion-dollar range. Most of the growth was from supermarket operations.

Sam Steinberg joined his mother in the first store at age 11, and maintained all voting control of the firm until his death in 1978. He also exercised close managerial rule over all its major decisions, at least until the 1960s, when the firm began to diversify into other forms of retailing.

In more than years, the company underwent only two forms of major strategic reorientation. One was in 1933, when Steinberg's moved into self-service: One of the firm's eight stores was incurring unacceptable losses, so Sam Steinberg closed the store on a Friday evening. Over the weekend, he converted it to self-service, changed the name from Steinberg's Service Stores to Wholesale Groceteria, slashed prices by 15–20 percent, printed handbills and stuffed them into neighborhood mailboxes, and reopened on Monday morning. The new strategy worked. The ideas were bold, the execution deliberate.

Steinberg's ability to change strategies was rooted in an intimate understanding of the grocery industry.

But this strength was also a source of failure. When success in the core business encouraged diversification into new ones (new regions, new forms of retailing, new industries), the organization moved beyond the ability of the founder's comprehension. In short, "Strategy-making became more decentralized, more analytic, in some ways more careful, but at the same time less visionary—less integrated, less flexible, and ironically, less deliberate."[32]

	Entrepreneurial Organization[33]	Intrapreneurial Organization
Model	Visionary Model	Grassroots Model
Strategy	o Often visionary process, broadly deliberate but emergent and flexible in details o Leader takes on many responsibilities o Organization thrives in protected niches	o Primarily a learning, or "grassroots," process o Largely emergent, evolving through a variety of bottom-up processes, shaped rather than directed by management o Strategic focus has characteristic cycles of convergence and divergence
Issues	o Responsive, sense of mission BUT o Vulnerable, restrictive o Danger of imbalance toward strategy of operations **(Mintzberg on management, 116–130)**	o Combines more democracy with less bureaucracy, so the structure is fashionable o Effective at innovation (an extraordinary configuration) BUT o Effectiveness achieved at the price of inefficiency o Also faces human problem of ambiguity and the danger of a possibly inappropriate transition to another configuration

Mintzberg's Key Points

6.1. The entrepreneurial organization and the innovative (intrapreneurial) organization have fundamentally different structures, and they flourish in different contexts.

6.2. An entrepreneurial organization has a "visionary model" for strategy formation: strategy is bold, and wrapped up in the founder's vision, with a precise execution method. By contrast, the innovative (intrapreneurial) organization has a "grassroots model": Unconventional strategies respond continuously to a complex, unpredictable environment.

Chapter 7

Gordon Redding: The Spirit of the Overseas Chinese Entrepreneur

The Overseas Chinese make up one of the world's most effective economic cultures. Always seemingly capable of being successful middlemen, they have blossomed in the last 30 years....

—Gordon Redding[1]

Introduction to Gordon Redding

Name	Gordon Redding
Title	Professor and Director
Affiliation(s)	Professor Emeritus, University of Hong Kong; Visiting Professor, University of Manchester; Director, Euro Asia and Comparative Research Center, INSEAD, Fontainebleau, France
Education	Ph.D., University of Manchester Ph.D. (Hon.), Stockholm School of Economics

Experience	o 11 years practical managerial experience as an executive in the UK department store industry o Founded and directed the University of Hong Kong Business School, where he spent 24 years o Consultant to large companies on matters connected with organizing for business in the Asian region and internationally
Notable Publications	o *The Spirit of Chinese Capitalism* (1990) o *The Future of Chinese Capitalism* (2007)

Biographical Highlights

- ⊙ Redding is the world's leading expert on the unique aspects of Overseas Chinese entrepreneurship, having studied, worked with, and written about the phenomenon for more than years.

- ⊙ He is a prodigious researcher at a world-leading institution, and the author of 10 books and more than 100 research papers.

- ⊙ He wrote *The Spirit of Chinese Capitalism,* a seminal and often-quoted work on the unique nature of Overseas Chinese entrepreneurship.

- ⊙ He is a pioneer in the study of management, having been a professor of management studies and director at the University of Hong Kong Business School for 24 years.

- ⊙ He has a unique international perspective, being British-born and British-educated, having lived and worked in Asia for much of his working career, and now being based at INSEAD in Fontainebleau, France.

7.1 The Overseas Chinese Diaspora

The Overseas Chinese Diaspora (or network) is one of the most successful—and least studied and understood—networks of entrepreneurs in the world, and it is a model of success in spite of significant social and economic obstacles.

The group of people Redding terms the Overseas Chinese is the most-important and least-understood network of high-energy entrepreneurs in the world. Who are they? First, we need to distinguish the "Overseas Chinese" from other Chinese people. In the countries around the South China Sea, and in certain Western communities such as Toronto, Vancouver, San Francisco, Paris, Sydney, and so forth, there are people whose families left China throughout the past 150 years and settled into the local citizenship of their host countries. These people, however, retain a sense of belonging to Chinese culture, and of sharing its heritage. The phrase _Overseas Chinese_ does not imply that they are citizens of the People's Republic of China; rather, they are simply ethnically and culturally Chinese. They are, in fact, almost all citizens of the countries where they now live, and it is often risky to identify them separately.

The Overseas Chinese consist of approximately 40 million people in the countries of Southeast Asia, and more recently in Canada and the United States.[2] These 40 million people have per capita incomes in the range of $20 to $30 thousand, 10 times those of their PRC cousins.

The most obvious cases of Overseas Chinese dominance are in Hong Kong, Taiwan, and Singapore. Hong Kong has long been revered as a minute, economic powerhouse, with virtually no natural resources, thriving primarily on ingenuity, hard work, and determination. However, most of Hong Kong's success can be attributed to the ethnic Chinese, who make up 99 percent of the population. Similarly, Singapore, though more cosmopolitan than Hong Kong, is still dominated by a Chinese population of approximately 75 percent. The Chinese presence there is so strong that Mandarin Chinese is an official language, and Confucianism is part of the educational curriculum. Moreover, Singapore originated in 1965 as part of the ethnic Chinese desire to peacefully opt out of the union with the predominantly Muslim and non-Chinese states that formed Malaysia in its post-colonial transition. Taiwan is also included among the Overseas Chinese countries, as its most significant business leaders are émigrés from China after the Communist Revolution in 1949, and their social and business norms are similar to those of other Overseas Chinese.

The Overseas Chinese have also been influential in Southeast Asian countries where they are a minority, namely Indonesia,

Malaysia, Thailand, and the Philippines. In Indonesia, for example, they have a population base of 4 percent and yet control 75 percent of the private domestic capital.[3] As well, the Overseas Chinese became close, if unobtrusive, allies of the two key areas of influence: the government and the military.

In Malaysia, the Overseas Chinese are 37 percent of the population and likely control 55–60 percent of commerce and manufacturing. In Thailand, the Overseas Chinese are 8.5 percent of the population, but own 90 percent of all local investments in the commercial sector, 90 percent of all local investments in the manufacturing sector, and 50 percent of all local investments in the banking and finance sector.[4] Lastly, in the Philippines, the Overseas Chinese are only 1 percent of the population, but they account for 67 percent of the sales volume in the commercial sector of the economy.[5]

There are four host environment influences that molded the nature of the Overseas Chinese. First, the host countries' social environments were often resentful or openly hostile to people of Chinese ethnicity, and frequently enacted specific laws to curb Chinese cultural influence. Second, the external threats caused heightened cooperativeness within the Overseas Chinese group; thus, working together ensured everyone's survival. Third, the conflict with the host countries reinforced a natural tendency to identify with China as a possible counterweight. Fourth, the values of economic survival, such as a strong work ethic, thrift and pragmatism, were reinforced as a result of being sojourners.[6]

One of the unique characteristics of the Overseas Chinese is their considerable staying power. Redding notes: "The sense of Chinese-ness, based as it is on the immense weight of Chinese civilization, seems to diminish remarkably little over distance or with the passage of time. It is the cynosure of the Overseas Chinese, and also their definition."[7]

The Overseas Chinese have retained their unique identity even in environments where they are a distinct minority.

There are several reasons for this phenomenon: The Overseas Chinese feel resented for their success, so they band together defensively; they perceive the Chinese culture as superior to its alternatives; and, as with many, they prefer the comfort of their own kind.[8] One practical barrier is the Chinese language. Redding observes that "for a Chinese person to give this up is a major sacrifice," and "for a foreigner to learn it is a major challenge."[9] In short, the Overseas Chinese have distinct characteristics as a subcultural group.

7.2 The Spirit of Overseas Chinese Capitalism

> The spirit of Overseas Chinese capitalism is rooted in a drive to get rich, the desire to protect ideas, secrecy regarding business affairs, and a paternalistic organizational structure.

Do the Overseas Chinese have a unique approach to entrepreneurship? Can their experience teach others how to succeed?

Redding notes that, as a caveat, it is hard to find a "typical entrepreneur" among the Overseas Chinese, because there is a great amount of variety. At the same time, there are certain central, shared ideals that are remarkably common among the Overseas Chinese.[10] These entrepreneurial traits are at the heart of Redding's analysis: "The spirit of Chinese capitalism is that set of beliefs and values which lies behind the behavior of Chinese businessmen."[11] Redding's context is a general study of capitalism, but the participants are overwhelmingly entrepreneurs.

To understand "the spirit of Chinese capitalism," we must distinguish between *what* they do and *how* they do it. There are two aspects to the "what" of Overseas Chinese business-people's behavior. First, in Redding's view, the Overseas Chinese are "opportunity seeking at a level of intensity higher than most other cultures."[12] Second, they are looking for a formula, a "magic solution which they can then replicate and expand."[13] Redding explains that the Overseas Chinese "will experiment endlessly until they solve the particular problem and find the formula. The formula could be something fairly simple, like a new method of distribution for a product, or something quite complex, such as a new marketing or supply system."[14] The Overseas Chinese are quite sophisticated in thinking through the components of an opportunity and stitching together a solution that no one else has thought about. However, Redding notes that it is difficult to generalize further about the "activities" of the Overseas Chinese, as they do so many things in so many different ways.

Next, there are four aspects with respect to "how" the Overseas Chinese pursue entrepreneurship. First, there is "a very powerful drive to get rich."[15] Money is a measuring stick for an individual's self-esteem, and status symbols are a coveted display of wealth. For years, Hong Kong has had the most Rolls Royces and Mercedes per capita of any city in the world. In addition, designer labels and brand name boutiques proliferate. Hong Kong residents are familiar with the various classes and designations of Mercedes, as a form of determining economic pecking order. A sense of moral duty to one's family name is a powerful motivation for the accumulation of money.

Money-mindedness is generally associated with the southern Chinese of Guangdong Province, which neighbors Hong Kong. Interestingly, Redding notes that money-minded behavior "has commonly, in Chinese culture, been attributed to Southerners, and been seen as part of their somewhat outlandish and uncultured deviance from the central civilization."[16] The motivation to make money affects the kind of people the Overseas Chinese trust, as well as how hard they work, what they do with their money, and the type of people they will employ.

Second, the Overseas Chinese are very protective and proprietary regarding ideas. In the Overseas Chinese context, information in itself is valuable. There are limited circles of trust, which are very critical to building refined and useable information. Also, the Overseas Chinese often work in a volatile environment with heavy political interference from government forces. As a result, they emphasize the importance of knowing government officials in order to have access to necessary licenses when regulations change.

Because policies are continually in flux, the Overseas Chinese must be very politically aware. Often these environments are weak in quality information, however, so information becomes critical and strategic. In short, Redding remarks, "Relationships are often built for the bartering of information on the grounds of mutual exploitation with a limited set of friends."[17] By contrast, "ideas are a dime a dozen" in Western countries, and "like a bus, another one will come by in 10 minutes." The root concept is that an idea is distinguishable from an opportunity, and that the execution required to turn the idea into an opportunity is a critical part of the equation.

Third, the Overseas Chinese are secretive with respect to their business affairs. One common joke in Hong Kong is that a Chinese entrepreneur has three sets of financial books: one for himself, one for his wife, and one for the tax authorities. Of course, all three sets are different. The Western notion of "transparency" does not exist among Overseas Chinese; in fact, it would be viewed as incomprehensible. Instead, the secretive approach is another means of exercising close controls of the organization.

Overseas Chinese entrepreneurs tend not to want to go public, because they fear they will lose control of their company. This feature may be true of entrepreneurs in the United States, also, but many proceed regardless. Not so among the Overseas Chinese. Overseas Chinese generally prefer to raise money among friends, from retained earnings, or through short-term bank borrowing—all situations where they can maintain control. They become uncomfortable if they expose themselves to too much public scrutiny. The issue of trust is relevant. One consequence of their secretive nature is that this limits the scale and scope of their organizations.

Fourth, the organizational style of the organization is paternalistic; in other words, there is a "father figure" founder who dominates the management team and the entire work force. This results in a high centralization of decision-making, which means that the organization can take advantage of opportunities when required to do so, because its capacity to move at lightning speed is very well-developed. The founders can also speak on behalf of their organization with total authority, and therefore cut deals very fast. Redding explains that these people carry a lot of weight in negotiations and "they don't need any one else's permission to commit the resources of the organization, so it makes the system very agile, very fast moving, very responsive, and highly personal in its kind of architecture."[18] This structure may exist in the United States, but it is much more common among the Overseas Chinese.

7.3 The Overseas Chinese Family Business

> The family business is intertwined with the aspirations of the present and future generations of a family, is a preferred way of doing business, and is not simply a transition stage in a firm's evolution to professional management.

In Western countries, the "family firm" is often the originator, but not the goal, of businesses. Many view a family business as a mom-and-pop operation that, if truly successful, would have transitioned to so-called professional management. Indeed, the emphasis in the United States has been on the transfer of power to professional managers, and the separation of control and ownership. By contrast, family businesses imply a degree of nepotism: family members on a board of directors, a spouse as president, and unemployable cousins sprinkled in line jobs are all cause for suspicion. Further, a "paternalistic" structure implies a condescending, meddling atmosphere subject to the personal discretion of the founder—as opposed to an objective meritocracy. There are, of course, successful family firms in the United States, but they are less common and suffer more scrutiny. The cliché is that the family business is run into the ground by the third generation.

But nepotism and paternalism do not carry the same negative connotations for the Overseas Chinese. To them, the interests of a family and its business are intertwined; the survival and prosperity of one is tied to the other. The overwhelmingly consistent theme in discussions about Chinese executives' organizations is patrimonialism. That word as such is not used by them, but it is the only word which captures adequately "the themes of paternalism, hierarchy, responsibility, mutual obligation, family atmosphere, personalism, and protection."[19] (According to Redding, personalism is "the tendency to allow personal relationships to enter into decision making."[20])

The very nature of patrimonialism causes Westerners to bristle, as it smacks of a male-dominated hierarchy. There is a glass ceiling to be concerned about; women are rarely even in the room yet. To some extent, the notion of patrimonialism resembles the "social contract" that existed between employer and employees in the

United States in past generations: Spend your career with the firm and you will be rewarded with job security and a good pension. In other words, there is a form of mutual loyalty.

For the Overseas Chinese, the phrase "run your family as a business, and your business as a family" has a ring of truth. The family and business are intertwined for historical reasons. As part of the sojourn of the Overseas Chinese, the family has become the basic survival unit, and families do not fuse naturally into the general community. Moreover, Redding asserts, the members of the family are "motivated by the pragmatic exigencies of protecting and enhancing the family resources on which they in turn are very dependent."[21] Whereas the United States is preoccupied with "family values" and "the breakdown of the family," the Overseas Chinese view family as the bedrock of their lives, the anchor in a world with competing interests. The notion of family "extends beyond its members to encompass its property, its reputation, its internal traditions, its ancestors' spirits, and even its unborn future generations."[22]

Redding writes that the family unit does business as follows:

> …[I]t establishes a network of the necessary connections, and to make such networks operate reliably, Chinese society has come to attach central importance to the notion of trust. What is Chinese about this trust, however, is that it is very specifically circumscribed. It is limited to partners in the bond. It works on the basis of personal obligations, the maintenance of reputation and face, and not on any assumption that a society's shared faith makes all who share it equally righteous regardless of whether you know them or not.[23]

Thus, a Chinese entrepreneur based in Hong Kong will enlist the help of siblings in far-flung places to assist in the family enterprise. An older brother, for example, will summon his younger brother back from a career in Canada because his help is needed back in Hong Kong. Or, a Hong Kong entrepreneur expanding into the Los Angeles market will seek a cousin to provide trusted input, even if he is not an expert in the particular industry. Blood comes before expertise. Though perhaps not wise from a Western perspective, the Overseas Chinese put their primary emphasis on trust (particularly for critical decisions) rather than on professional, independent expertise.

There may be similarities to the Western model, although the Overseas Chinese model remains distinct. Redding explains: "The answer as to its special nature is that it retains many of the characteristics of small scale, such as paternalism, personalism, opportunism, flexibility, even to very large scale. It does not follow the Western pattern of professionalization, bureaucratization, and neutralization to anywhere near the same extent."[24]

In other words, in a Western context the family business is a transitory stage, whereas for the Overseas Chinese the family business model is a preferred way of doing business.

For the Overseas Chinese, Redding notes, the family provides roots: "It is hard for a Westerner to understand the extent to which the Chinese depend on family; how they look out and see the vacuum of no-man's-land—traversed as it may be by the networks they construct—but no man's land nonetheless."[25] Within the culture, the family business is a credible way of running a business. And, as noted previously, there are clearly some advantages to the family business model, namely responsiveness, flexibility, networking, and trust relationships.

7.4 Overseas Chinese Network Capitalism

> The use of "guan-xi" is a fundamental aspect of doing business among Overseas Chinese people; a network of close friends and associates is considered a critical competitive advantage in a cutthroat environment.

One frequently cited feature of *The Spirit of Chinese Capitalism* is "network capitalism." This is one of the most effective forms of economic systems that exists in the world, and is rooted in the notion of "guan-xi" (close interpersonal trust bonds; pronounced "guan-shee"). The Overseas Chinese build these personal networks for three reasons: to gather information, to stabilize sources of supply and markets, and to cement certain key relationships in an organization.[26] For example, a quick survey of goods in any department store in the world will reveal that about two-thirds of them were manufactured in China. But, the manufacturing facilities in China are often controlled by Overseas Chinese in Hong

Kong (and elsewhere) who have international connections in addition to relationships within China. The manufacturing pre-eminence of China is not an accident, as it owes much to the trading and technical expertise acquired by China's international cousins in the post-war decades. The Overseas Chinese, however, have developed a system based on a remarkable formula that efficiently delivers what the customer wants.

How do they produce goods so effectively? According to Redding, the "essential source of that efficiency is the reduction of transaction costs down to a point where they are minimized by the use of guan-xi in circumstances where the society suffers from endemic mistrust."[27] Paradoxically, this mistrusting society is able to "construct bonds and trust between specific individuals in a network which are absolutely cast iron, solid, unbreakable, lifetime reliable—but very specific."[28] The bonds do not apply to everyone, but just the particular people with whom they have been established. This reduces transaction costs because Overseas Chinese business-people do deals "across the network at lightning speed, without contract, without law, without documentation very often, and with an ability to change and adjust over time on the basis of a moral understanding that the obligation to the other person is sacred."[29]

The efficiency of guan-xi is something very few societies can match. In the United States, businesspeople will build up a network of contacts, but these are built on a house of cards compared to the Overseas Chinese—this is the difference between deep-seated bonds versus relationships of immediate convenience. Entrepreneurs are accustomed to considering transaction costs as part of every deal. The complaints of high legal costs are routine in the United States; to some extent, lawyers and contracts are an insurance policy against individuals breaking their agreements or not being amenable to alterations in the event of unforeseen circumstances. The law underwrites the risk, and the law is expensive. In other societies, such as Latin America, the Middle East, and India to some extent, this mistrust is so endemic that an entrepreneur cannot circumvent it. There is no equivalent of the Chinese notion of moral obligation within the network, except in subcultures (usually ethnic) within the larger society. Thus, the Overseas Chinese subculture works apart from societal norms of legal agreements.

This is the "secret weapon" of the Overseas Chinese. It produces a very low level of transaction costs and, therefore in turn, a very high efficiency in stitching things together and exemplifying the flexibility that customers demand. For example, overseas customers (such as Wal-Mart or Home Depot) who want to fine-tune the production of goods for the U.S. market will have a very quick turnaround time.

> **Friends Do Business**
> ...[Overseas] Chinese people will not do business with people they do not know, and network building for purposes of business deals has a high priority in their behavior.[30]

Relationships with individuals are a key element of Overseas Chinese society. Redding observes, "The Chinese are loyal to people, less so to principles or ideas. It is people who can most easily give them what they want in exchange for the highly focused form of loyalty which they are prepared to offer in exchange."[31]

7.5. The Overseas Chinese and Western Models of Entrepreneurship

> The use of "guan-xi" is a fundamental aspect of doing business among Overseas Chinese people; a network of close friends and associates is considered a critical competitive advantage in a cutthroat environment.

What can the Overseas Chinese model of entrepreneurship teach us about being entrepreneurs in North America? This question requires further clarification of the Overseas Chinese model. One must recognize an important distinction between the paradigm of the private sector presently in China and that of the Overseas Chinese people. In fact, these are two very different viewpoints. The private sector in China is subject to governmental regulations and their loosening over time, along with the creation of a legal system and the entry of the country into the world trading community (such as acceptance into the World Trade Organization on December 11, 2001).

The Overseas Chinese, by comparison, grew up in a unique fashion, apart from the Mother Country, and (aside from those in

Hong Kong, Taiwan, and Singapore) as a minority in an unfriendly environment. With respect to the Overseas Chinese model, Redding states, "It's a child of its upbringing, a product of its context—and what is Chinese about it is the particular pattern of response to a context. This response takes on a distinct Chinese form as a result of the social history in which the phenomenon is embedded."[32]

Next, we must examine the meaning of "entrepreneurship" for Overseas Chinese people. The starting point is to separate the three universal aspects of entrepreneurship from the social interpretations of entrepreneurship in a particular society. The first universal aspect of entrepreneurship is innovation—putting together new combinations of existing products, processes, or services. Second, there is usually domination by a single individual, the entrepreneur. Third, there is a strong drive among entrepreneurial organizations to be successful, because of the dominance of the entrepreneur's own personal ideology. These are three universal aspects of entrepreneurship; most other aspects of entrepreneurship will be shaded by local circumstances.

Then, there are "distinct social interpretations of how those aspects are to be brought to life and made real."[33] How are the universal principles of entrepreneurship applied in the case of the Overseas Chinese? It is almost a historical accident that their common form of business unit was particularly well suited to the conditions of Hong Kong and Taiwan in the second half of the 20th century and China at present. Redding reveals that in Hong Kong and Taiwan, for example, "the commanding heights of those economies were looked after by multinationals or governments; that left the rest of the economies to be run by small and medium-sized enterprises."[34]

In the case of Hong Kong and Taiwan, and now China, that opportunity coincided with a restructuring of world markets that was well suited for nimble and responsive small and medium enterprises to fit world market patterns, such as the endless demand for OEMs (original equipment manufacturers). The demand occurred because Western markets were looking for low-cost sourcing, and these small- and medium-sized firms could meet the demand. Most of these firms happened to be controlled by Overseas Chinese families that were better organized than their competitors in the Philippines, Indonesia, Thailand, and Malaysia. These factors coalesced to produce the so-called Asian economic miracle.

Thus, it is accurate to say, as Redding does, that there is a "special Overseas Chinese interpretation of the universals of entrepreneurship which happens to fit perfectly into the current opportunities based on world trade patterns."[35] What are the implications for understanding how entrepreneurs do business in other countries, and how one should relate to them? One is simply recognizing the nature of Overseas Chinese entrepreneurs when doing business with various aspects of the Chinese Diaspora.

What are the comparables to the United States? American entrepreneurship operates in a social structure with a number of distinct characteristics that do not apply in other countries, specifically "the extreme concentration on the individual as the core unit of society; the extreme obsession with competitive success; the extremely easy access to capital in exchange for disclosure; and a highly developed and systematized free market."[36] Not one of those conditions applies in China, or other countries, for that matter. Thus "American entrepreneurship" is unique on a global scale.

But the Overseas Chinese model is relevant in any nation where the environment is uncertain and heavily politicized—which covers many countries throughout the globe. If an entrepreneur works in those two conditions, then the response formula of the Overseas Chinese model is a perfect adaptation. Redding remarks that the Overseas Chinese "have raised the exchange of information and the sacred nature of information to a very high level of significance in their system, which includes the secrecy about it."[37] Further, he believes the Overseas Chinese have "learned to play the political game by focusing power within their system on the key players in the game, who can then co-opt political support, if necessary."[38] This relevant scenario may not apply in the U.S. context, where information is less secretive and environments are more predictable. Ironically, Redding records that one of the reasons Overseas Chinese often feel that they cannot make money in the United States is that the American system is too orderly: "There are no opportunities to develop, since everyone has the same information—so where's the sport in that?"[39]

The uniqueness of the Overseas Chinese model of entrepreneurship is how it responds to its particular conditions. With this knowledge, one can then examine the potential to apply lessons from the Overseas Chinese model to other international conditions or situations.

3 Inspirational Overseas Chinese Entrepreneurs

Li Ka Shing (1928–) is the wealthiest person in Hong Kong and East Asia, and the richest person of Chinese descent in the world. (The February 26, 2004, issue of *Forbes* ranked him 19th in the world, at $12.4 billion.) He has interests in 90 countries in the world, and he controls 12 percent of all container port capacity in the world. He has extensive interests in property development, telecommunications and energy.

He is unique because of his ability to trust other people, including Western professionals, to an extent far more than any other Chinese businessperson I know would do. He learned that very early. In addition, Li Ka Shing has immense personal entrepreneurial skill in spotting opportunities, and in coordinating a very large complex organization.

Sir Y.K. Pao (1918–1991) built the world's largest fleet of cargo vessels; by the 1970s he had 21 million tons and 200 ships (Aristotle Onassis had 3 million tons). Pao expanded into property, communications, media, and aviation. At his death, he was worth $1.3 billion, and was Hong Kong's first global businessman.

He is unique for his ability to create the 1950s world of "bare boat" chartering, meaning the chartering of an empty boat to a corporation for their use in moving goods around—and he would run the boat. Nobody ever thought of that before, but that was a stroke of genius in terms of entrepreneurship, and he was able to build the biggest ship-building company in the world.

Gordon Wu (1935–) founded Hopewell Holdings in 1964 and was listed on the Hong Kong Stock Exchange in 1972.

Hopewell is engaged in the development of properties, hotels, power stations and superhighways in Hong Kong, China, the Philippines, Indonesia, and Thailand.

Wu is an extraordinary innovator. His "slip form" method of construction enables one high-rise floor to be erected every three days. His power station in Guangdong, PRC, set a world record of sending the first electricity in month 22 after groundbreaking.

Redding's Key Points

7.1. The Overseas Chinese Diaspora (or network) is one of the most successful—and least studied and understood—networks of entrepreneurs in the world, and it is a model of success in spite of significant social and economic obstacles.

7.2. The spirit of Overseas Chinese capitalism is rooted in a drive to get rich, the desire to protect ideas, secrecy regarding business affairs and a paternalistic organizational structure.

7.3. The Overseas Chinese family business is intertwined with the aspirations of the present and future generations of a family, is a preferred way of doing business, and is not simply a transition stage in a firm's evolution to professional management.

7.4. The use of "guan-xi" is a fundamental aspect of doing business among Overseas Chinese people, with a network of close friends and associates being viewed as a critical competitive advantage in a cutthroat environment.

7.5. The Overseas Chinese model has two implications: First, Americans need to understand the model to do business with Overseas Chinese businesspeople; second, the model demonstrates how an entrepreneur can succeed in a volatile environment with limited access to information.

Chapter 8

Howard H. Stevenson: The Dimensions of Entrepreneurship

At Harvard we define entrepreneurship as the pursuit of opportunities without regard for the resources controlled.
—Howard H. Stevenson[1]

Introduction to Howard H. Stevenson

Name	Howard H. Stevenson
Title	Sarofim-Rock Professor of Business Administration
Affiliation(s)	Harvard University (Cambridge, Massachusetts)
Education	B.S. (Stanford) M.B.A; D.B.A. (Harvard)

Experience	o Sarofim-Rock Professor since its inception in 1982 o Chairman of the Owner/President Manager Program in Executive Education o Founder and the first president of the Baupost Group, Inc., which manages partnerships investing in liquid security for wealthy families (Its assets exceeded $400 million when he resigned as president)
Notable Publications	o Authored, edited, or coauthored 12 books and 42 articles, including *New Business Ventures and the Entrepreneur* (with Michael J. Roberts and H. Irving Grousbeck), *Just Enough* (with Laura Nash), and *The Entrepreneurial Venture* (with William Sahlman) o Authored, coauthored, or supervised more than 150 cases at Harvard Business School

Biographical Highlights

⊙ Stevenson has steered the study of entrepreneurship education at Harvard, which has more than 30 faculty members in its Entrepreneurial Management Unit. (Harvard, one of the world's most elite business schools, has been a leading institution for entrepreneurial education since the 1930s.)

⊙ Stevenson coauthored one of the leading textbooks in the field, *New Business Ventures and the Entrepreneur,* through six editions.

⊙ He has combined his academic expertise with the practical experience of being a founder, the first president, and now cochair of the advisory board, for Baupost, Inc., an $8 billion registered investment company.

The Entrepreneurial Culture at Harvard Business School

What are the goals and objectives of Harvard in terms of its entrepreneurial programs?[2] Harvard's approach to teaching entrepreneurship is rooted, quite naturally, in its well-known case-method approach. The school, which requires its 900 first-year students to take a course called "The Entrepreneurial Manager," and offers nearly 20 elective courses in entrepreneurship to second-year students,[3] also develops case-method resources. Since 1999, Harvard's Entrepreneurship Unit has developed nearly 600 sets of course and curricular material, including nearly 400 teaching cases. A total of 1,800 cases on myriad aspects of entrepreneurship are now available.[4]

"There are many different mechanisms that we integrate into our teaching of entrepreneurship," Howard Stevenson describes. He goes on to say:

> We use exercises, field studies, case studies, and participant-centered learning….I recently ran a course for 60 Eastern European teachers of entrepreneurship. They came in thinking they knew the case study method as a means of business school teaching, but their eyes were opened to the fact that the requisite knowledge, skills, and attitudes are acquired through how people really learn, rather than how we typically teach them."[5]

Such unique methods draw attention to the entrepreneurship program.

In fact, Harvard promotes entrepreneurship as something that should be considered by all students. Stevenson notes:

> One of the critical things we do in developing courses is to introduce people who aren't larger than life, with whom students can identify. Very early, we build cases around both female and male entrepreneurs of all types and all ages. The opportunity to provide a course where students can identify with the protagonists in a case is an important part of the pedagogy.[6]

At Harvard, students learn that entrepreneurial management is a viable and promising option.

"What we are trying to do at Harvard Business School is plant a 'time bomb' that will go off in 10–15 years," Stevenson explains.[7] In other words, when opportunities arise for MBA students, they will know how to exploit them. Stevenson continues, "If we can infuse the students with the right attitude, we will have a tremendous impact on their ability to make a difference."[8]

In saying this, he places entrepreneurship under the umbrella of Harvard's institutional mission: to train leaders who make a difference in the world. Not only is entrepreneurship under the umbrella: It seems to help hold up the umbrella. Stevenson notes that it is "an important part"[9] of Harvard's international mandate.

One of Stevenson's three tenets of teaching entrepreneurship at Harvard is to convey to students that entrepreneurship is an opportunity-focused orientation to general management, one that is applicable in many situations, regardless of near-term career aspirations.[10] He encourages students that an entrepreneurial career may be a more interesting alternative to a standard-issue investment banking or management consulting job. According to his philosophy, students can learn that "controlling your own life is something an entrepreneur does."[11] Stevenson believes students need to be exposed to an entrepreneur-friendly culture and positive entrepreneurial role models.[12]

> Entrepreneurship is like having children: it requires a moment of enthusiasm, followed by decades of hard work, in order to be successful.[13]

As Stevenson expresses, Harvard Business School teaches three simple attitudes: "Every situation can be improved; you can make a difference, no matter how minimal your power or your current resources; and, experts and experience may be wrong."[14] Stevenson believes these attitudes have helped Harvard generate more high-profile, successful entrepreneurs than any other school. He also notes that Harvard had a high share of the MBA market in 1945, and that many of these individuals have achieved great success through time. (Since 1945, however, the number of MBA programs has multiplied and Harvard's proportionate share of the MBA market has dropped significantly.)[15]

According to Stevenson, the core of Harvard's approach is this: "While the world has its share of problems, if I solve them for other people, I will make money—and just because I don't presently have the resources, doesn't mean I shouldn't try to solve the problem."[16] In essence, his teaching approach is, "Don't tell me what you would do if you were God; instead, what are you going to do as a product manager with inadequate power and resources?"[17] He also advises students, "If somebody tells you it hasn't been done that way before, treat that as good news rather than bad news."[18]

Stevenson likens many so-called trade publications to diet books: Both offer recycled easy paths to success, but at best have only a minimal effect. "How many people actually lose weight?" he states frankly. "It is easier to buy the book than it is to go on the diet!"[19] Similarly, he cautions students to remember that entrepreneurship is very complicated, and they shouldn't look for simple solutions.

Instead, Stevenson points students to the fundamentals of the entrepreneurial process. With a witty sense of humor, he remarks, "I tell students not to start a business, because the only one they are qualified to start right now is a lemonade stand."[20] Instead, he recommends, "Learn an industry, get known in your field, get people to respect you, and then when you are ready to launch a venture, you can do so in a high potential field."[21]

By "high potential field," he means "[a business] that has a chance of actually making a difference to you and to the world."[22] In his view, "We are dealing with students who are gifted, otherwise they wouldn't be at Harvard. We are trying to help them think that one of the right things they might do is enjoy entrepreneurship."[23] Though his approach may not be suitable for all aspiring entrepreneurs, it reflects the outlook of one of the world's most prominent and accomplished institutions.

8.1 The 6 Dimensions of Entrepreneurial Management

> The six dimensions of entrepreneurial management are: strategic orientation, commitment to opportunity, commitment of resources, control of resources, management structure, and compensation and reward policy.

Stevenson's succinct definition of entrepreneurship, as noted in the Introduction, is "the pursuit of opportunities without regard to the resources controlled."[24] He focuses on the process, not the person. Furthermore, he highlights a "behavioral phenomenon" of entrepreneurship with relation to the following six critical dimensions of business practice: strategic orientation, commitment to opportunity, the resource commitment process, control over resources, the concept of management, and the compensation policy.[25]

Stevenson argues that these six dimensions of business practice reveal a range of behavioral responses, with two types of individuals on opposite ends of the spectrum. At one extreme is the "promoter," who "feels confident of his or her ability to seize opportunity, regardless of the resources under current control."[26] At the other extreme is the "trustee," who "emphasizes the efficient utilization of existing resources."[27]

Stevenson's definition sees entrepreneurship within the context of existing business practices. In addition, he individually characterizes entrepreneurs, based on their tendencies toward certain ends of the spectrum. Thus, he sees entrepreneurship as similar to, rather than different from, conventional business.

"I think part of Harvard's success is that we don't say entrepreneurship is different," he observes. "What we say is that entrepreneurship is the pursuit of opportunity beyond the resources you control—and that is absolutely critical for every organization. A start-up needs to do this, as does a larger company."[28]

Stevenson's 6 Dimensions

1. Strategic orientation.

Strategic orientation is "the factors that drive the firm's formulation of strategy."[29] In this context, the promoter is *opportunity-driven* concerned with new possibilities and not constrained by lack of resources. The trustee, on the other hand, is *resource-driven* focused on best utilizing the resources under his or her present control.

Stevenson points out that this dimension of business practice has led many people to see entrepreneurship as innovation. However, in Stevenson's definition, entrepreneurs include those who are not only innovators, but also those who pursue opportunity through a "new mix of old ideas or the creative application of traditional approaches."[30]

Stevenson refers to a collection of "pressures" that pull a firm to one of two "sides" of behavior, either entrepreneurial (promoter) or administrative (trustee). The pressures that pull a firm to the entrepreneurial side of behavior are consumer economics, social values, diminishing opportunity streams, rapid changes in technology, or political roles. Conversely, the pressures that pull a firm to the administrative side are the "social contract" (a responsibility to use existing people and resources), performance criteria (rewards for growth or for resources utilization), and planning systems and cycles. (Can new opportunities change the allocation of resources in a three- or five-year plan?)

Strategic orientation addresses the entrepreneur's situational reality and motivating factors. It asks what resources are attainable, and how a person could best manage them. Stevenson illustrates, "If you have $500 million, your best opportunity is to figure out how to invest that money wisely. But most entrepreneurs who start a firm do not have $500 million at their disposal."[31] Many entrepreneurs start with limited resources, and their desire to pursue an opportunity often arises from a practical standpoint—from their ability to exploit the current situation.

Stevenson gives examples: "If you are a black person from the inner city, you may have started playing baseball or basketball. And if you were a Jew living in the early 1900s, you weren't going to join a bank and rise to the top, because they didn't let you."[32] The challenge for Stevenson is to convince talented Harvard MBA students that entrepreneurship opportunities are worth pursuing, despite the parallel option to join secure investment banking and consulting firms.

2. Commitment to opportunity.

This second dimension of business practice steps beyond strategic orientation and begins a process of practical implementation. Stevenson comments, "There are innovative thinkers who never get anything done; it is necessary to move beyond the identification of opportunity, to its pursuit."[33]

A promoter, who is willing to pursue an opportunity quickly and with gusto, may not be as committed to the project as a trustee, who moves deliberately and with great thought. The promoter's commitment level depends heavily on initial results.

Pressures that pull a firm to the promoter side of the spectrum include action orientation, short decision windows, flexible deployment of financial resources, and limited decision constituencies. By contrast, a firm moves to the trustee side because of multiple decision constituencies, strategy dependent upon compromise and evolutionary agreement, study and analysis to reduce risk, or projects needing to fit existing corporate resources.

3. Commitment of resources.

A third dimension of business practice that separates promoters from trustees is the commitment of resources. Promoters attempt to maximize value by committing the minimum amount of resources for the greatest possible return. Their perspective, as Stevenson affirms, is, "Entrepreneurial management requires that you learn to do a little more with a little less."[34] Promoters straddle a fine line between exploiting an opportunity and having barely enough resources to do so.

Trustees, on the other hand, deploy resources after careful analysis and large-scale commitment.[35] The pressures on the trustee side of the spectrum are lack of predictable resource needs (the entrepreneur commits less up front so more will be available later on), lack of long-term control, and the ability to allocate resources when required. In a large company, the trustee faces pressures related to resource intensity, such as personal risk reduction (through increased resources), incentive compensation (because excess resources increase short-term returns), managerial turnover, capital allocation systems (designed for one-time decision making), and formal planning systems.[36]

4. Control of resources.

With respect to the control of resources, an entrepreneur must be able to deploy resources when necessary, instead of retaining control through ownership. In other words, a promoter only needs to bring resources together at deal time; otherwise, the resources are a drain on overhead. Thus, a promoter has a very utilitarian view of the resources required to run a business or complete a deal.

High-tech companies, in their early stages, may employ a "CEO in a box"—a person with a level of expertise that the young company cannot afford, but who works on a part-time basis. As the company grows, they can then transition their CEO to a full-time position. Thus the pressures toward the entrepreneurial side of the spectrum come from increased resource specialization, risk of obsolescence, and the demand for increased flexibility.

The trustee, on the other hand, prefers to control his or her own resources, as this enhances certainty of planning. The pressures toward the trustee side of the spectrum are the distinct appeal of power, status, and rewards (may be determined by resource control and ownership); the advantage that ownership facilitates a quick response (as control, rather than negotiation, is critical); the ability to maximize profit (by capturing all proceeds associated with an operation); inertia and the cost of change (control of resources reduces risks); and industry structures (ownership prevents preemption by competition).

5. Management structures.

A promoter functions through an array of informal relationships, called upon when necessary, in order to pursue possibilities and facilitate the use of supplies. As a result, he or she does not delegate authority, but rather assembles resources. On the contrary, the trustee views relations more formally, with specific rights and obligations attached to particular positions. Only owned resources can be organized in a hierarchy.

Does being a good manager (trustee) preclude someone from being an effective entrepreneur (promoter)? Stevenson explains, "Although the managerial task is substantially different from the entrepreneur's, management skill is nonetheless essential [in entrepreneurship]. The variation [between the two] lies in the choice of appropriate tools."[37]

Thus, "entrepreneurial management" is an effective combination of both skill sets. It is also a result of several pressures: for promoter-types, the need to coordinate resources outside the firm, the desire for flexibility through a flat organization, and the fact that employees accept authority based on competence and persuasion; for trustee-types, the need for clearly defined authority and responsibility, and the desire for organized culture and clearly-specified reward systems.

6. Reward philosophy.

The last dimension of business practice that distinguishes the promoter from the trustee is differing approaches to reward and compensation. Entrepreneurial firms focus on generating capital and providing a return to shareholders that is commensurate with the perceived risk of the venture. Moreover, entrepreneurial firms tend to reward all those who create value. They attain their goals, opportunities to sell the business or go public, when the rewards are sufficient. And if this occurs, the entrepreneur is typically confident that he or she can start another venture subsequently; thus, he or she has no loyalty to the existing business.

The trustee, on the other hand, makes decisions based on a desire to protect his or her position, which is his or her career and personal sense of security. An individual's compensation may be tied to specific targets within the established hierarchy; his or her success and longevity may exist, to some extentm, apart from the overall health of the organization. Moreover, compensation may be tied to increased responsibility within a firm, rather than specific value creation, which can be more difficult to quantify.

The pressures toward the promoter end of the spectrum include the following: individual compensation in proportion to contribution; investor expectations of immediate returns; and increased demand for talented individuals requires adequate compensation. The pressures toward the trustee side are as follows: Loyalty to an organization is a counterweight to a focus on compensation; individual contribution to value creation may be difficult to segment out of an organizational structure; and public shareholders may resist perceived excessive compensation.

The six dimension of business practice, and the promoter and trustee ends of the spectrum, are summarized in the following chart. Stevenson's approach is that entrepreneurship is more than the behavior model of individual traits and is not only an economic function—instead it is a "cohesive pattern of managerial behavior."[38]

In his opinion, entrepreneurship is an approach to management that can be applied in start-ups or in large corporations, although in view of the spectrum established, it is more difficult in a "trustee" environment. A practical point emphasized by Stevenson is that entrepreneurial management involves a lot of perspiration and not just inspiration: "You actually have to run the numbers. You learn to tell a bad deal from a good deal."[39]

A Process Definition of Entrepreneurship[40]

ENTREPRENEUR	KEY BUSINESS DIMENSION	ADMINISTRATOR
Driven by Perception of Opportunity	**Strategic Orientation**	Driven by Resources Currently Controlled
Quick Commitment	**Commitment to Opportunity**	Evolutionary with Long Duration
Multistage with minimal exposure at each stage	**Commitment Process**	Single-stage with Complete Commitment Upon Decision

Episodic use of Rent of Required Resources	**Control of Resources**	Ownership or Employment of Required Resources
Fiat with Multiple Informal Networks	**Management Structure**	Formalized Hierarchy
Value-Based & Team-Based	**Reward System**	Resource-Based; Individual and Promotion Oriented

8.2 Ethics and Entrepreneurship

> An ethical approach to the six dimensions of business practice is a critical success factor for entrepreneurial management.

Stevenson explains that in view of his definition of entrepreneurship, a finely tuned sense of ethics is critical to individual and organizational success. If entrepreneurship is about pursuing opportunity beyond the resources you presently control, then "unless you create a sense of real trust with others who control resources, then [you] will never succeed."[41] It is critical that an entrepreneur have a sense of fair dealing and a sense of just proportion when dealing with other people.

Taking this high road will not necessary make you successful: "That doesn't mean you cannot succeed by cheating."[42] But, the bottom line is that, for most people, "When you are going out to raise money or launch a venture, [you have] to develop both an implicit and explicit sense of trust among those people—and if you do not, you will not be able to access their resources."[43]

Stevenson argues that most entrepreneurship texts do not place a sufficient emphasis on the role of ethical behavior.[44] In fact, the notion of ethics needs to permeate the entire curriculum. One outcome of a lack of ethical sensitivity relates to business plan competitions routinely held at universities. Many of these are fundamentally flawed. The objective, in Stevenson's opinion, is to "hide the fatal flaw."[45] In a sense, students are operating on the premise that they can "fool the person who is only going to spend an hour reading the business plan."[46] This is not good ethical training. As Stevenson points out, "That's absolutely not the way the world works and it's certainly not the way you succeed.

If you find a fatal flaw and you don't disclose it, you are going to be the one that bears most of the consequences."[47] Entrepreneurs (or promoters, as Stevenson calls them) need to be even more sensitive to ethical matters than managers (trustees).

However, entrepreneurs, with their greater degree of personal responsibility for the success of the business venture, also suffer the greater temptation to cut corners. Because they will benefit from an increased upside, they feel a strong pressure that does not exist for trustees in their more stable environment. In fact, entrepreneurial trade publications often gleefully recount the tales of now-successful entrepreneurs who launched themselves through deception, misleading suppliers as to their financial creditworthiness, making involuntary financiers of creditors, and exaggerating their backgrounds, financial capabilities, and connections.

Stevenson affirms: "When things are going badly for an entrepreneur, there is a natural inclination to think about cutting closer to the line."[48] As the past financial shenanigans on a grand scale, exemplified by companies such as Enron and Worldcom, have demonstrated, large companies have ethical issues. Stevenson notes, "The [entrepreneur's] internal pressure…of being personally at risk creates a lot of ethical tension."[49]

Although being an ethical person is not a recipe for success, it is a better way to live with oneself and others. And Stevenson believes the majority of successful entrepreneurs are those who indeed maintain a good sense of ethical behavior:

> Most of them who succeed in the long run, and this isn't the Donald Trumps of the world, actually do have a very strong sense of ethics, because they know that their ability to do a deal twice depends on treating people fairly the first time. I don't think that's naïve, although some might say it is. I don't think it's "the reputation effect;" rather, you operate on the basis that "our paths will likely cross again."[50]

To some degree, good ethics is an extension of knowing how to treat people properly—not attempting to manipulate or mislead others. In other words, ethical people ask what the other person wants and how they can help him or her succeed.

In an organizational setting, successful companies look at failure in a unique way. Stevenson advises that a successful manager must distinguish between moral, personal, and uncontrollable failure. Moral failure is "a violation of internal trust or of societal rules."[51] Individuals who violate the internal trust mechanisms set up within an organization (through deception, thievery, or other moral transgression) affect not only their own relationships but also those existing among others. Successful organizations treat these transgressions seriously even if the goal was noble and the results positive to the bottom line. A moral failure is difficult to remedy, and typically has permanent consequences for the transgressor—who almost always leaves the organization.

Personal failure, on the other hand, results from a lack of skill, dedication, or application. Because there may be ways for both the organization and the individual to readjust the work performed and the set of expectations, there is scope to rethink how to move forward together. Lastly, an "uncontrollable failure" is one caused by external factors, such as a parent corporation reshifting resources; in this instance, the organization will have to exercise extreme fairness in assessing the performance of the manager.

Practice and Theory as Recounted by Howard Stevenson[52]

The Entrepreneur to the Professor: "If you're so smart, why aren't you rich?"

The Professor to the Entrepreneur: "If you are so rich, why aren't you smart?"

Frank Batten of the Weather Channel[53]

One of the most inspirational entrepreneurs I have come to know is Frank Batten, who founded The Weather Channel in 1982. He's created a number of very successful businesses, but more importantly he's created an organization that functions well. He's not a guy where it all has to be about him.

Frank often says that the most important thing for employees to remember is that they serve customers at a profit. And both parts of this statement are very critical. We have to serve our customers well, because if we don't, we won't have them. But we have to do so at a profit, or we won't be in business. I think that simply reflects a very clear understanding of the reality of being in business every day.

Frank Batten, the entrepreneur behind The Weather Channel, faced almost certain failure in the venture's first year of operation.

His cable channel, which delivered weather information and forecasts 24 hours a day, was losing $1 million a month.

Yet unwilling to concede defeat, and confident in his idea's potential, Batten convinced cable system operators to keep him on the air. Now, just more than 25 years later, The Weather Channel is a booming success. It has more than 80 million viewers across North America.

After graduating from the University of Virginia and spending time in the U.S. Merchant Marine, Batten went to Harvard for an MBA. When he finished his MBA in 1952, he returned to Norfolk, Virginia. There he worked for his family's media business, Landmark Communications, Inc. In 1954, when Batten was 27, he became the publisher of two of his family's newspapers, the *Norfolk Ledger-Dispatch* and the *Virginian-Pilot*.

Landmark Communications purchased a cable television system in 1964, and later acquired several more cable systems. In the three years that followed, Batten himself (under the umbrella of Landmark Communications) was responsible for starting or buying 10 daily newspapers, numerous television stations, and more than 100 non-daily newspapers and magazines. He also started Trader Publishing Co. (a national publisher of classified advertisements) in partnership with Cox Enterprises.

Batten created The Weather Channel in 1982. It became international (moving into Europe and Latin America) in 1996, and today it is also connected with the Website *weather.com,* which has more than 300 million page views per month. The growth of The Weather Channel is a testament to Batten's perseverance and his wisdom as an entrepreneur.

8.3 Enduring Success

Success is not about maximization, but about balancing your work and life; this can be managed through an approach of "just enough," which will create enduring success.

Is an all-consuming focus on business, with little regard for the rest of life, a necessary part of entrepreneurial success? Entrepreneurs generally acknowledge that the one-dimensional pursuit of financial success does not make for a content person. More commonly, during the past decade or so, work and life have become viewed as inseparable. The compartmentalization of the past is no longer acceptable to businesspeople, and workers are more self-focused. The corporate employer will no longer look after them for the long term, so the individuals take on that responsibility. The "free agent" mentality of employees, lack of allegiance from company to employee, the independence afforded by the Internet, and the on-going growth of entrepreneurship have allowed workers to carve out their own career goals and seek a balance between work and life.

Stevenson (and coauthor Laura Nash) state in the preface to *Just Enough,* "You cannot separate individual success from the success of the organizations in which we are embedded: family, work, community, and the world. Our goal is to enhance your ability to handle legitimate performance difficulties in today's business environment and to help you to understand how this skill depends on deeper commitments to an authentic view of success."[54] Thus, work and life are truly intertwined; the "whole person" sits at his cubicle or in her corner office every day.

Furthermore, each person needs ongoing, achievable success in multiple forms. Nash and Stevenson define four important outcomes in order to generate enduring success: achievement, happiness, significance, and legacy.[55] Achievement means striving toward the extraordinary in some form. This is an ideal of excellence, an innovation, a personal stretch, an expanded capacity beyond that of your competitors without the frustration at partial victory. Second, happiness is experiencing pleasure or contentment in and about your life. Third, significance is giving value to others, contributing something valued by society and the people you care about. And finally, legacy is the sustained impact that will build other people's success. This is not a flash in the pan achievement, but is about having an impact beyond your present influence on the lives of others.

Within this framework, Nash and Stevenson propose a "kaleidoscope strategy"[56] to address goals in each of the four categories without shortchanging other goals. This is a method for allowing individuals and business to "switch" and "link" between the goals. Nash and Stevenson assert that enduring successes are people who are actively engaged in hitting moving targets, and yet do it in such a way that they create a coherent set of satisfactions for themselves and others. The outcome, according to Nash and Stevenson, is, "When you achieve these goals, success feels satisfying and worthwhile: Just enough."[57]

In addition, Nash and Stevenson stress two major themes in *Just Enough*. First, they "caution against the assumptions of celebrity and thinking that what you expect from success can be gained by putting your all into the One Right Target."[58] Although bookstore shelves are replete with titles that highlight the power of focus, Nash warns that this type of approach is likely to create an imbalanced life and an unstable basis for financial performance over the long term.[59] Second, the coauthors argue "that everyone needs to construct a success framework."[60] Those who do not think through their priorities and how to manage them are likely to be subsumed by society's stilted notions of success. They become slaves to the demands of short-term shareholders or to expectations of overconsumption in one's personal life.

A significant point raised in *Just Enough* is that lofty goals are great for motivational purposes, but may be debilitating in the long term if they are not considered in light of the total picture of success. Setting your sights unrealistically high may lead to severe disappointment. The enthusiastically uttered aphorism that "what the mind can believe, the mind can achieve" sounds quite nice when cannonading from the front of an auditorium to an adoring audience, but it is a tad impractical the next morning. As a result, Nash and Stevenson affirm, "It's important to bring your goals down to the admired but possible reality."[61] An important tool is the self-definition of success, according to one's individual commitments, rather than as defined by external norms.

In terms of practical applications, Nash states that the book can be used on a personal and organizational level. First, *Just Enough* has a fractal value. There is the *private application* of the book, whereby an individual can use the tools for his or her personal life management. An individual, depending upon his or her role within an organization, will have differing degrees of control as to how to implement the concepts in *Just Enough*. An entrepreneur in charge of a small, high-growth company could structure his or her lifestyle around a suitable balance; on the other hand, a mid-level manager might be fighting against the culture of his or her department or organization in order to achieve a balanced life. For the latter group of people, solutions will have to be explored in the domain of life outside work—or the job must change. In either scenario, the individual takes the initiative to create a work and life equilibrium.

In *systematic application,* an organization strives to create a work environment in which the multiple dimensions of a person's being are recognized. This approach can be very useful, because an imbalanced leader might normally expect his or her executive team to live with a similar imbalance. Using this approach, though, he or she will recognize the differences in others. Nash mentions, "If you are an uberachiever who puts your own interests first, last, and always and you are leading a company, you will sap other people's ability to develop beyond a supporting role—if you don't burn them out first."[62] Such leadership is "not a sustainable model."[63] After all, few executives want to sacrifice everything for a company they have not founded, in which they do not have a strong ownership stake, and for which their entire ego is on the line.

Overall, Stevenson emphasizes that success should not be achieved through personal aggrandizement. We live in community. An orientation to the needs of others will serve entrepreneurs best in the long term:

> I think anybody who thinks it's all about me by studying economics has got it wrong. And I think almost all people who are successful have an understanding that it's about more than them. That includes an ethical approach to other people. It also includes a notion that we are all servants to other people in terms that we will only succeed when we meet other people's needs. It's also the relationship to our employees. In short, I believe we must teach that entrepreneurship is not just an economic transaction with the purpose of making money. We need to teach that it's not all about you.[64]

Stevenson's Key Points

8.1. The six dimensions of entrepreneurial management include: strategic orientation, commitment to opportunity, commitment of resources, control of resources, management structure, and compensation and reward policy.

8.2. An ethical approach to the six dimensions of business practice is a critical success factor for entrepreneurial management.

8.3. Success is not about maximization, but about balancing your work and life; this can be managed through an approach of "just enough," which will create enduring success.

Chapter 9

Jeffry Timmons:
New Venture Creation

During the past 30 years, America has unleashed the most revolutionary generation the nation has experienced since its founding in 1776. This new generation of entrepreneurs has altered permanently the economic and societal structure of this nation and the world, and it has set the "entrepreneurial genetic code" for future generations. It will determine, more than any other single impetus, how the nation and the world will live, work, learn, and lead in this century and beyond.

—Jeffry Timmons[1]

Introduction to Jeffry Timmons

Name	Jeffry R. Timmons
Title	Franklin W. Olin Distinguished Professor of Entrepreneurship
Affiliation(s)	Babson College (Babson Park, Massachusetts)
Education	A.B. (Colgate) M.B.A.; D.B.A. (Harvard)

Experience	Investor, director, and advisor for public and private companies including Cellular One in Boston, New Hampshire, and Maine, the Boston Communications Group, BCI Advisors, Inc., Spectrum Equity Investors, Internet Securities, Inc., and Chase Capital Partnersada
Notable Publications	*New Venture Creation, 6th Ed.* (2003) *The Entrepreneurial Mind* (1989)

Biographical Highlights

- ⊙ Jeffry Timmons pioneered entrepreneurship programs in the early 1970s, when the field of study hardly existed. Inc. Magazine dubbed him "the Johnny Appleseed of entrepreneurship."[2]

- ⊙ With Timmons as a leading light, Babson College (Wellesley, Massachusetts) has consistently been ranked the number-one entrepreneurship program in the world.

- ⊙ Timmons has held simultaneous professorships at Babson College and Harvard Business School. He is currently at Babson full time, and in 1995 the school named him the first Franklin W. Olin Distinguished Professor of Entrepreneurship.

- ⊙ Timmons has authored several books, including the leading entrepreneurship textbook *New Venture Creation, 6th Ed.* (2003).

- ⊙ Timmons' writings are infused with practical insights, as he has nearly 30 years of immersion in the world of entrepreneurship, as an investor, director, and advisor for private companies.

9.1. The Entrepreneurial Revolution

> The "entrepreneurial revolution" is creating historically unique opportunities for individuals to amass wealth for themselves and their communities.

Change creates opportunity. With a society's transitioning likes and dislikes, and new developments in technology, some products are rendered obsolete as niches for others grow. One of the most notable changes in recent yearsare the arrival of the internet which is highlighted in the dotcom boom of the late 1990s, only to be followed by the "dot bomb," which began in March 2000.

Another area of recent societal transformation is the music industry: Technology has dramatically transformed how people record, distribute, and listen to music. In a few decades, we have evolved from record albums to eight tracks, and from eight tracks to cassettes—and from there to CDs, then MP3s, and then to Internet downloading and the iPod. As a result, the music industry, from producers to artists, has also changed to meet new demands. Similarly, the lifeblood of the entrepreneur and his or her organization is anticipating and responding to change. This requires an organization that can act and react quickly.

Sometimes small, nimble organizations exist, but not necessarily. The Internet has created a handful of household company names, and huge accompanying stock market valuations, within a few short years. Amazon.com is legendary as a new distribution-based powerhouse that grew from nothing. Another example is eBay, which bills itself as "The World's Online Marketplace" and boasts more than 100 million registered members. This San Jose-based company was founded in 1995, and by 2005 had a market capitalization of approximately $55 billion.[3] Now eBay is one of the 50 largest companies in the United States. It has local sites in approximately 20 countries, and is continually expanding into new markets to sustain its rapid growth.[4] So, why was eBay's dramatic emergence possible? Jeffry Timmons's answer: because of the changing technological landscape.

In _New Venture Creation,_ Timmons (speaking of the sea change since the 1970s) claims, "America has unleashed the most revolutionary generation the nation has experienced since its founding in 1776."[5] His reasoning is that "this new generation of entrepreneurs has altered permanently the economic and social structure of [the United States] and the world, and it has set the 'entrepreneurial genetic code' for future generations."[6] He predicts, "It will determine, more than any other single impetus, how the nation and the world will live, work, learn, and lead in this century and beyond."[7] In other words, individuals such as Jeff Bezos, Michael Dell, Bill Gates, Steve Jobs, and others have set a standard of innovation, success, and prominence that acts as an entrepreneurial beacon. Their stories—for example, the one about Michael Dell building computers in his dorm room at the University of Texas—inspire other entrepreneurs.

The cumulative impact of these high-profile entrepreneurs, who provide modern-day variants of the Horatio Alger tales, has enormously altered the economic landscape of the United States and the world. Unlike in Europe, for example, few Americans talk of "old money"; after all, past fortunes can be dwarfed in a matter of years by the fast-rising entrepreneurs. Timmons points out, "[M]ore than 95 percent of the wealth in America today has been created by this entrepreneurial generation ('E-generation') of revolutionaries since 1980."[8] This entrepreneurial class is a self-made, self-generating elite, as opposed to an upper class coasting on momentum and borrowed time. There is complete social mobility within the entrepreneurial class—entry is a reflection of economic success rather than race or creed.

Mr. K[9]

Ewing Marion Kauffman, or "Mr. K.," as Timmons calls him, founded the pharmaceutical company Marion Labs in 1950—with five thousand dollars, in the basement of his Kansas City home. He had experienced previous success with another company, but when the president cut back Mr. K's commission, he quit.

His basement business venture paid off. Mr. K's work through four decades culminated in Merrill Dow's acquisition of his company in 1989, when it became "Marion Merrill Dow, Inc." The company had approximately $3 billion in revenues.

Timmons says one of Mr. K's core principles was to share created wealth with all those who have contributed to it, at all levels. Not only did Mr. K prosper, but more than 300 of his employees became millionaires when the company sold.

A second principle Mr. K. endorsed was to give back to the community. He established the Ewing Marion Foundation, which became one of only a dozen or so foundations in America with assets of over $1 billion. The Foundation has two missions: to make a lasting difference by helping at-risk youth, and to encourage leadership in all aspects of American life. Kauffman also established a Center for Entrepreneurial Leadership in Kansas City.

The entrepreneurial revolution is creating unique opportunities for individuals to amass wealth and build organizations on a previously unimaginable scale. Individuals who can create technical innovations in the midst of a rapidly changing environment are able to join the entrepreneurial elite—open to all, based on success in the marketplace. These entrepreneurial leaders can significantly impact their communities with the monetary resources they acquire.

9.2. The Entrepreneurial Mind

Effective pursuit of opportunities starts with an *entrepreneurial mind,* composed of six acquirable "core" attributes and supplemented by four not-as-acquirable "desirable" attributes.

Although we may be in the midst of an "entrepreneurial revolution," few people take heed. Why do some individuals see opportunities where others see none? Timmons defines entrepreneurship as "a way of thinking, reasoning, and acting that is opportunity obsessed, holistic in approach, and leadership balanced."[10] Such methodical action identifies and pursues a particular opportunity with a concentrated team effort.

Who, then, is the protagonist at the center of the entrepreneurial process? He or she is not necessarily an entrepreneur, but an individual who acts and thinks with an entrepreneurial mind. The notion that people are born entrepreneurs has long been discounted, but perhaps it bears repeating that, instead, entrepreneurs are individuals who adopt a certain pattern of behavior. If this were not the case, the only point of educating people would be to hone preexisting proclivities.

Timmons's research and synthesis of more than 50 studies has revealed six dominant attitudes and behaviors that characterize the entrepreneurial mind. The rate at which individuals acquire these attitudes and behaviors depends on their motivation and level of perseverance, but the attributes are at least available to all. Moreover, people have an amazing capacity for change and growth.

ATTRIBUTES[11]	
Core (Acquirable)	Desirable (Not Acquirable)
Commitment and determination	Energy
Leadership	Health and emotional stability
Opportunity obsession	Creativity and innovation
Tolerance of risk, ambiguity, and uncertainty	Intelligence
Creativity, self-reliance, and adaptability	
Motivation to excel	

First, the entrepreneur will require *commitment and determination* to overcome inevitable obstacles and challenges. Timmons notes, "Almost without exception, entrepreneurs live under huge, constant pressures, first for their firms to survive startup, then for them to stay alive, and finally for them to grow."[12] Thus, entrepreneurs need to channel their energy. They must make personal sacrifices, often risking all of their own worth in order to grow the company. Further, they should have the discipline to persist in a well-ordered method of solving problems.

A second desirable and acquirable core attribute is *leadership*: Entrepreneurs inspire themselves and others to achieve lofty goals. Timmons explains, "They are self starters, and have an internal locus of control with high standards. They are patient leaders, capable of instilling tangible visions and managing for the longer haul."[13] Much of their ability to lead comes from exerting power without formal control—they inspire others to work together, rather than demanding support through hierarchical dominance.

A third desirable/acquirable attribute is *opportunity obsession*. The successful entrepreneur typically focuses on a single opportunity and pursues it with passion. An entrepreneur realizes that, although there are many ideas in the marketplace, there may be few opportunities, particularly ones that fit the entrepreneur's skills. Thus, when there is a good fit, the entrepreneur pursues the opportunity passionately.

Fourth, entrepreneurs must develop a *tolerance of risk, ambiguity,* and *uncertainty*. The entrepreneurial mind is quite different from the mindset of many managers and professional workers. Entrepreneurs are constantly assessing risks and determining which opportunities to pursue, all the while putting a good portion of their net worth on the line. Ambiguity is high—entrepreneurs must often make choices without knowing all the facts; thus, they learn to exploit available information as much as possible, and to reach decisions without having all the details, as an opportunity may vanish with prolonged deliberation. They must also face the disconcerting possibility of failure, since the outcomes of entrepreneurial actions are impossible to foresee. Managers and company workers, by contrast, prefer predictable tasks, a regular salary, minimal risk, and foreseeable results.

A fifth set of acquirable and desirable attributes is *creativity*, *self-reliance*, and *adaptability*. Entrepreneurs need to envisage new ways of doing things, and they need to arrive at solutions. The pioneering process requires them to be self-reliant, because they present innovations in a world where change is not always welcomed. With that in mind, entrepreneurs obviously have to welcome and adapt to new environments, even when others pine for the way things have always been.

Finally, entrepreneurs should cultivate a personal *motivation to excel*. Timmons notes, "Entrepreneurs are self starters who appear driven internally by a strong desire to compete against their own self-imposed standards and to pursue and attain challenging goals."[14] This motivation is critical, because entrepreneurs have something to prove: namely, that they can start a business, that the product will work and succeed, and that those who doubted them and/or their technology were wrong. For most entrepreneurs, money is a way of keeping score rather than a motivation in and of itself. Instead, entrepreneurs feel the compelling need to meet and surpass a challenge. Thus, even when they have already built a large company—and accumulated a seemingly inexhaustible amount of wealth—they keep moving forward, propelled by further challenges.

Timmons presents other desirable behaviors as well, but these are not as acquirable: energy; health and emotional stability; creativity and innovation; and intelligence.[15] Energy levels vary with an individual's physical health; there is a limit to one's ability to bypass this fact. In addition, emotional stability is, of course, an asset. The stresses of the entrepreneurial process can frazzle an entrepreneur with a fragile psychological disposition, and thus can undercut his or her efforts.

Finally, not everyone demonstrates high levels of creativity or intelligence—such as having the ability to write software code, invent new mechanical devices, or cure cancer. And indeed, these capabilities are not prerequisites for entrepreneurship; however, entrepreneurs that are not exceptionally creative or intelligent need to consciously play to their strengths and supplement their weaknesses.

9.3 The Entrepreneurial Process

Aspiring entrepreneurs will swing the odds of success in their favor by mastering the *entrepreneurial process*, which seeks to achieve an appropriate balance between one's opportunity, team, and resources.

How does someone with an entrepreneurial mind master the entrepreneurial process? Timmons states, "At the heart of the process is the creation and/or recognition of opportunities, followed by the will and the initiative to seize these opportunities."[16] In his mind, a recognized opportunity without initiative is a tripod with two legs. The entrepreneurial process is the method by which an individual with an entrepreneurial mind is able to assess risks, distinguish an idea from a viable opportunity, and gather resources to pursue this niche in the market.

What precisely does the entrepreneurial process involve? In general, ventures with a substantially higher success pattern are:

1. Opportunity-driven.
2. Creative and resource parsimonious.
3. Guided by a lead entrepreneur and an entrepreneurial team.

4. Examples of appropriate balance between these elements.
5. A good fit for the opportunity.
6. Integrated and holistic.

First, the process starts with an opportunity—not money, strategy, networks, team, or the business plan.[17] In plain terms, no other factors are relevant until one finds an appropriate prospect to pursue and determines a valid starting point. The opportunity should also receive support from investors (which is frequently a point of failure or struggle). Then, the size and scope of the opportunity will dictate the necessary amount of resources, the nature of the team, and the strategy required.

After an entrepreneur secures the initial opportunity, the process must control resources with ingenuity and prudence. Sharing office space and equipment, swapping small bits of equity in the company for advice from key advisors, traveling on stand-by, and designing your own logos are ways to minimize cash outlays. Money is one necessary resource, but it should be supplemented by sources of information, professional advisors, and a range of industry relationships. The most common misconception among inexperienced entrepreneurs is that nothing can be accomplished without money.

Timmons reflects, "If you grabbed 100 people on the street at random and asked them, 'Does it take money to make money?' they would all say, 'Yes!'"[18] He goes on: "[Most people think] entrepreneurs who have a lot of money have a higher chance of success than those who don't. But you can dispel that as a myth," he observes, "because it has been erroneous, and just dead wrong, and backwards so many times. Get people to look at cases where you buy a $40 million business for a buck. It happens all the time."[19]

Timmons considers this delusion—that "money is the most important start-up ingredient"—so prevalent that he lists it among his fifteen main myths of entrepreneurship.[20] He has seen that not every opportunity requires money. Instead, the entrepreneurial process succeeds through creative use of *all* resources, which may include money, but is by no means limited to it. In other words, securing funding is not the single key to establishing a business.

After the first two considerations (the opportunity, followed by the creative, parsimonious use of resources), the third element of the entrepreneurial process is developing a team. A great entrepreneurial leader who stands alone can attain some level of success—but typically not enough to build an organization that achieves sustained growth. A company with a single leader is a commercial cult; if the entrepreneur leaves, the company (which exists independently in name, but not in fact) will simply implode. For obvious reasons, this is not the finely tuned organization model investors prefer.

Thus, one entrepreneurial imperative is to demonstrate the existence of a team and system that can ride through difficult patches and replace key players along the way. As the popular saying goes, investors prefer a Grade-A team with a Grade-B idea over the reverse. The Grade-A team will figure out a way to make the business work and will overcome the challenges of a sudden change in circumstance or direction.

Fourth, the venture must arrive quickly at a balance between the key elements of opportunity, resources, and team, and must properly determine where each element fits in the overall picture. For example, if a large opportunity has insufficient resources, the business is likely to fail. Similarly, if a team is too big for the opportunity, dissension will fester among the ranks. Thus, the entrepreneur needs to keep these three elements of the model in balance.

What about the "fit"? Timmons addresses this question by asking, "This is a fabulous opportunity, but for whom?"[21] The entrepreneurial process will only succeed if the opportunity, resources, and team fit the particular circumstances. People can only exploit an opportunity if they have the expertise to do so. Therefore, investors in one country may forego opportunities in an emerging market, such as China, because they lack familiarity with the investment dynamics. The opportunity may have been a good one, but it was not an appropriate fit for the team and resources available.

Finally, an entrepreneur's approach to the process must be "integrated and holistic."[22] He or she must integrate multiple factors to determine how an opportunity should be pursued. For example, ambiguity and uncertainty may exist in the external environment. Yet at the same time, internal decisions will affect the venture: The company requires funding, so it needs to satisfy the requirements and expectations of investors. In the midst of this swirl of considerations and uncertainties, the entrepreneur has to apply leadership, creativity, and good communication skills. Furthermore, Timmons emphasizes that he or she must do this in a "holistic" manner: Specifically, the entrepreneur must step back and assess each opportunity in light of all constituent factors. Timmons comments, "This integrated, holistic balance is at the heart of what we know about the entrepreneurial process and getting the odds in your favor."[23]

9.4. Sustaining an Entrepreneurial Culture

> Entrepreneurs achieve success by sustaining an entrepreneurial culture. This requires both entrepreneurial and managerial competence. A supportive community will further enhance an organization's prosperity.

The entrepreneurial process concentrates on establishing a venture, but how can one maintain the business once the wheels are set in motion? An entrepreneur's chances of long-term success will increase as he or she develops competence, not just as an entrepreneur, but also as a manager. External factors—such as the overarching culture or subculture—will also affect entrepreneurial achievement.

Will the entrepreneurial culture that gave birth to the company continue as human and financial resources grow? According to Timmons, this is the fundamental question. Unfortunately, entrepreneurs are often authors of their own demise. They struggle to pass on the company's reins to a manager, whose goal would be to build the culture around the company as an institution (rather than around the entrepreneur as an individual). For the entrepreneur, this can seem the same as raising a child until he or she is 6 years old, and then sending him or her off to a residential boarding school that claims it will do a better job of raising him or her to adulthood.

As I observed from my own experience as an advisor to high-growth companies, most entrepreneurs naively assume that the same skills required in the initial growth stage will also help the company expand later. Based on their company's previous development, these entrepreneurs have too much confidence in their management skills. Also coloring the equation is the fact that entrepreneurs of small, high-growth companies have a huge personal stake in the enterprise. Of course, there are well-known examples of founders such as Bill Gates and Michael Dell who have grown start-up companies right through to multi-billion-dollar organizations, but these are the exception rather than the norm.

Timmons concludes that an individual can, indeed, transition from being an entrepreneur to being a manager in order to sustain an entrepreneurial culture. But, one thing is apparent: "Growing a higher-potential venture requires management skills."[24] Timmons explains, "Organizations at different stages [of their growth cycle] are characterized by differing degrees of change and uncertainty, and are therefore more-or-less entrepreneurial or more-or-less administrative."[25] Thus, the entrepreneur's managerial skills will vary accordingly. A start-up venture exists in a fluid environment, with limited staff and resources. On the other hand, a more established company, in a mature market, primarily focuses on serving its customer base. Nevertheless, it must maintain aspects of an entrepreneurial culture so that the drive for innovation will be self-perpetuating. The tendency is for complacency to set in, and for managers to douse the original entrepreneurial spark with an overemphasis on maintaining operations instead of growing them.

Entrepreneurial and managerial cultures can differ significantly. In an entrepreneurial culture, managers "appear unconcerned about status, power, and personal control. They are more concerned about making sure tasks, goals, and roles are clear than they are about guaranteeing that the organizational chart is current or that their office and rug reflect their current status."[26] This entrepreneurial culture can exist in big and small organizations, although the entrepreneurial spirit within a larger and more bureaucratic organization is typically referred to as "intrapreneurship" in place of classic "entrepreneurship."

Timmons stresses the importance of sustaining an entrepreneurial culture in a large company. He states, "[Entrepreneurs] who build substantial companies that grow to more than $10 million in sales, and have 75 to 100 employees, are good entrepreneurs and good managers."[27] Why? Because they create an entrepreneurial culture with "a belief in and commitment to growth, achievement, improvement, and success, and [they foster] a sense among members of the team that they are 'in this thing together.' Goals and the market determine priorities, rather than those whose territory or prerogatives are being challenged."[28] This is the opposite of the classic company bureaucracy, which focuses on position, job description, reporting structures, and self-preservation.

The likelihood of maintaining an entrepreneurial culture within a company will be significantly affected by the surrounding societal culture. Timmons cites Native Americans as an example:

> I've done a lot of work with Native Americans. Interestingly enough, when I first started working with Native Americans about 13 years ago and they found out about Mr. Eugene Kauffman, one of them gasped and blurted out in my seminar, "He must have been a Native American!" Kauffman's principles, like theirs, included sharing wealth with everyone who helped create it, giving back to your community, and treating other people as they like to be treated. These are wonderful principles of leadership and company building.[29]

Timmons is a pioneer in his analysis of the Native American community from an entrepreneurial perspective. His focus on a self-contained ethic group facilitates a study of the relationship between individual entrepreneurial activity and the broader societal culture.

He describes his experience:

> When I first started working with Native Americans on reservations, the casino owners were the only apparent kinds of entrepreneurs! It didn't make sense to me. They could not have survived the past 150 years without an enormous amount of raw survival tactics.
>
> However, I would describe their self-preservation from an entrepreneurial perspective: bootstrapping, bartering with an absolute paucity of resources, being resilient, being very creative, and being very team-oriented in the things they do.
>
> Some Native Americans believe these entrepreneurial practices are uncommon. They argue that there are, instead, huge conflicts between Native American-run businesses on reservations and the surrounding Native American community.
>
> In my experience, this is not the case. Native Americans are figuring out how to get both constituencies together. There is probably a greater groundswell of interest and support

for entrepreneurship—as a community development and an economic development strategy—among Native Americans today than there ever has been, by a long, long shot.[30]

Timmons makes the point that individual Native American entrepreneurs, who do include more than merely high-profile casino operators, would not be able to sustain their business endeavors without a supportive societal environment.

Thus, there are two parts involved in sustaining company growth. On one level, there are the controllable factors: An entrepreneur needs to create an entrepreneurial culture within his or her own company, to instill in others the values that gave birth to the company. As well, the creation of this culture requires the lead individual to evolve from possessing pure entrepreneurial skills to acquiring the skills of a manager, without losing an entrepreneurial orientation. On another level, however, the context in which the company operates will affect the creation and maintenance of this entrepreneurial culture, as demonstrated by the example of the Native American community. This factor is often not under the company's control.

Timmons's Key Points

9.1. The "entrepreneurial revolution" is creating historically unique opportunities for individuals to amass wealth for themselves and their communities.

9.2. Effective pursuit of opportunities starts with an *entrepreneurial mind*, composed of six acquirable "core" attributes and supplemented by four not-as-acquirable "desirable" attributes.

9.3. Aspiring entrepreneurs will swing the odds of success in their favor by mastering the *entrepreneurial process*, which seeks to achieve an appropriate balance between one's opportunity, team, and resources.

9.4. Entrepreneurs achieve success by sustaining an entrepreneurial culture. This requires both entrepreneurial and managerial competence. A supportive community will further enhance an organization's prosperity.

Chapter 10

Karl H. Vesper:
New Venture Experiences

School is limiting, in that it doesn't give you the most important learning tool you need for success in a venture, which is op-
portunity- and venture-specific knowledge. [The experienced,
school-of-hard-knocks entrepreneurs] instinctively grasp that the
key of entrepreneurship is to deliver something good enough that
people are willing to pay a premium for it. [Then] you can make a
satisfactory return.

—Karl H. Vesper[1]

Introduction to Karl H. Vesper

Name	Karl H. Vesper
Title	Professor of Business Administration, Mechanical Engineering, and Marine Studies
Affiliation(s)	University of Washington
Education	Ph.D., Stanford University (1969) M.S.M.E., Stanford University (1966) M.B.A., Harvard University (1960) B.S.M.E., Stanford University (1955)

Experience	o Gave testimony to U.S. Congress on entrepreneurship and national policy o Spearheaded an intrapreneurship program at Westinghouse Electric o Started entrepreneurship program at the University of Illinois o Developed an entrepreneurship program and research conference at Babson College
Notable Publications	o *New Venture Strategies* (Prentice-Hall, 1980) o *New Venture Mechanics* (Prentice-Hall, 1993) o *New Venture Experience: Cases, Text and Exercises, Revised Edition* (Vector Books, 1996)
Website(s)	*www.bschool.washington.edu*

Biographical Highlights

⊙ Vesper is the world's leading chronicler of entrepreneurship research and education programs worldwide, as well as the designer and evaluator of entrepreneurship cultivation programs since their origins in the 1970s.

⊙ He holds a joint appointment in the Faculty of Business and the Faculty of Engineering, a feat which is rarely achieved or permitted, and this gives him a unique interdisciplinary perspective.

⊙ He founded the entrepreneurship division of the Academy of Management.

⊙ He is the first professor to hold a chair in entrepreneurship studies at Babson College (Wellesley, Massachusetts).

⊙ He generated the idea of the annual "Frontiers of Entrepreneurial Research Conference" at Babson College in 1981, which has now evolved into one of the leading conferences in the world.

10.1.The Experience: Failure, Survival, and Success

An individual embarking on an entrepreneurial venture must realize that the experience involves the emotional implications of differing levels of failure, survival, and success throughout the growth process.

Vesper asserts that the entrepreneurial life is an emotional roller coaster of failure, survival, and success. Just as professional athletes must learn to be both good losers and gracious winners, entrepreneurs must learn to be equally magnanimous in victory and defeat, knowing that on any given day the outcome could be reversed.

Consequently, whereas some professionals' main source of value is their technical competence, entrepreneurs have to develop both specialized skills and emotional resilience. Traits such as determination, enthusiasm, hard work, energy, and passion are important components of an entrepreneur's success. Moreover, he or she should be prepared to face many emotional risks throughout the course of each venture.

Vesper recognizes that one dominant emotional risk for the entrepreneur is the frightening possibility of failure. He writes, "The price of [pursuing the entrepreneurial career path] can be high. If the venture fails, the entrepreneur may lose everything."[2] In many cases, the entrepreneur has the added stress of taking financial risks that require a personal guarantee, and the pledging of all assets, as security for his or her undertaking.

Although estimates vary, the failure rate among entrepreneurial ventures, especially start-ups, is significant. According to Vesper, recent studies indicate that failure rates for new ventures average around 50 percent each year following inception, and that the rate depends greatly on the line of business.[3] He cites a study claiming that, though it is difficult to explain the direct cause and effect of failure, there are certain directions of the causality: First, rapid growth tends to propagate structural errors; second, due to limited resources, a few bad decisions can be fatal; third, training can be very expensive; and fourth, the early days of the venture may not allow one the luxury of learning how to succeed.[4] Yet, despite the reality of failure, a number of start-ups do stay alive.

At the same time, mere survival (although a short-term relief) is not a sustainable status for a company. Thus, the entrepreneur must also endure the emotional challenge of overcoming this stage. To aid a company's growth, and avoid unnecessary stress, Vesper recommends eliminating possible competition by establishing appropriate barriers early in the venture.

First, a company should have the foresight to stake its claim to an idea—before other companies catch on. Patenting a desirable product or process, or having a trade secret, will create a high level of return. Second, an entrepreneur should use experience or special knowledge about his or her venture to the company's advantage. Third, proper capitalization of the enterprise, through staying power, economies of sale, and production expertise, is critical to a venture's success. Lastly, the company must be able to persist until its wares are established in the marketplace. Taking these steps will help an entrepreneur minimize the emotional unpredictability of a company's journey.

At any rate, the tension between failure, survival, and success is akin to the circle of life for the entrepreneur, a pattern similar to "the thrill of victory and the agony of defeat" used the former ABC show *The Wide World of Sports*. And, as one could expect, the resulting range of experiences involves a strong emotional component. The entrepreneur has little room for theorizing; all decisions hit close to home.

10.2. Thinking Through Ventures

There are four types of knowledge: (1) generalized business knowledge; (2) general entrepreneurship knowledge; (3) opportunity-specific knowledge; and (4) venture-specific knowledge. Opportunity- and venture-specific knowledge, which are critical to entrepreneurial success, are primarily discerned in the marketplace rather than in an educational context.

What aspects of entrepreneurship can actually be learned? Vesper believes the difficulty in answering this question is that most people measure entrepreneurial success in a financial way, and there is no uniform method for attaining wealth. In fact, a person's own circumstances may even contradict any generalization offered. Though one entrepreneur may have benefited from an MBA with a specialization in entrepreneurship, another may have been a high-school dropout who pursued a particular interest and became financially prosperous. Then there is the school-of-hard-knocks entrepreneur who slowly clawed his or her way to success, against all odds, and cannot fathom learning the lessons of the marketplace in a classroom.

Along those lines, Vesper notes that experienced entrepreneurs "may be pre-occupied with their own knocks"[5] and not appreciate that a generalized knowledge base is useful to an aspiring entrepreneur. He believes a variety of experience—in both the classroom and the marketplace—is beneficial:

> I remember…a group of highly successful restaurant entrepreneurs who combined their experience, brilliance, and creativity to come up with a killer restaurant—one that would feature the best of their know-how, talent, and gifts. It was a total flop!
>
> How does that happen? Partly because there is luck in the game, and partly because hard knocks teach you some things. But, while you are learning specific lessons, [entrepreneurs around you] are learning other ones [that you may not know]. So, [learning from] a variety of experiences is important.[6]

In order to make sense of the issue, Vesper identifies two broad categories of knowledge: the knowledge that can be learned in the classroom, and the knowledge that must be learned through experience.

General business knowledge, which is part of the first category, involves the conventional areas of business, such as marketing, finance, human resources, and business law. Individuals may have various levels of exposure to these areas, and their shortcomings can be remedied by hiring outside consultants or professionals. Indeed, issues will inevitably arise in these functional areas as the start-up venture grows, and the entrepreneur must learn to cope with these problems—either before the venture begins, or during the process. (Presumably everyone would recognize the benefit of doing some preparation before embarking on the process.)

Vesper points out the challenges of a "learn-only-when-needed approach" to business knowledge: "(1) to a person without knowledge, the need for it may not be apparent, and (2) when he or she desperately needs the knowledge, he or she may not have enough time to seek it out."[7] Thus, while such prior knowledge alone will not make a venture successful, it will lower the marketplace tuition involved in expanding the entrepreneur's knowledge base.

A second type of knowledge entrepreneurs can learn in the classroom is *general entrepreneurship knowledge*. This is more specialized information within each of the functional areas of business, especially applicable to start-ups. For example, entrepreneurial finance is significantly different from traditional corporate finance. Entrepreneurial concepts involve innovation and breaking new ground, which are frustrating ideas for a significant group of financiers who expect to see a track record. Unfortunately, entrepreneurship does not provide comfort for the banking community.

General entrepreneurship knowledge teaches the entrepreneur how to stretch his or her resources, pursue bootstrapping, and fundraise. It also teaches the entrepreneur how to sell his or her vision, and who to sell it to. Because the entrepreneur relies on a different spectrum of financing sources, he or she needs to know where to look for funds—the local bank may simply be an exercise in frustration. Again, this specific entrepreneurship knowledge will not guarantee a successful venture, but it will assist the entrepreneur in focusing his or her efforts prudently and securing financial support.

Unlike the other two types of knowledge mentioned, *opportunity-specific knowledge* develops only through marketplace experience. Vesper affirms, "This is probably the most important knowledge for starting a company, and you can't find it in a school." He describes it as "business savvy related to the particular type of business you wish to start,"[8] and notes that it is "possessed by a person who knows about the existence of a specific opportunity."[9] Vesper explains, "The school can't give you [opportunity-specific knowledge,] because the opportunity isn't in school—it's out in the marketplace."[10] When experienced entrepreneurs discredit the possibility of entrepreneurial education on a university campus, they often have this type of knowledge in mind.

A second type of experience-based knowledge, *venture-specific knowledge*, is the other half of opportunity-specific knowledge. It is the know-how that allows people who recognize an opportunity to capitalize on it.[11] Vesper explains that if an entrepreneur believes there is a market for a new radio station, he or she will need information on how to obtain a license—that information is the venture-specific knowledge.[12]

Vesper highlights three ways of acquiring venture-specific knowledge: First, take a job in the business you are interested in, and learn it as an insider; second, undertake a start-up venture and learn the step-by-step requirements; or third, develop a business plan for the venture through study and analysis.[13]

He summarizes candidly:

Unfortunately...[opportunity- and venture-specific knowledge] are usually by far the least teachable in school, and usually little described in books or periodicals. Possibly they can be learned in advance of the venture through work experience or deliberate investigation. But often it is not clear in advance what must be learned. The need for these types of knowledge is idiosyncratic to the individual person, time and circumstance.[14]

Vesper explains this dynamic in relation to what experienced entrepreneurs appreciate instinctively. A school of engineering can teach its students the principles that govern physical nature, but the school cannot teach the students how to have a financially viable engineering office. The students only learn this by going to work for another company, or by identifying a niche in the marketplace after years of work. In that sense, Vesper agrees, "School is limiting in not giving you the most important learning you need to succeed in a venture."[15]

The experienced, school-of-hard-knocks entrepreneur discovers this truth very quickly. He or she instinctively grasps that "the key of entrepreneurship is to deliver something good enough that people are willing to pay a premium for it. [Then] you can make a satisfactory return."[16] His or her experience puts a university program in its proper context. An education can do many valuable things, such as provide a base of contacts, or give a vantage point from which to observe and understand before jumping in, but it cannot realistically offer opportunity- and venture-specific knowledge.

10.3. Selling for Start-Ups

One of the core skills of an entrepreneur is the ability to sell a product or service to a consumer, or a business proposal to a venture capitalist. There are five ways to sell to an enterprise: respond to customer requests, advertise, open a store, personally "hit the road," or pay others to do the selling.

Very few entrepreneurship courses include any instruction on selling. Vesper, however, teaches his classes a unit on cold-calling. He believes the ability to develop contacts will expand an individual's potential for entrepreneurship: "Developing contacts is useful, and being able to develop contacts with people you don't know is even more useful. So, I welcome the opportunity for students to practice that activity. It's not easy for a class of students."[17]

Indeed, marketing and research courses are not enough to give aspiring entrepreneurs exposure to one of the core skills of an entrepreneur: the ability to sell, whether a product to a consumer or a business proposal to a venture capitalist. Vesper classifies five practical approaches to sales: responding to customer requests, advertising, opening a store, personally hitting the road, or paying others to do the selling.[18]

The first approach is reactive: responding to a customer's request. This has been the genesis of various ventures. People ask a business for a product that it doesn't presently provide, and the business makes a move to satisfy the particular need.

The second way to generate sales is to advertise, whether in the Yellow Pages, through different Internet-related options (such as Google searches or Web page ads), in a variety of newspapers, or elsewhere. Proactive sales in this category may utilize public relations techniques to develop a strategy for an advertising campaign.

The third sales method is simply to open a physical location. This can range from an independent retail location to a kiosk at fairs, shows, and malls. When you have a physical location, customers can peruse your product line with relative ease.

A fourth, and challenging, approach to sales is to engage in personal selling. This is often a key requirement for getting a start-up venture off the ground. Personal selling is hard, but rewarding. In Vesper's words, it "calls for self-discipline and initiative.... [I]t is vital to decide with care who to go after, what to seek from him or her, how much effort to apply in each attempt, and how to assess results [when you are] planning [your] next action."[19]

The last approach is to pay others to do the selling for you. Of course, resources will be limited in a start-up situation—and thus may not be available. In that case, it is doubly important for the founder to remain closely attuned to the process. The entrepreneur, rather than viewing it as a supplement for his or her own efforts, needs to coordinate the process. Paying people to sell the product/idea will involve a range of activities such as hiring salespeople as employees, engaging independent representatives, or selling to brokers, wholesalers, or retailers.[20] Each choice has benefits and disadvantages. For many entrepreneurs in the early stages of a venture, however, close contact with the customer is crucial.

Vesper's Key Points

10.1. An individual embarking on an entrepreneurial venture must realize that the experience involves the emotional implications of differing levels of failure, survival, and success throughout the growth process.

10.2. There are four types of knowledge: (1) generalized business knowledge; (2) general entrepreneurship knowledge; (3) opportunity-specific knowledge; and (4) venture-specific knowledge. Opportunity- and venture-specific knowledge, which are critical to entrepreneurial success, are primarily discerned in the marketplace rather than in an educational context.

10.3. One of the core skills of an entrepreneur is the ability to sell a product or service to a consumer, or a business proposal to a venture capitalist. There are five ways to sell to an enterprise: respond to customer requests, advertise, open a store, personally "hit the road," or pay others to do the selling.

Part III

The Pursuit of Entrepreneurial Excellence

Chapter 11

3 Steps to Pursue Entrepreneurial Excellence

In order to pursue entrepreneurial excellence, I propose a three-step process that asks three basic questions: What is your starting point? What can you learn? And, with those questions in mind, how do you pursue entrepreneurial excellence? I have devised the framework of this process based on many years of personal, practical experience in the field of entrepreneurship. The three-step process reflects my own discoveries, as well as those of the many entrepreneurs I have advised and worked with. In keeping with the nature of this book, I have integrated the insights from the entrepreneurship experts as applicable throughout the various steps of the model.

---

3 Steps to Pursue Entrepreneurial Excellence

Step 1: What Is Your Starting Point?
- ⊙ Jeffry Timmons: Breadth of Experience
- ⊙ Henry Mintzberg: Depth of Experience

Step 2: What Can You Learn?
- ⊙ Gordon Redding: The Scope of Teachable Content
- ⊙ Larry Farrell: Learn From the Practicing Masters

> Step 3: How Can You Learn to Pursue Entrepreneurial
> Excellence?
>   ⊙ Henry Mintzberg: Practicing Entrepreneurship
>   ⊙ Henry Mintzberg: Cultivating an
>   Entrepreneurial Imagination

Step 1: What Is Your Starting Point?

A starting point for the three-step process begins where it should: with the learner. Sometimes conventional learning methods emphasize what teachers are conveying rather than what students are receiving. In the field of entrepreneurship, however, the value of the learning process is heavily influenced by what the student has experienced prior to starting a specific learning program (whether executive education courses or an MBA).

Entrepreneurial learning is also unique because it is a practice, as explained in the Introduction. A practice is different from a profession, such as law or medicine, where a person may begin his or her education with no direct experience, and have only tangential or indirect exposure to the field. By contrast, individuals interested in entrepreneurship often seek to learn about it before pursuing it as a field of study, and many have already had previous—and, possibly, financially successful—prior experience. Consequently, a small group of entrepreneurial learners may have widely discrepant levels of previous experience.

With that in mind, self-assessment is the first necessary task. The views of the following two entrepreneurship experts provide a useful frame of reference for performing a successful self-assessment. In this regard, I distinguish between breadth of experience (exposure to a variety of entrepreneurs and entrepreneurial situations) and depth of experience (personal experience in founding and operating one's own company). Jeff Timmons's comments explain the importance of entrepreneurs' breadth of experience in their own self-assessments: Where people start determines what they need to learn. Henry Mintzberg's observations are relevant to entrepreneurs' depth of experience:

People's previous experience will direct where and how they can learn about entrepreneurship.

Jeff Timmons: Breadth of Experience

Jeff Timmons describes how the learning process varies considerably, depending on the starting point of the student's own frame of reference:

It depends a great deal on the background of each student. Let's take two extremes. Let's take a kid who grows up in a family where parents, grandparents, aunts, uncles, or present neighbors have never owned a business of any kind. In fact, they don't know anyone who has ever owned his own business! The other extreme is someone who grew up with all of this.[1]

What the two students learn will be very different: "The kids that have had very little exposure to entrepreneurship can learn a ton about whether this life path is for them. What are the risks and rewards? Who does it? Who seems to thrive on it? Why do they seem to thrive on it?"[2] Timmons explains that the students' life experiences and firsthand exposures to entrepreneurship form a filter through which they assess risks and opportunities. For example, differences in mindset, attitude, values, and orientation to risks and ambiguities can make the formation of a new venture either fun, challenging, and rewarding, or terrifying and discouraging. Timmons recognizes that these differing viewpoints are formed through experiences students have accumulated before they arrive in his classes. He states, "I think they learn this by testing themselves."[3]

In Timmons's classes, the process of self-assessment is facilitated by expanding students' breadth of experience. Timmons has students analyze cases involving actual businesses and real entrepreneurs, so they develop some of their own benchmarks. His objective is to have students simulate the experience of entrepreneurs who must test their ideas in the marketplace—without making students risk money.

Part of the self-discovery process occurs through exposure to organized knowledge in the form of books. But also of great value are encounters with real-life entrepreneurs who share stories from the trenches. According to Timmons, such entrepreneurs give students "a real texture and feel for who these people are, how they think, why they did this, how they look at the risk and reward, how they look at the sacrifices, and how they look at the joys and satisfactions when they find them."[4] Timmons continues: "I think this real-time benchmarking gives students the anchors and the criteria for them to start to figure these things out."[5]

From this exercise, Timmons notes that two important elements of self-assessment are, first, to understand the process, and secondly, to determine if entrepreneurship is the direction one wishes to pursue. The entrepreneurial path is not necessarily for everyone, but it is best to make an informed decision. Timmons describes, "You try to say, 'this is not for everybody, and I don't know if it's for you or not. It's very important that you try and figure this out as you dive into it.'"[6]

As indicated earlier, an important aspect of entrepreneurial learning is direct experience—what could be likened to a form of apprenticeship. Timmons refers to this as "50,000 chunks of experience."[7] He recounts:

> When one looks at successful entrepreneurs, one sees profiles rich in experience....They have acquired ten or more years of substantial experience, built contacts, garnered the know-how, and established a track record in the industry, market, and technology niche, within which they eventually launch, acquire, or build a business.[8]

Thus, part of an entrepreneur's learning process is to keep increasing knowledge by benefiting from each experience. One of the key components of learning is to avoid making too many expensive mistakes; as the cliché goes, the objective is to "keep the tuition low."

Timmons believes another aspect of self-assessment is understanding basic business concepts: "What's the difference between a good idea and a good opportunity? Where do you focus your time? What do investors, bankers, customers, and suppliers look for? How do you invest in these things? How do you build a brain trust?"[9] Aspiring entrepreneurs often have not spent enough time considering the elements necessary for creating a successful business.

How the entrepreneur interacts with other people is a further factor. Timmons avers that being an entrepreneur "is not like being a solo, lone wolf, star entertainer—it's not a rock-star thing. It's much more complex and has much more texture around the whole constellation of people that you surround yourself with."[10]

Moreover, students must realize that successful entrepreneurship requires hard work. Timmons says:

> Students sometimes expect me to have some magical insight or secret that can tell them whether their business ideas will be a raging success or not—and whether or not they will be a raging success as an entrepreneur. It's almost the wrong question. No one can know the answer to that....The most powerful parallel that I share with students when they ask this question is as follows: How predictive is the National Football League draft in telling you who is going to be the next great star quarterback, or receiver, or running-back? And the realities are that it's not terribly accurate![11]

With that in mind, entrepreneurial learning (and unlearning) requires frank self-assessment. Individuals must carefully consider whether or not an entrepreneurial path is for them. If so, the learning process depends on the individual's starting knowledge and experience base.

Some aspiring entrepreneurs have been exposed to the dynamics of the marketplace through their supper conversations at home. Others may have had parents who were lifelong employees with consistent pay and minimal disruption. As well, many may need to unlearn certain lessons. In any case, this journey of learning and unlearning must be undertaken through practical experience as well as in a classroom. The classroom does not have a monopoly on entrepreneurial education; the bottom line is that expanding one's breadth of experience will enhance self-assessment.

Henry Mintzberg: Depth of Experience

A second element of self-assessment is individual depth of experience (as Timmons alluded to previously when he emphasized the value of 50,000 chunks of experience). Mintzberg's writings focus on the importance of actual experience as a foundation for learning about management, and by extension also about entrepreneurship. Mintzberg notes that the starting point is critical for a person being educated. If the person has length and depth of work experience, this will greatly advance his ability to understand the practical dimension of important business concepts.

Mintzberg's insights in the field of management, as noted previously, have many parallels to entrepreneurship education. Timmons agrees, "A lot of things that Mintzberg talks about are very applicable to how you would approach entrepreneurship."[12] For example, Mintzberg discusses the fact that you can't really train a manager, because a manager needs to have a wealth of experience, and you can't just take a recent university graduate and teach him how to lead a bunch of other people.[13] Likewise, with entrepreneurship, it is difficult to train a young, inexperienced student how to be successful. Timmons also concurs with Mintzberg that entrepreneurship education should be "more practice-oriented, by bringing in people who are employed already and mining out their experience."[14]

Mintzberg observes a significant difference between teaching young, inexperienced undergraduates and teaching practicing managers who "are used to doing what they do."[15] Specifically, teaching untrained students requires a more content-centered paradigm than that required for students with professional experience. As a result, Mintzberg notices that instructors generally favor dictation over a hands-on, interactive approach:

> You have your whole ritual worked out. Case study teachers are probably the most rigid of all because they have to be in control of that classroom from beginning to end. In other words, instructors are used to teaching as if students have no experience worth integrating into class; as a result, the emphasis is on dispensing information rather than on a shared learning process.[16]

The three-step process, by contrast, is a learner-centered paradigm. Mintzberg notes that practitioners (non full-time teachers) are often "strong where regular academics tend to be weak—for example, in skill development and classroom facilitation. They can provide effective bridges to practice." [17] Mintzberg's conclusion: The learning process improves greatly when professors mine the insights of experienced students in their classroom who can divulge personal discoveries in a thoughtful manner. From the perspective of self-assessment analysis, an individual with experience will provide a more detailed, accurate and comprehensive self-evaluation.

Step 2: What Can You Learn?

What aspects of entrepreneurship, then, are learnable? This relates to the discussion in the Introduction, and the example of Jim Pattison, CEO of the Jim Pattison Group. Can educators teach a person to have an inner drive for success, a knack for selecting the most advantageous business opportunities, or an ability to divine the timing of market maneuvers? The answer is no. On the other hand, can they teach people due diligence, how to assess possible employees, and how to structure a company? Yes. To define learnable content, and highlight the method through which one teaches such information, I examine the approaches of experts Gordon Redding and Larry Farrell.

Gordon Redding: The Scope of Teachable Content

One starting point for determining the scope of teachable content is to distinguish between the various types of knowledge. While using different terminology, Gordon Redding comes to the same conclusion that Karl H. Vesper describes in Chapter 10. As Vesper explained, Redding believes there are two types of knowledge—general business knowledge and general entrepreneurship knowledge—that can be taught; on the other hand, he maintains that venture- and opportunity-specific knowledge are not teachable in a formal education context.[18] Gordon Redding provides an analysis of the scope of teachable content from his own perspective:

> First, there is a set of techniques which you need to have to be a manager. A good administrative manager, for example, needs to keep a clean and tidy company that's not going to go bankrupt; [he needs to] build and retain staff, be able to organize a market and assess a situation, or whatever. These are techniques of management that entrepreneurs need to have just as much as senior professional executives. You need to be able to read a profit and loss account and a balance sheet, you need to lay out a factory floor, you need to design a Human Resources Management system, you need to be able

to design a marketing strategy, etc. These are requirements of any good businessman, whether he or she is an entrepreneur or a standard executive. These technical skills are very useful, and that is in fact what most of the MBA programs teach.

Second, you can teach individuals that entrepreneurs find new combinations of things, seek opportunities, monitor the environment for opportunity, and network with key suppliers of capital and information technology. You can tell them that, but you cannot make them understand the drive, the passion—the greed, as it were—or the hunger of the entrepreneur. You simply cannot teach that. You can throw out examples, you can say, "why don't you try it?" and you can encourage it when you see it, but you can't develop it if it's not there already. So a large percentage of the average class would never have this drive. In fact, very often the number of people who have it, and the particular ones who have it, are surprising, as they may be the weakest academically.[19]

Redding concludes that there is a clear distinction between technical skills—which, of course, can be taught—and personal drive and ambition—which cannot.

Larry Farrell: Learn From the Practicing Masters

Larry Farrell's perspective is unique, as noted earlier, in that he is an independent consultant who has researched the practices of more than 2,000 working entrepreneurs, most through firsthand interviews. Farrell's core ideas are rooted in entrepreneurial basics learned directly from the practicing masters of entrepreneurship. From that standpoint, he emphasizes what entrepreneurs need to learn: Primarily, they must know how to do or make something. Further, they must be experts at that process, and possess detailed knowledge of how their products or services will appeal to a customer. Then, to this core customer/product knowledge, entrepreneurs must add the skills required to build a business.

Where can one acquire these skills? Farrell adamantly asserts that the business schools of the world are not the place to receive an entrepreneurial education.[20] In this regard, Farrell and Mintzberg are kindred spirits. In fact, Farrell claims that business schools can be a hindrance to entrepreneurial success, because they teach management skills, but fail to teach students how to create a great product or service.

According to Farrell, two prevalent entrepreneurial myths are that "getting an MBA is the way to go," and that "business schools will teach you how to be an entrepreneur."[21] Farrell stresses, "This is just not true!"[22] His analysis states:

The majority of the business schools in North America are followers. Because entrepreneurship has become hot and acceptable and part of our folklore culture in the United States and Canada, entrepreneurs are heroes now, whereas they weren't 25 years ago. So all these business schools and their professors are racing around, saying, "How do we teach this? How do we add this to our curriculum?"[23]

Farrell remarks that business schools do not teach product knowledge. Moreover, many business school students are angling for careers as investment bankers and management consultants, rather than seeking to create a company from scratch around a new product or service.

However, Farrell is optimistic about a new trend that has appeared on the educational landscape: Entrepreneurship centers at universities in the United States are beginning to teach entrepreneurial principles across the university. One notable example is Wharton School of Business at the University of Pennsylvania, which the *Financial Times* survey has ranked as the number-one MBA program in the world for five years in a row, starting in 2003.[24] Farrell recounts:

Ian MacMillan [coauthor with Rita McGrath, who is featured in Chapter 5], at Wharton, University of Pennsylvania, said that the reason they started the Snider Entrepreneurship Center was that they did a survey of the alumni of the whole University of Pennsylvania and—shockingly—they found out that students from the general university, studying history, biology, mathematics, are two to three times more likely to become entrepreneurs than graduates of the business school![25]

The university's conclusion was that graduates of other faculties developed product knowledge in their own fields, and then needed entrepreneurial skills to pursue their business ventures. Conversely, students in business schools had little product knowledge.

In recognition of this dynamic, Farrell states, "The business schools are okay, if they will reach across the disciplines and teach entrepreneurship to those in other fields of study, such as biology and chemistry students."[26]

Farrell's advice for the universities:

We wouldn't have a biotech industry if it were left up to MBA kids. The biotech industry, probably the most exciting industry in the world today, is completely based on people who have Ph.D.s in biology and chemistry. We have to be sensible about this. It is fine to teach entrepreneurship in the universities, but not to business students. Let the MBAs go out and become the professional managers of the world, which we need, but they are not going to learn how to make anything that the world needs, like a biochemist would. [We have to] start teaching entrepreneurship across the disciplines, to everybody. At least give them a brief, introductory course to let them know that it is an honorable and possible career path, and that you do not have to work for Merck if you are a biology major.[27]

This analysis is consistent with the customer/product vision included in Farrell's entrepreneurial basics. An individual's entrepreneurial potential is typically grounded in technical expertise, which remains unexplored in business schools.

Farrell advises that the best way to add entrepreneurial skill to technical expertise is to learn from specialized trainers who offer workshops and seminars on entrepreneurial growth practices.[28] These short courses (one or two days) teach practical principles, rooted in the dynamics of the marketplace, that aspiring entrepreneurs can apply to their start-ups. The success of Farrell's organization reflects the importance of this kind of coaching. The Farrell Company has provided training to almost one million individuals worldwide—more than any business school.

Step 3: How Can You Learn to Pursue Entrepreneurial Excellence?

Now that we understand a good starting point, and the scope of learnable content, we can address the final question: How can you learn to pursue entrepreneurial excellence? There are, of course, many ways to learn about entrepreneurship: learning by doing, experimenting, working with family, finding mentors, buying a business, turning a hobby into a new venture, and so on. However, in the North American context, the vast majority of individuals learn about entrepreneurship in the context of formal education programs. More specifically, university MBA programs are the single largest delivery system for entrepreneurship education.

Entrepreneurship was first taught in the United States in 1947 at Harvard Business School. Since that time, the American infrastructure has grown to offer 2,200 courses at more than 1,600 schools, 277 endowed positions, 44 English-language refereed journals, and more than 100 centers.[29]

Mintzberg critiques the method in which learning about entrepreneurship occurs within MBA programs. His comments provide a context for how to pursue entrepreneurial excellence.

Henry Mintzberg: Practicing Entrepreneurship

Mintzberg, as noted previously, views management and entrepreneurship as a practice, complemented with an element of craft. He argues that learning management (and, by extrapolation, entrepreneurship) requires more than just a gloss on the current MBA programs.

"Some schools have tried to simulate entrepreneurship," he comments. "The students pretend to create businesses (sometimes they really do), work out strategies, draw up plans, even present them to investment bankers for comment."[30] He is not impressed: "It has been said of bacon and eggs that the chicken is involved, but the pig is committed. MBA students play chicken in these projects, not pig."[31]

In light of his criticism, can established educational institutions innovate and adopt practice as a foundation for learning? "In some ways it is obviously easier to break new ground in a new school," he concedes, "although if the school is not known, it may live in mortal fear of acceptance."[32]

"But," he continues, "there is a short answer to your question: we've done it in five established schools. So we are able to do that kind of teaching in an established business school, even though the other things going on may be more conventional. McGill does not apologize to me. They do what they do—and very well."[33]

Mintzberg is the driving force behind what is called the "International Masters Program in Practicing Management" (IMPM; *www.impm.org*). He began the program with the assistance of colleagues from other universities. It consists of a series of two-week modules spread over 16 months and five countries, and the participants include McGill University in Montreal, Lancaster University in the United Kingdom, INSEAD University in France, Bangalore University in India, and a consortium of faculty in Japan and Korea. The five modules are: Managing Self, the reflective mindset; Managing Relationships, the collaborative mindset; Managing Organizations, the analytic mindset; Managing Context, the worldly mindset; and Managing Change, the action mindset.

The modules are rooted in seven propositions for developing management education: management education should be restricted to practicing managers; the classroom should leverage the managers' experience in their education; insightful theories help managers make sense of their experience; thoughtful reflection on experience in the light of conceptual ideas is the key to managerial learning; "sharing" competencies raises managers' consciousness about their practice; beyond reflection in the classroom comes learning from impact on the organization; and, all of the above should be blended into a process of "experienced reflection."

"I make the case [in *Managers, Not MBAs*] that it is critical to have a very thoughtful atmosphere," Mintzberg remarks. "And you can have a thoughtful atmosphere in a company, of course, but you can also do some very interesting things. So I think any university that is smart about it can offer tremendously interesting stuff."[34]

He goes on:

The essential idea behind the IMPM is that managers learn best in their natural contexts. There are better and worse routes to an IMPM classroom, but only those that bring managers able to learn in context are acceptable. Indeed, we have had many single managers and entrepreneurs from small businesses in India, which has worked fine (although being able to work in class with several colleagues from one's company is preferable).[35]

Mintzberg appreciates the applicability of these concepts to entrepreneurship training: "I have often thought we could do a short program of the IMPM for entrepreneurs to discuss among themselves: dealing with banks, staffing, creating an organization, marketing, etc."[36]

Moreover, he agrees that the elements are relevant to entrepreneurship: "An IMPM class of, say, entrepreneurs, should work well—indeed, be fascinating—because they would relish sharing their experiences (although my suspicion is that most would prefer something shorter than our degree version)."[37]

Entrepreneurs have thus far participated successfully in the IMPM program. "A number of participants from India have been entrepreneurs, and some from Canada have been involved,"[38] Mintzberg recalls. He affirms, "I think that the experience of entrepreneurs is very powerful."[39]

Mintzberg also notes that a number of graduates of the IMPM are entrepreneurs: "We have had entrepreneurs in the program and they have been comfortable with the IMPM approach—to the extent they will sit still for anything!"[40] Mintzberg remembers a man in their second IMPM group who is now one of the hottest entrepreneurs in India: "His name is Gopi and he has created a discount airline that is getting huge amounts of attention. He has $1.5 billion in planes on order; 17 months ago he had none!"[41]

Mintzberg, the Entrepreneur, and the IMPM Program[42]

"The design of the IMPM was the front part, and was rather easy. As a team among the participating institutions, we were very creative and had a lot of ideas. It went smoothly—and building up around the world came easily. The tricky part was the marketing, because this was something new and different. Some people get it right away and are enamored; for other people, it takes a lot of explaining. That has always been the trickiest part.

"I see no reason why any EMBA program anywhere could not learn from our experience. We are building a health-care version of the IMPM at McGill that will start in June 2006 (www.imhl.com). We have also run the McGill-McConnell program for voluntary sector managers. [Plus,] we have been doing two Advanced Leadership

versions (www.alp-impm.com), and we have been doing great. We are looking at expanding the IMPM itself.

"We have a fixed partnership that is not negotiable—it's working fine. We are not looking to replace anyone. There have been expressions of interest and we have worked with other groups in various ways. The Japanese module is run partly in Korea.

"There are not necessarily unique aspects to developing the IMPM from an entrepreneurial dimension—how to get started, marketing something new, etc. I see it as an adhocracy, the ultimate devolved project management organization: there are no subordinates or superiors; there is no lead school. It's a collegial relationship that has been quite smooth, perhaps because it is set up in a way that everyone feels like part of it."

Mintzberg believes universities can play a vital role in management and entrepreneurship education, because they can combine elements of practical orientation with an oasis of reflection. "What managers desperately need today is to step back from the hectic nature of managerial work and be able to reflect in a thoughtful atmosphere," he muses, "and nobody can create as thoughtful an atmosphere as universities, when they are attuned to what these managers need." He pauses. "That is why I think the idea of coming to university and being under high pressure is so laughable. These people have to slow down and not be kept at the same pace [as their work environment]."[43]

According to Mintzberg, the instruction of entrepreneurs is still best suited to the university rather than to a technical school. The university, through its own track record of advanced scholarship, can attract people interested in serious learning.

Mintzberg warns:

The...stuff we are doing is not trivial kind of trade school things. When you get together a group of serious, intelligent managers—because obviously you want to screen for intelligence—you are going to get quite a high level of discussion. We don't spend our time trying to figure out how you can market your deodorant. We spend our time talking about the fundamental notions of business, including some marketing issues, but on a rather high plane.[44]

Henry Mintzberg: Cultivating an Entrepreneurial Imagination

Apart from emphasizing the integration of practice, Mintzberg believes methodologies for teaching entrepreneurship should incorporate more creativity. In his view, there should be more emphasis on the notion of *craft*, and the related role of *art*, in fostering the entrepreneurial imagination. He comments, "You can observe art. You can be voyeuristic about art. You can bring it into the classroom for observation, but you can't teach it."[45]

Maintaining that this element belongs in the educational process, he remarks, "How do you bring in creativity? There are plenty of people in business schools who are creative. But those people are overwhelmed by all the technocrats."[46] Furthermore, "An arts undergraduate degree may be better than one in a technical area, such as science or engineering, since it teaches a lot of nuance."[47]

So, how does someone foster creativity? Mintzberg's answer: in ways that run contrary to the present business school model. Business schools often place a higher degree of emphasis on its applicants' technical skills, favoring science, engineering, and math graduates who have a high degree of mathematical proficiency. Mintzberg notes, "Many business school professors will tell you that the undergraduate students tend to be more creative and energetic than the MBAs, and also more inclined toward entrepreneurship.... This suggests that a broad, idea-based education may serve them, and society, better than a limited technical one."[48]

In *Managers, Not MBAs*, Mintzberg quotes Robert Chia with respect to "Cultivating the Entrepreneurial Imagination."[49] Chia argues that the cultivation of an entrepreneurial imagination is the singular most important contribution university business schools can make to the business community. This requires a radical shift in pedagogical priorities, from teaching analytical problem-solving skills to cultivating a paradigm-shifting mentality. Chia further argues that recourse to literature and the arts provides the best means of stimulating the "powers of association" in young, fertile minds. Whereas the traditional scientific mentality emphasizes the simplification of the complex multiplicity of our experiences into principles, literature and the arts emphasize the tasks of complicating our thinking processes and sensitizing us to nuances.

In short, Chia promotes that one facet of pedagogy would be to incorporate diverse sources of learning in order to stimulate more creative thinking.

Continual Growth

As noted, the three-step process begins with self-assessment, a learner-focused method of analysis. From every nascent entrepreneur's unique breadth of experience comes a distinctly personal frame of reference. As a result, determining the role that entrepreneurship has played in one's past is a pre-requisite for understanding the perspective through which one views the entrepreneurial landscape. Honest self-assessment lets individuals determine if entrepreneurship is a direction worth pursuing.

Secondly, understanding what people can and can't learn about entrepreneurship allows an upcoming entrepreneur to adequately prepare for a venture, both through educational means and understanding inherent strengths and weaknesses.

Finally, attaining a level of entrepreneurial excellence requires individuals to cultivate an entrepreneurial imagination—to continually nurture creativity and integrate an artistic consciousness into entrepreneurial life. If you (the potential entrepreneur) are doing pre-MBA studies, then you should seek a liberal arts style of education, which presents a wide base of knowledge in an array of disciplines, rather than a "limited" technical education. If you are presently in the workforce, perhaps working for a larger company, you should seek to get outside your comfort zone and take on new and different tasks, travel to new countries, or meet a different circle of business associates, all with the intent of stimulating your creativity.

Entrepreneurs, similar to artists, never stop learning. Thus, these three steps are not a one-time success analysis test; rather, they are a continual course of reflection and growth. The moment an entrepreneur becomes stagnant in his training, he is in serious trouble. Indeed, as the experts in this chapter have advised, entrepreneurship requires a deep level of thought, anticipation, and creativity. Furthermore, entrepreneurship is, by definition, a field on the forefront of society's discoveries; we should not be surprised, then, that those who stop exploring beyond their current boundaries soon find themselves left behind.

Part IV

Conclusion

Conclusion

Where Do I Go From Here?

Is the pursuit of entrepreneurial excellence for everyone? Though I would like to think so, my experiences as a consultant and educator tell me it is not. Skydiving is fun, too—but not for everyone! Some of my students recoil at the thought of the emotional and economic risk, the psychological toll, and the high degree of time and effort required to build a successful venture. These are all intimidating realities, to say the least. In addition, as prior chapters affirm, an entrepreneurial venture demands creativity, passion, perseverance, and continual growth.

Who, then, is ready for such an undertaking? And do all entrepreneurial efforts require the same personal strengths and sacrifices? To address these questions, I draw on the insights of three of the entrepreneurship experts: Rita McGrath, Karl Vesper, and Irv Grousbeck.

McGrath discusses the different types of entrepreneurs, and how career aspirations vary accordingly. Karl Vesper outlines the types of career departure points (and the respective challenges involved) for individuals considering entrepreneurship. Lastly, Irv Grousbeck discusses the relationship between an entrepreneurial career and a risk threshold.

Rita McGrath: 3 Entrepreneurial Career Alternatives

According to McGrath, entrepreneurial expectations and experiences do indeed vary, depending upon the individual entrepreneur's objectives. She identifies three different types of entrepreneurs:[1]

1. High-growth entrepreneurs.
2. Lifestyle entrepreneurs.
3. "In-and-outer" entrepreneurs.

Each of the three types has a unique notion of success; likewise, stress and uncertainty levels are different for all of them.

The High-Growth Entrepreneur

A high-growth entrepreneur is the stereotypical individual featured on magazine covers: a high-energy, almost frenetic individual, pursing a niche with gusto and passion, and constantly promoting his idea in hopes of building a fast-growing enterprise. This individual is bent on building a company around his product or service, expanding into new markets, and eventually either selling the business, merging, or taking the company public.

The aspiring high-growth entrepreneur has an entrepreneurial frame with a register of opportunities that he must assess in relation to his present circumstances. McGrath provides a very practical model: These people should look for opportunities that provide double their present income within two to three years.[2] Would-be entrepreneurs should adopt this premium to take into account the risk of starting a business. The guideline is also a measuring stick with which to review the opportunity register. If a potential entrepreneur is earning $250,000 per year at a fast-track investment banking or management consulting firm, then his equation differs from that of a recently laid-off sales manager who was earning $50,000 per year.

The Lifestyle Entrepreneur

A second type of individual is the lifestyle entrepreneur, for whom the entrepreneurial frame is very different. The lifestyle entrepreneur's primary motivation is personal control over his own destiny: the ability to do what he wants, when he wants to do it. Other than that, these individuals are content simply earning a living. Sometimes corporate executive refugees, they put personal lifestyle ahead of profit.

McGrath cites the example of a lifestyle entrepreneur in one of her classes:[3] Among the first to create a winery in the former potato fields of Long Island, New York, he and his wife were completely passionate about the actual business of making wine, particularly because it allowed them a certain manner of living. Their goal was not to achieve the highest possible economic returns. Rather, as do many artists, they felt content earning a comfortable living and producing a product they found inwardly satisfying.

The In-and-Outer Entrepreneur

A third type of entrepreneur is the "in-and-outer," someone who regularly transitions between being an independent entrepreneur and working within a company. Of course, if a high-growth entrepreneur is successful, he inevitably grows a large business within which intrapreneurship becomes critical. Thus, the line between the two types is very blurry. After all, in today's society, an individual rarely makes a single, all-defining career choice at a particular age and sticks with it for the rest of his life.

Although people sometimes have in their minds the stereotype of a figure such as John Hershey, who relentlessly perfected his chocolate business and built an empire, such is not the norm for all entrepreneurs.[4] Instead, for the in-and-outer, the entrepreneurial frame fluctuates over time: At one point he may pursue start-up opportunities, and at another time he may be content working within a large organization.

Karl H. Vesper: Career Departure Points

Karl H. Vesper adopts a slightly different, but equally beneficial, perspective with respect to the evaluation and application of entrepreneurial options. After making an extensive professional career of studying the entrepreneurial process, Vesper believes there are myriad departure points for an entrepreneurial career.[5] These options are too vast and variable to generalize; a safer route is simply to categorize the range of experiences. Of course, a categorical approach has less predictive value, but it more accurately depicts the nature of the entrepreneurial experience. After all, almost anyone can start a business—and many people do.

Many new ventures are in basic industries, namely retailing and services. Often prior work experience will prompt someone to start his own venture in the same field. People most frequently start such ventures when they are in their 30s and 40s, but (of course) some well-known entrepreneurs—Bill Gates, for example—started ventures in their early 20s. More recently, there is the tale of Mark Zuckerberg, who started Facebook (*www.facebook.com*) at age 19; three years later he was apparently turning down $1 billion offers from Yahoo and Viacom.[6] From a practical standpoint, the older entrepreneurs presumably have more experience and resources; however, younger entrepreneurs may have critical opportunity-specific knowledge.

As well, individuals pursue different types of entrepreneurial jobs. Not all wish to be on the track of a high-growth technology company. As McGrath mentioned, there are lifestyle entrepreneurs who wish to escape the stresses of a corporate environment and pursue something they view as more meaningful. In response to their dreams, they might buy out an existing business, start a new venture, work with several partners, or act as an independent consultant.

Does this range of options reveal definable success patterns? Vesper cites an extensive study (involving almost three thousand entrepreneurs) that compared common characteristics of successful entrepreneurs with the traits of entrepreneurs who had failed a start-up after three years: The study showed that the successful entrepreneurs (1) were more likely to be college graduates, (2) started their ventures with more capital, (3) were less likely to have continued to hold other jobs, (4) were more likely not to be in retail, and (5) were less likely to have left prior jobs out of dissatisfaction.[7] Vesper also comments that the claim that successful entrepreneurs tend to come from homes with self-employed parents is contradicted by research.[8] Moreover, studies that search for a psychological link between entrepreneurs have proven to be inconclusive.

According to his research, Vesper maintains that prosperous entrepreneurs have a wide variety of qualifications and attributes; however, he has found that some prior work experience is important in preparation for entrepreneurship. Vesper concludes that founders "not only tend to start companies that are in the same industries as their prior employment, but [they] also tend to have concentrated their work experience on fewer jobs."[9] In retrospect, his conclusion is common sense, because previous experience allows an individual to see needs in the marketplace, to improve skills, and to wait for the right opportunity.

Vesper summarizes: "Work provides practice against standards required to compete, and thereby hones excellence. It helps a would-be entrepreneur judge [if] he could truly compete with an independent venture, and adds to [his] self-confidence in making a venture choice."[10]

Though there are stories of individuals resolving to make their millions by a certain age—and they occasionally do just that—most entrepreneurs find their career departure point through the outcome of their circumstances. Some get an idea in the workplace and then decide to pursue it; others may feel forced into entrepreneurship if they get outsized or downsized with a severance package and minimal future prospects; yet, ultimately, the drive to entrepreneurship is a function of someone having the ability, interest, and inclination to chase opportunities. This, of course, can occur at any time in a person's career.

Vesper also observes that today's technology allows an entrepreneur to have much more flexibility regarding the place and nature of work. DSL lines, wireless Internet, laptops, and cell phones allow people to work in a virtual office, whether at home, while driving (though this is a dangerous idea), or from the deck of a private yacht.

Vesper recalled one contact in Southern California who worked part-time as a dentist, and used his earnings to invest in real estate—which had doubled in value over the past five years.[11] The man, in essence, evolved into a lifestyle entrepreneur, earning a base of income from an established professional practice, which he then channeled into other investments and items for personal enjoyment. Vesper remarked, "He is balancing his life between his dental practice and playing around with his toys, such as his airplane and motorcycle."[12]

One aspect of pursuing an entrepreneurial career is deciding whether it is financially worthwhile in view of the risks involved. Besides monetary risks, there are also personal and emotional risks associated with the experience. Not everyone wishes to expose himself to the emotional highs and lows of the process. In addition, the entrepreneurial life can take a toll on the entrepreneur's family and friends. Working for a company, on the other hand, can provide comfort, security (depending on the organization), benefits, and predictability, and can liberate a person from the stressful risk of losing it all.

The choice is not easy. Vesper cites the conclusion of one study: It claims that those who (1) accept modest—rather than too lofty—goals initially, (2) seek partners with industrial experience, and (3) start to prepare for a venture earlier in life, have higher odds of leading a start-up company.[13]

Part of the entrepreneur's duty is not only to maintain an emotional equilibrium, but also to be continually positive. As opposed to an employee in a company environment, where the individual may be one cog in a large machine, the entrepreneur who leads a start-up is the barometer of enthusiasm for everyone else involved. Hence the popularity of entrepreneurial self-help volumes and periodicals: Entrepreneurs routinely read these books as a way of maintaining enthusiasm in the face of less-than-positive suppliers, bankers, and partners. The entrepreneurial career path requires a continual recharging of mental and emotional batteries.

H. Irving Grousbeck: Demystifying the Entrepreneurial Career

With myriad options leading into the unknown, how can an individual determine which way to embark on a career in entrepreneurship? According to H. Irving Grousbeck, the journey begins by identifying the personal concerns of the entrepreneur, apart from those related to the business. He elaborates, "[Entrepreneurship] is a career that we attempt to demystify— [we want people to] hold it up against other careers and make an informed choice."[14] Grousbeck continues: "We try to show students that one can think reasonably, logically, and calmly about an entrepreneurial career, and decide to pursue that career if he chooses to."[15]

But not every venture succeeds. What is the option for an individual who has depleted all his resources, only to have his business fail? Hopefully the person has taken this possibility into consideration from the beginning.

Indeed, entrepreneurs must begin by considering the potential cost of their venture and preparing themselves to accept all possible outcomes. A personal analysis depends on the individual's particular circumstances, in relation to age, financial resources, and aspirations: What is the extent of his career risk? What is the worst thing that can happen? And, if the venture fails, will he be able to get another job?

Entrepreneurs retain their skills, and they are presumably wiser for having gone through the entrepreneurial process. Yet, Grousbeck identifies one risk related to the emotional impact on the entrepreneur. Some would-be entrepreneurs become "constitutionally unemployable" in the sense that, as Grousbeck mentions, "It becomes emotionally difficult to go back to work for another company."[16] Once having tasted the entrepreneurial life, these people wish to keep persisting in some entrepreneurial form—the same way chronic gamblers hope success is waiting around the next corner.

Grousbeck notes that aspiring entrepreneurs in his classes at Stanford can proactively reduce some elements of personal risk by analyzing their post-graduate career strategy: How do they plan to pursue an entrepreneurial career?

His context is a graduate business school environment where the average student is about 26 years old, although ages range from 22 to 42. A typical student has obtained an undergraduate degree over four years, worked for another four years, and obtained his MBA in the following two years. So, these students may consider taking the entrepreneurial plunge at about age 28 (upon graduation), possibly without a spouse and children.

Grousbeck counsels his students that, although their downside risk may be less at this stage of life than in 10 or 20 years, they should still consider a number of factors. "There are some [options] that mitigate [students'] risks in a relatively short amount of time, without affecting their present risk profiles," he notes. "For example, they can buy an existing business if they are intent on running a business right away. Alternatively, they can get an operating job—a so-called 'doing job'—such as sales, so they can acquire some experience."[17] These suggestions are a challenge, since the gilt-edged Stanford degree is a ticket to high-paying jobs as management consultants, venture capitalists, and investment bankers.

Charting Your Own Course

Inasmuch as all entrepreneurs face challenges, risks, and sacrifices, the intensity levels of such demands vary widely from person to person. The intimidating realities of high-growth entrepreneurship differ significantly from the stakes and goals of a part-time or lifestyle entrepreneur. Along similar lines, the future of every venture is uncertain: A tiny hamburger chain could become the next fast-food phenomenon—or it could fail miserably. Or, as noted earlier, a simple online tool for connecting people (initially with minimal overhead costs) could explode into one of the most-trafficked sites on the Internet.

With that in mind, Vesper's and Grousbeck's strategies for minimizing unnecessary risk are valuable ideas to ponder. Finding a venture with low risks and high potential is always ideal—and often those opportunities arise in areas of personal interest, experience, and ability. Furthermore, using McGrath's measurement analyses, entrepreneurs can determine which style of entrepreneurship is right for them and decide if a new business enterprise is financially worthwhile. Taking these considerations into account from the beginning may diminish stress in the future and allow one to make an informed decision about which of the many entrepreneurial career paths to pursue.

In other words, if the thought of forging your own trail overwhelms you with terror, consider the stakes of your venture. Does the opportunity carry realistic potential for advancement or career satisfaction? Are you prepared to accept the risks involved? Do you have expertise, talent, and connections in the area you are pursuing? Are you willing to sacrifice the time, energy, and resources that your venture requires? In the end, every entrepreneur navigates an unknown course. However, those who are wise can, and will, equip themselves accordingly.

Pursuing Entrepreneurial Excellence

The final—and most demanding—call of every entrepreneur is to pursue excellence in all of his or her endeavors. As the experts have noted, excellence is a many-faceted term. It is a practice, a continual habit that shapes everything from critical business interactions to menial daily tasks. It is also an attitude, one that rejects mediocrity and refuses to accept an apathetic stance. Moreover, it involves taking the ethical high road, exercising wisdom through preparation and reflection, and continually embracing new challenges.

The journey is not easy, and it can be discouraging at times. After all, there is no set path: Entrepreneurs are explorers by definition. That being said, for those who bravely venture into the marketplace, the navigational tools they acquire—both from experts and personal experience—will prove an invaluable resource. The advice in this book cannot tell you what lies around the next bend, but it can help you stay your course through confusing and difficult terrain.

Obstacles are a reality for all entrepreneurs; you cannot avoid them. However, if you build your business on the practice of entrepreneurial excellence, you are much more likely to overcome them. Furthermore, as expert Gordon Redding noted at the beginning of the Introduction, the process involves making mistakes—but they are your opportunity to recalibrate and avoid future problems. The entrepreneurial path requires astute perseverance. Yet, along the way, you will find that failure is sometimes the first step toward success.

Appendix

The Selection Process: Finding the Experts and Choosing Key Points

Any selection process will be contentious: By its very nature, exclusion occurs. In this instance, there are many significant contributors to the field of entrepreneurship education, and selecting some does not minimize the contributions of others. This book does not claim to be a "top 10" or "best of all time" selection; such an approach would simply become a focus of tangential debate. Rather, the book assembles a collection of perspectives from a diverse group of leading experts.

During this book's review process, the bulk of reviewers concurred that the present grouping provides a stellar collection of insights from key influencers at the world's leading institutions. I can confidently claim that I am not aware of another book that gathers firsthand insights from such an esteemed and influential group of entrepreneurship experts.

How were the entrepreneurial experts selected?

The selection criteria for the interviewees in this book included a series of requirements. He or she must be: a recognized pioneer in business and/or entrepreneurship (mentioned in leading publications); head of a leading entrepreneurship center; author of an influential trade book or text in the field; an entrepreneurial instructor at a leading institution; and a leading educator whose expertise has been validated in the marketplace. Although the experts do not have to be based at a university, most of them are. (One, however, is an independent globetrotting consultant.) Overall, I believe the chosen individuals present a rich spectrum of wise and perceptive opinions.

What aspects of each expert's work were selected for inclusion in the book?

You will notice that each chapter is organized around three to five easily digestible points. These points are not meant to be all-inclusive; neither is this a survey book on entrepreneurship, of which there are many. Instead, I have included insights from the experts selectively, in order to make the book a concise, cohesive, and unified whole. Accordingly, I avoided overlapping insights as much as possible.

I cannot and do not claim that the key points attributed to various thinkers are their chief or only contributions to the field. I also readily acknowledge that each expert has a substantial body of work, which is impossible to reduce to a handful of pages. At the same time, I believe the points included in each chapter are important ones, and paint a fair representation of the individual's perspective. Essentially, this book adopts more of a seminar approach, studying different perspectives and gearing its message toward those who already have some type of foundation in entrepreneurship.

What was the process of identifying the entrepreneurial experts?

My purpose was to get a cross-section of experts, for a balanced and integrated treatment of entrepreneurship. As a result, the experts selected do not simply consist of educators at the leading two or three schools; this, of course, would result in a uniform perspective. Similarly, when selecting a national team for a professional sport, such as basketball, merely choosing all the top scorers for a "Dream Team" does not make an effective group (or guarantee a Gold Medal in a walkover). A wiser approach is to select a balanced team that includes so-called role players, such as defensive specialists.

Similarly, I integrated individuals who, though not known for entrepreneurship, provide important insights on the topic. For example,

Henry Mintzberg is a well-known management guru. He doesn't write on entrepreneurship specifically, but his insights on the craft and practice of management are quite applicable. Also, because most entrepreneurship education still exists within the confines of MBA programs, I believe the perspective of the world's leading critic of that delivery model is worth considering.

Why interview "academics?" Does this not provide a limited perspective on how entrepreneurship works?

Many leading lights in the realm of entrepreneurial academia are, in fact, practitioners. Daniel Muzyka, Dean of the Sauder School of Business, University of British Columbia, rails at "the false dichotomy" of pitting academics and practitioners against one another in the field of entrepreneurship education.[1] Muzyka explains that entrepreneurship education has developed as a field that is well-informed by practice, and educators are continually crossing over from working to teaching.[2] Along those lines, all of the experts I have selected have practical experience, either as corporate consultants or leaders of their own start-up ventures. Perhaps the best example is H. Irving Grousbeck of Stanford, who cofounded Continental Cablevision and helped it grow to a multi-billion-dollar corporation. He is now also one of four managing partners of the fabled Boston Celtics. In addition, he is a founding director of Asurion, Inc., a thriving wireless communications company with 6,000 employees and more than $1.3 billion in revenue.

Another example is Howard H. Stevenson of Harvard, who was a founder and the first president of the Baupost Group, an $8 billion registered investment company. And from a different angle, Henry Mintzberg is a highly sought-after consultant to the largest corporations in the world. He is quite an innovator as well, having pioneered a program called the "International Masters Program for Practicing Management," with five institutions, plus his own at McGill.

This list highlights the balance of theory and practice among great educators. The advantage of gleaning their advice (as opposed to that of others) is that they know how to teach. Not all great entrepreneurs have the skill required to coach someone.

In short, the experts assembled in this book are far from being "ivory tower academics." They practice what they teach, and teach what they practice—and they pursue both of these endeavors with excellence.

Notes

Introduction

1. Gordon Redding, telephone interview with the author, February 16, 2005.
2. Jim Pattison, telephone interview with the author, October 6, 2005.
3. Ibid.
4. Ibid.
5. See *www.jimpattison.com.*
6. Stevenson, "Why Entrepreneurship."
7. Bhide, Grousbeck, and Stevenson, *New Business Ventures,* p. 4.
8. This is the first of Stevenson's "Three tenets of the Harvard Business School approach to teaching entrepreneurship." See *www.hbs.edu/entrepreneurship.*
9. Bhide, Grousbeck, and Stevenson, *New Business Ventures,* p. 5.
10. H. Stevenson, telephone interview with the author, August 8, 2005.
11. Barringer and Ireland, *Entrepreneurship*
12. Drucker, *The Executive* p. 247.
13. Ibid.
14. Ibid.
15. Ibid., p. 248.
16. Gordon Redding, telephone interview with the author, February 16, 2005.
17. Mintzberg, *Managers, Not MBAs,* p. 1.
18. Ibid.
19. Ibid., p. 11.
20. Henry Mintzberg, interview with the author, September 27, 2004.
21. Ibid.
22. Ibid.
23. Merriam-Webster Online.
24. Schank, *Coloring Outside,* p. xx.

Chapter 1

1. Drucker, *The Executive,* p. 248.
2. Maciariello *Daily Drucker.*
3. Crainer, *Ultimate Book,* p. 50.
4. Numerous telephone conversations and e-mail communications with Joseph Maciariello from May to September, 2005, and a review of this chapter in June

2007. At the same time, I take full responsibility for the shortcomings and limitations of this brief summary of Professor Drucker's insights on innovation and entrepreneurship.

5. Karl H. Vesper, telephone interview with the author, August 8, 2005.

6. Ibid.

7. Ibid.

8. Ibid.

9. Drucker, *The Executive*, pp. 277–8.

10. Ibid., p. 280.

11. Ibid., p. 285.

12. Ibid.

13. Ibid., p. 317.

14. Ibid.

15. Ibid., p. 318.

16. Ibid., p. 321.

17. Ibid., p. 322.

18. Ibid., p. 285.

19. Ibid., p. 345.

20. Ibid.

21. Ibid., p. 350.

22. Ibid., p. 357.

23. Ibid., p. 384.

24. Ibid.

25. Ibid.

26. Ibid., p. 386.

27. Ibid.

28. Ibid., p. 387. Also see Randall E. Stross's *The Wizard of Menlo Park: How Thomas Alva Edison Invented the Modern World* (New York: Crown Publishers, 2007) for a recent and comprehensive biography of Edison.

29. Drucker, *The Executive*, p. 261.

30. Ibid., p. 264.

31. Ibid., p. 400.

32. Ibid.

33. Ibid., p. 402.

34. Ibid., p. 424.

35. Ibid., p. 425.

36. Ibid.

37. Ibid., p. 460.

38. Ibid., p. 469.

39. Ibid., p. 462.

40. Ibid., p. 471.

41. Ibid.

42. Ibid., p. 477.

43. Ibid., p. 478.

44. Ibid., p. 479.

45. Ibid., p. 483.

46. Ibid.

Chapter 2

1. Larry C. Farrell, telephone interview with the author, December 9, 2004.

2. Ibid.

3. Farrell, *Getting Entrepreneurial!*, p. 9.

4. Larry C. Farrell, telephone interview with the author, December 9, 2004.

5. Ibid.

6. Ibid.

7. Farrell, *Getting Entrepreneurial!*, p. 8.

8. Larry C. Farrell, telephone interview with the author, December 9, 2004.

9. Farrell, *Getting Entrepreneurial!*, p. 43.

10. Ibid., pp. 12–3.

11. Ibid., p. 39.

12. Larry C. Farrell, telephone interview with the author, December 9, 2004.

13. Farrell, *Getting Entrepreneurial!*, p. 59.

14. Ibid., p. 71.

15. Ibid., p. 75.

16. Ibid., p. 13.

17. Ibid.

18. Ibid., p. 108.

19. Ibid., p. 125.

20. Ibid., p. 122.

21. Ibid., p. 14.

22. Ibid., pp. 150–1.

23. Ibid., p. 176.

24. Larry C. Farrell, telephone interview with the author, December 9, 2004.

25. Ibid.

26. Ibid.

27. Ibid.

28. Ibid.

29. The source for this material is the Farrell telephone interview (previously cited), except for the Jannie Tay quote, which is from page 185 of Farrell's *Getting Entrepreneurial!*

30. Larry C. Farrell, telephone interview with the author, December 9, 2004.

31. Ibid..

32. Farrell, *Getting Entrepreneurial!*, p. 200.

33. Ibid., p. 209.

34. Larry C. Farrell, telephone interview with the author, December 9, 2004.

35. Farrell, *Getting Entrepreneurial!*, p. 209.

36. Ibid., p. 210.

37. Ibid., p. 213.

38. Ibid.

39. Larry C. Farrell, telephone interview with the author, December 9, 2004.

40. Ibid.

41. Farrell, *Getting Entrepreneurial!*, p. 216.

42. Ibid., p. 217.

Chapter 3

1. H. Irving Grousbeck telephone interview with the author, August 5, 2005.

2. Center for Entrepreneurial Studies, Stanford Graduate School of Business. *www.gsb.stanford.edu/ces/*.

3. Devlin and Gray, "Heroes."

4. H. Irving Grousbeck telephone interview with the author, August 5, 2005.

5. Ibid.

6. Ibid.

7. Ibid.

8. Ibid.

9. Ibid.

10. Ibid.

11. Ibid.

12. Grousbeck, "You Gotta Have."

13. Ibid.

14. Ibid.

15. Ibid.

16. Ibid.

17. Ibid.

18. H. Irving Grousbeck telephone interview with the author, August 5, 2005.

19. Grousbeck, H. Irving. Doctor of Humane Letters.

20. H. Irving Grousbeck telephone interview with the author, August 5, 2005.

21. Ibid.

22. Ibid.

23. Grousbeck, "You Gotta Have."

24. "An Entrepreneurial Journey."

25. Media One Website.

26. H. Irving Grousbeck telephone interview with the author, August 5, 2005.

27. eBay Website. "About eBay."

28. eBay Website. "About eBay."

29. Grousbeck, "eBay."

30. Grousbeck, "eBay."

31. H. Irving Grousbeck telephone interview with the author, August 5, 2005.

32. Ibid.

33. Ibid.

34. O'Toole, "Basketball Barons" AND "Investment Group."

35. Bhide, Grousbeck, and Stevenson, *New Business Ventures.* (See, by contrast, Chapter 11 in Timmons's *New Venture Creation (6th Ed).*)

35. H. Irving Grousbeck telephone interview with the author, August 5, 2005.

36. Ibid.

37. Ibid.

38. Ibid.

39. Ibid.

40. Ibid.

41. Ibid.

42. Ibid.

43. Ibid.

44. Ibid.

45. Ibid.

46. Ibid.

47. Ibid.

48. Ibid.

49. Ibid.

50. Ibid.

51. Ibid.

52. Ibid.

53. Ibid.

54. Ibid.

55. From the Skoll Foundation Website.

56. H. Irving Grousbeck telephone interview with the author, August 5, 2005.

57. Ibid.

58. Ibid.

Chapter 4

1. Tom Hockaday, telephone interview with the author, June 11, 2007.

2. Ibid.

220

Entrepreneurial Excellence

3. Cook, "Isis Innovation."

4. Attributed to Ralph Waldo Emerson, philosopher and poet (1803–82).

5. Dwek, "Commercializing."

6. From the Oxford University Press Website.

7. Hockaday, "Starting a Spin-out," p. 3.

8. Stanislaw and Yergin, *Commanding Heights,* pp. 105–13.

9. Tom Hockaday, telephone interview, June 11, 2007.

10. Ibid.

11. See *www.isis-innovation.com.*

12. "Isis Innovation."

13. A "spin-out" is a type of "spin-off" where a company splits off from its root organization to become a separate legal entity. The spin-out company takes intellectual property and technology from the parent organization. For example, Isis will have a spin-out (such as Oxonica Materials plc [see section 4.3]) enter into agreements to transfer the key technology and licensing agreements to the University, in exchange for permission to use the "Oxford" name. In most instances the University (through Isis) is a part owner of the spin-out company, arranges professional and consulting services, and possibly provides physical office/research space for the company.

14. See www.isis-innovation.com.

15. Tom Hockaday, interview with the author, July 16, 2007.

16. Ibid.

17. Tom Hockaday, telephone interview, June 11, 2007.

18. Cook, "Isis Innovation."

19. Dwek, "Commercializing." For further reference, view summary at *www.loc.gov/today/cyberlc/feature_wdesc.php?rec=4056.*

20. These organizations are sometimes referred to as a "Technology Licensing Office" or a "University-Industry Liaison Office."

21. See, for example, Barringer and Ireland's *Entrepreneurship,* p. 39.

22. Although the basic premise of patent law in the United States and the UK is the same—the protection of an invention for a specified period of exploitation by the originator—there are some significant differences. The Isis booklet, *Guidelines to Researchers[:] Intellectual Property, Patents and Licences,* notes: "Patent provisions in the USA are different (they operate a first to invent system, rather than the first to file system), and if the invention has been disclosed, Isis and its patent attorneys will advise as to whether it is still possible for the valid patent protection [ion the UK] to be secured in the USA." (p. 6). The guide points out another distinction: "In the majority of countries patent applications are published 18 months after they are filed. US patents are not published until they grant – which may be many (2–15) years after filing" (p. 7).

23. "General Information Concerning Patents (Revised January 2005)." U.S. Patent and Trademark Office. *www.uspto.gov/web/offices/pac/doc/general/index.html.*

24. "Isis Innovation."

25. Hockaday, "Starting a Spin-out," p. 3.

26. Tom Hockaday, telephone interview with the author, June 11, 2007.

27. Ibid.

28. Ibid.

29. Ibid.

30. Hockaday, "Starting a Spin-out," p. 3.

31. Cook, "Isis Innovation."

32. Ibid.

33. Ibid.

34. Ibid.

35. Ibid.

36. In *New Venture Creation (7th ed.)*, author Jeff Timmons (featured here in Chapter 9) notes that there are good reasons why "outside professionals" (p. 227) should not write the business plan.

37. Hockaday, "Starting a Spin-out," p. 6.

38. Ibid., p. 4.

39. Tom Hockaday, interview with the author, July 16, 2007.

40. Hockaday, "Starting a Spin-out," p. TK.

41. Ibid., 5.

42. Ibid., p. 10.

43. Tom Hockaday, interview with the author, July 16, 2007.

44. Ibid.

45. The abbreviation "plc" stands for "public limited company" and is equivalent to the U.S. abbreviation "Ltd." for "Limited."

46. To clarify, as per my "Author's Note" at the start of this chapter, that this summary of Oxonica is prepared by myself; other than Hockaday informing me of the company, none of the comments in this section should by attributed to him.

47. From the Foresight Nanotech Institute Website: *www.foresight.org/nano/whatisnano.html.* The site also explains: "Many fields of endeavor contribute to nanotechnology, including molecular physics, materials science, chemistry, biology, computer science, electrical engineering, and mechanical engineering. Due to the extreme breadth and generality of this definition, many prefer to use the term 'nanotechnologies.' For clarity, it is also useful to differentiate between near-term and long-term prospects, or to segment the field into first-generation through fourth-generation stages."

48. "Dr. Kevin Matthews."

49. Kevin Matthews, telephone interview with the author, June 11, 2007.

50. Ibid.

51. "Dr. Kevin Matthews."

52. Kevin Matthews, telephone interview with the author, June 11, 2007.

53. Ibid.

54. Ibid.

55. **Venture Capital Trusts** are "quoted limited companies whose purpose is to invest shareholders' funds in smaller unquoted trading companies, (including AIM listed stocks) having potential for growth, with a view to mak[e] profits. Most VCTs are run by investment managers and raise their funds from private investors." From *www.is4profit.com/is4money/savings-investments/venture-capital-trusts.html.*

56. Kevin Matthews, telephone interview with the author, June 11, 2007.

57. "Commercial Solutions." from Nanotechnology, PowerPoint Presentation. March 19, 2007. Retrieved from *www.oxonica.com.* on June 21, 2007.

58. Tom Hockaday, telephone interview, June 11, 2007.

59. Ibid.

59. Ibid.

60. Ibid.

61. Ibid.

62. Ibid.

63. Ibid.

64. Ibid.

65. Kevin Matthews, telephone interview with the author, June 11, 2007.

66. Ibid.

67. Tom Hockaday, telephone interview with the author, June 11, 2007.

68. Tom Hockaday, interview with the author, July 16, 2007.

Chapter 5

1. Rita Gunther McGrath, telephone interview with the author, March 29, 2005.

2. Both books were coauthored with Ian MacMillan.

3. MacMillan and McGrath, *The Entrepreneurial Mindset,* p. 1.

4. Ibid., p. 2.

5. Rita Gunther McGrath, telephone interview with the author, March 29, 2005.

6. Ibid.

7. Ibid.

8. MacMillan and McGrath, *The Entrepreneurial Mindset,* p. 2.

9. Ibid., p. 3.

10. Ibid.

11. Ibid.

12. Ibid.

13. Ibid., p. 11.

14. Ibid.

15. Ibid., pp. xiv–xv.

16. Rita Gunther McGrath, telephone interview with the author, March 29, 2005.

17. Ibid.

18. Ibid.

19. MacMillan and McGrath, *The Entrepreneurial Mindset*, p. 232.

20. Ibid., p. 236.

21. Ibid.

22. Ibid.

23. Ibid., p. 237.

24. Ibid., p. 238.

25. Ibid., p. 241.

26. Ibid.

27. Ibid.

28. Ibid., p. 242.

29. Ibid., p. 243.

30. Ibid.

31. Ibid., p. 246.

32. Ibid., p. 310.

33. Ibid., p. 163.

34. Rita Gunther McGrath, telephone interview with the author, March 29, 2005.

35. Ibid.

36. Ibid.

37. Ibid.

38. Ibid.

39. Ibid.

40. Ibid.

41. MacMillan and McGrath, *Market Busters*, p. 5.

42. Ibid., p. 77.

43. Ibid., p. 80.

44. Ibid., p. 122.

45. Ibid., p. 155.

46. Ibid.

47. Rita Gunther McGrath, telephone interview with the author, March 29, 2005.

48. Ibid.

Chapter 6

1. Mintzberg, *Managers, Not MBAs*, p. 131.

2. Mintzberg, *Mintzberg on Management*, p. 117.

3. Ibid., p. 120.

4. Ibid., p. 128.

5. Ibid., p. 117.

6. Ibid., p. 118.

7. Ibid.

8. Ibid., p. 120.

9. Ibid., p. 196.

10. Ibid., p. 199.

11. Mintzberg, *Mintzberg on Management*, pp. 117 and 198.

12. Mintzberg, et. al., *The Strategy Process*, p. 9.

13. Mintzberg, *Mintzberg on Management*, p. 26.

14. Mintzberg, *The Rise and Fall*, p. 410.

15. Ibid.

16. Ibid.

17. Henry Mintzberg, telephone interview with the author, April 20, 2005.

18. Ibid.

19. Mintzberg, *Mintzberg on Management*, p. 125.

20. Ibid.

21. Ibid., pp. 128–9.

22. Ibid., p. 128.

23. Mintzberg, *The Rise and Fall*, pp. 408–9.

24. Mintzberg, *Mintzberg on Management*, p. 210.

25. Ibid.

26. Ibid.

27. Ibid.

28. Ibid.

29. Ibid.

30. Ibid.

31. Culled from Mintzberg, *Mintzberg on Management*, pp. 116–30.

32. Mintzberg, *Mintzberg on Management*, p. 125.

33. Ibid., pp. 116–30.

Chapter 7

1. Redding, *The Spirit*, 223.

2. Ibid., p. 22.

3. Ibid., p. 25.

4. Ibid., p. 32.

5. Ibid., p. 29.

6. Ibid., p. 35.

7. Ibid., p. 34.

8. Ibid., p. 57.

9. Ibid., p. 58.

10. Redding uses as part of the starting point of his analysis the well-known book by Max Weber, _The Protestant Ethic and the Spirit of Capitalism._ In short, the Protestant ethic is defined by Weber as a moral code stressing hard work, asceticism, and the rational organization of one's life in the service of God.

11. Redding, _The Spirit_, p. 79.

12. Gordon Redding, telephone interview with the author, February 16, 2005.

13. Ibid.

14. Ibid.

15. Ibid.

16. Redding, _The Spirit_, p. 70.

17. Gordon Redding, telephone interview with the author, February 16, 2005.

18. Ibid.

19. Redding, _The Spirit_, p. 155.

20. Ibid., p. 135.

21. Ibid., p. 53.

22. Ibid.

23. Ibid., p. 67.

24. Ibid., p. 3.

25. Ibid., p. 129.

26. Ibid., p. 112.

27. Gordon Redding, telephone interview with the author, February 16, 2005.

28. Ibid.

29. Ibid.

30. Redding, _The Spirit_, p. 113.

31. Ibid., p. 130.

32. Gordon Redding, telephone interview with the author, February 16, 2005.

33. Ibid.

34. Ibid.

35. Ibid.

36. Ibid.

37. Ibid.

38. Ibid.

39. Ibid.

Chapter 8

1. Howard H. Stevenson, telephone interview with the author, August 8, 2005.

2. For more information, see Jeffrey L. Cruikshank's _Shaping the Waves: A History of Entrepreneurship at Harvard Business School_ (Boston: Harvard University Press, 2005).

3. According to the Arthur Rock Center for Entrepreneurship, Harvard Business School.

4. "Entrepreneurship Program."

5. Howard H. Stevenson, telephone interview with the author, August 8, 2005.

6. Stevenson quotation from the Arthur Rock Center for Entrepreneurship, Harvard Business School archives. *hbswk.hbs.edu/archive/2905.html*.

7. Howard H. Stevenson, telephone interview with the author, August 8, 2005.

8. Ibid.

9. Ibid.

10. Ibid.

11. Ibid.

12. This is the second tenet of Stevenson's approach to teaching entrepreneurship.

13. Howard H. Stevenson, telephone interview with the author, August 8, 2005.

14. Ibid.

15. Ibid.

16. Ibid.

17. Ibid.

18. Ibid.

19. Ibid.

20. Ibid.

21. Ibid.

22. Ibid.

23. Ibid.

24. Bhide, Grousbeck, and Stevenson, *New Business Ventures*, p. 5.

25. Ibid.

26. Ibid., pp. 5–6.

27. Ibid., p. 6.

28. Howard H. Stevenson, telephone interview with the author, August 8, 2005.

29. Bhide, Grousbeck, and Stevenson, *New Business Ventures*, p. 6.

30. Ibid.

31. Howard H. Stevenson, telephone interview with the author, August 8, 2005.

32. Ibid.

33. Bhide, Grousbeck, and Stevenson, *New Business Ventures*, p. 7.

34. Howard H. Stevenson, telephone interview with the author, August 8, 2005.

35. Bhide, Grousbeck, and Stevenson, *New Business Ventures*, p. 9.

36. Ibid., p. 10.

37. Ibid., p. 13.

38. Ibid., p. 15.

39. This is the third tenet of Stevenson's approach to teaching entrepreneurship.

40. Stevenson, "Why Entrepreneurship."

41. Howard H. Stevenson, telephone interview with the author, August 8, 2005.

42. Ibid.

43. Ibid.

44. Ibid.

45. Ibid.

46. Ibid.

47. Ibid.

48. Ibid.

49. Ibid.

50. Ibid.

51. Stevenson with Jarillo-Mossi, "Preserving," p. 20.

52. Howard H. Stevenson, telephone interview with the author, August 8, 2005.

53. The first two paragraphs here come from Stevenson's August 8, 2005, telephone interview with the author. The remaining material is paraphrased from *Frank Batten: Thriving on Challenge*, cited in the Bibliography.

54. Nash and Stevenson, *Just Enough*, p. xii.

55. Ibid., p. xviii.

56. Ibid.

57. Ibid.

58. Ibid., p. 277.

59. Laura Nash, telephone interview with the author, June 16, 2004.

60. Nash and Stevenson, *Just Enough*, p. 278.

61. Ibid., p. 209.

62. Laura Nash, interview with the author, June 16, 2004

63. Ibid.

64. Howard H. Stevenson, telephone interview with the author, August 8, 2005.

Chapter 9

1. Timmons with Spinelli, *New Venture Creation*, p. 3.

2. "Registry."

3. According to the eBay Website.

4. Ibid.

5. Timmons with Spinelli, *New Venture Creation*, p. 3.

6 .Ibid.

7. Ibid.

8. Ibid., p. 4.

9. Ibid., pp. 245–6.

10. Ibid., p. 47.

11. Ibid., pp. 249–56.

12. Ibid., p. 250.

13. Ibid., p. 251.

14. Ibid., p. 254.

15. Ibid., p. 255.

16. Ibid., p. 47.

17. Ibid., p. 56.

18. Jeffry Timmons, telephone interview with the author, November 17, 2004.

19. Ibid.

20. Timmons with Spinelli, *New Venture Creation*, p. 67.

21. Ibid., p. 62.

22. Ibid., p. 56.

23. Ibid.

24. Ibid., p. 274.

25. Ibid.

26. Ibid., p. 279.

27. Ibid., p. 281.

28. Ibid., p. 279.

29. Jeffry Timmons, telephone interview with the author, November 17, 2004.

30. Ibid.

Chapter 10

1. Karl Vesper, telephone interview with the author, August 8, 2005.

2. Vesper, *New Venture Experience*, p. 10.

3. Ibid., p. 11.

4. Ibid.

5. Karl Vesper, telephone interview with the author, August 8, 2005.

6. Ibid.

7. Vesper, *New Venture Experience*, p. 21.

8. Karl Vesper, telephone interview with the author, August 8, 2005.

9. Vesper, *New Venture Experience*, p. 22.

10. Karl Vesper, telephone interview with the author, August 8, 2005.

11. Vesper, *New Venture Experience*, p. 23.

12. Ibid.

13. Ibid., pp. 23–4.

14. Ibid., p. 24.

15. Karl Vesper, telephone interview with the author, August 8, 2005.

16. Ibid.

17. Ibid.

18. Vesper, *New Venture Experience*, p. 505.

19. Ibid., p. 511.

20. Ibid., p. 513.

Chapter 11

1. Jeffry Timmons, telephone interview with the author, November 17, 2004.
2. Ibid.
3. Ibid.
4. Ibid.
5. Ibid.
6. Ibid.
7. Timmons, *New Venture Creation*, p. 17.
8. Ibid., p. 259.
9. Jeffry Timmons, telephone interview with the author, November 17, 2004.
10. Ibid.
11. Ibid.
12. Ibid.
13. Henry Mintzberg, telephone interview with the author, April 20, 2005.
14. Jeffry Timmons, telephone interview with the author, November 17, 2004.
15. Henry Mintzberg, telephone interview with the author, September 27, 2004.
16. Ibid.
17. Mintzberg, *Managers, Not MBAs*, p. 408.
18. See Section 10.3 in Chapter 10.
19. Gordon Redding, telephone interview with the author, February 16, 2005.
20. Larry Farrell, telephone interview with the author, December 9, 2004.
21. Farrell, *Getting Entrepreneurial!*, p. 7.
22. Ibid.
23. Larry Farrell, telephone interview with the author, December 9, 2004.
24. Retrieved from *rankings.ft.com/rankings/mba/rankings.html* on August 13, 2007.
25. Larry Farrell, telephone interview with the author, December 9, 2004.
26. Ibid.
27. Ibid.
28. Ibid.
29. Katz, "The Chronology," pp. 1, 283–300.
30. Mintzberg, *Managers, Not MBAs*, p. 46.
31. Ibid., p. 45.
32. Henry Mintzberg, telephone interview with the author, September 27, 2004.
33. Ibid.
34. Henry Mintzberg, telephone interview with the author, September 27, 2004.
35. Ibid.
36. Henry Mintzberg, telephone interview with the author, April 20, 2005.
37. Mintzberg, *Managers, Not MBAs*, 364.

38. Henry Mintzberg, telephone interview with the author, April 20, 2005.

39. Henry Mintzberg, telephone interview with the author, September 27, 2004.

40. Henry Mintzberg, telephone interview with the author, April 20, 2005.

41. Ibid. See also: Mintzberg, "Gopi's Farm."

42. Henry Mintzberg, telephone interview with the author, September 27, 2004.

43. Ibid.

44. Ibid.

45. Ibid.

46. Ibid.

47. Ibid.

48. Mintzberg, *Managers, Not MBAs*, p. 387.

49. Ibid., p. 388.

Conclusion

1. Rita Gunther McGrath, telephone interview with the author, March 29, 2005.

2. MacMillan and McGrath, *The Entrepreneurial Mindset*, p. 10.

3. Rita Gunther McGrath, telephone interview with the author, March 29, 2005.

4. Ibid.

5. Karl Vesper, telephone interview with the author, August 8, 2005.

6. McGirt, "Hacker. Dropout. CEO.," pp. 74–81, 112.

7. Vesper, *New Venture Experience*, p. 656.

8. Ibid.

9. Ibid., p. 657.

10. Ibid.

11. Karl Vesper, telephone interview with the author, August 8, 2005.

12. Ibid.

13. Vesper, *New Venture Experience*, p. 664.

14. H. Irving Grousbeck, telephone interview with the author, August 5, 2005.

15. Ibid.

16. Ibid.

17. Ibid.

Appendix

1. Daniel Muzyka, interview with the author, February 19, 2007.

2. Ibid.

Bibliography

Alexander, M. (2002). "Wanted: A Company to Call Their Own." *Stanford Business;* 70(4). Retrieved August 2, 2005, from online archives: *www.gsb.stanford.edu/community/bmag/sbsm0208/ideas.html.*

Allen, Marc. *Visionary Business: Entrepreneur's Guide to Success.* Novato, Calif.: New World Library, 1995.

Alvesson, M., and K. Skoldberg. *Reflexive Methodology: New Vistas for Qualitative Research.* Thousand Oaks, Calif.: Sage, 2000.

Anderson, P. H., D. A. Beveridge, and T.W. Scott. *Threshold Entrepreneur: A New Business Venture Simulation.* Upper Saddle River, N.J.: Prentice Hall, 2000.

Archer, Jeffrey. *Not a Penny More, Not a Penny Less.* New York: HarperCollins, 1976.

The Arthur M. Blank Center for Entrepreneurship Website (Babson College). *www3.babson.edu/eship.* Viewed August 9, 2005.

Arthur Rock Center for Entrepreneurship Website, Harvard Business School. *www.hbs.edu/entrepreneurship.* Viewed August 15, 2005.

Asurion, Inc. Website. *www.asurion.com.* Viewed September 18, 2005.

Balderson, W.D. *Canadian Entrepreneurship & Small Business Management (6th Ed).* Toronto: McGraw-Hill Ryerson, 2005.

Baron, R. A., and S. A. Shane. *Entrepreneurship: A Process Perspective.* Mason, Ohio: South-Western, 2005.

Barringer, B.R., and R.D. Ireland. *Entrepreneurship: Successfully Launching New Ventures (2nd Ed.).* Upper Saddle River, N.J.: Pearson Prentice Hall, 2007.

Bell, J., I. Callaghan, D. Demick, and F. Scharf. "International Entrepreneurship: A Literature Review." *Internationalizing Entrepreneurship Education 2 (1–2),* 109–24.

Bennis, W.G., and J.O'Toole. "How Business Schools Lost Their Way." *Harvard Business Review* (online version). Retrieved August 1, 2005, from *www.harvardbusinessonline.hbsp.harvard.edu.*

Benthos, Inc. Website: *www.benthos.com.* Viewed September 13, 2005.

Bernstein, P. L. *Against the Gods: The Remarkable Story of Risk.* New York: John Wiley & Sons, 1996.

Bhide, A.V., H. I. Grousbeck, M. J. Roberts, and H. H. Stevenson. *New Business Ventures and the Entrepreneur (5th Ed).* New York: McGraw-Hill, 1999.

Birley, S., and D. Muzyka, Eds. *Mastering Entrepreneurship: Your Single-Source Guide to Becoming a Master of Entrepreneurship.* London: Pearson, 2000.

Blanchard, K., B. Hybels, and P. Hodges. *Leadership by the Book: Tools to Transform Your Workplace.* New York: William Morrow and Company, 1999.

Blenker, P., P. Dreisler, and J. Kjeldsen. "Entrepreneurship Education—The New Challenge Facing Universities: A Framework for Understanding and Development of Entrepreneurial University Communities." Department of Management, University of Aarhus, Denmark. Working Paper. 2006.

————. M. Faergemann, and J. Kjeldson. "Learning and Teaching Entrepreneurship: How to Reformulate the Question." 13th Global IntEnt Conference, Grenoble, France, September 8–10, 2003.

Bogatti, Steve. "Introduction to Grounded Theory." Retrieved on March 18, 2006, from *www.analytictech.com/mb870/introtoGT.htm.*

Bolles, R. N. *What Color Is Your Parachute?* Berkeley, Calif.: Ten Speed Press, 2003.

Boyer, Ernest. "College: The Undergraduate Experience in America," in Templeton, J. Jr., Introduction. Retrieved June 10, 2004, from *www.collegeandcharacter.org/guide/introduction.html.*

Boyett, Joseph H. and Jimmie T. Boyett. *The Guru Guide to Entrepreneurship: A Concise Guide to the Best Ideas From the World's Top Entrepreneurs.* New York: John H. Wiley & Sons, 2001.

Brown, T., et al. *Business Minds: Connect with the World's Greatest Management Thinkers.* London: Pearson, 2002.

Bunyan, John. *The Pilgrim's Progress.* Grand Rapids, Mich.: Zondervan, 1967.

"Corporate Crime: The Reckoning." *BusinessWeek Online,* March 15, 2004. Retrieved on March 15, 2006, from *www.businessweek.com/magazine/content/04_11/b3874141_mz029.htm.*

Bygrave, W., and J. Timmons. *New Business Opportunities.* Amherst, Mass.: Brick House, 1990.

Bygrave, William D., and Andrew Zacharakis, eds. *The Portable MBA in Entrepreneurship, Third Edition.* New York: John Wiley & Sons, 2004.

Calloway, L J., and C.A. Knapp. "Using Grounded Theory to Interpret Interviews." Retrieved March 18, 2006, from *www.csis.edu/~knapp/AIS95.htm.*

"Can Entrepreneurship Be Taught? Ranking the Programs." *Entrepreneur.com.* Retrieved   July 25, 2005, from *www.entrepreneur.com/Magazines/Copy_of_MA_SegArticle.*

Canfield, J., M.V. Hansen, and L. Hewitt. *Power of Focus: How to Hit Your Business, Personal and Financial Targets With Absolute Certainty.* Deerfield Beach, Fla.: Health Communications, 2000.

Carnegie, Dale. *How to Win Friends and Influence People.* New York: Doubleday, 1937.

Carr, E. H. *What Is History?* London: Penguin, 1962.

Center for Entrepreneurial Studies Website, Stanford Graduate School of Business: *www.gsb.stanford.edu/ces.* Viewed June 11, 2007.

Chenier, Ron. *How to Become an Entrepreneurial Genius! Your Blueprint to More Money, More Respect and More Freedom.* Victoria, British Columbia: Trafford, 2000.

Ciulla, Joanne B. *Ethics, the Heart of Leadership.* New York: Praeger, 1998.

Collins, Jim. *Good to Great: Why Some Companies Make the Leap... and Others Don't.* New York: HarperCollins, 2001.

Collins, L.A., A. J. Smith, and P.D. Hannon. "Applying a Synergistic Learning Approach in Entrepreneurship Education." *Management Learning, 37 (2003),* 335–54.

"Commercial Solutions from Nanotechnology." PowerPoint presentation, March 19, 2007. Retrieved from *www.oxonica.com.* on June 21, 2007.

Conger, Jay A. *Spirit at Work: Discovering the Spirituality in Leadership.* San Francisco, Calif: Jossey-Bass, 1994.

Cook, Tim. "Isis Innovation." *Oxford Science Enterprise Centre Newsletter,* November 2004. Retrieved June 21, 2007 from *www.science-enterprise.ox.ac.uk/html/TimCook.asp.*

Cooper, A. C., J. A. Hornaday, and K. H. Vesper, K. H. "The Field of Entrepreneurship Over Time." *Frontiers of Entrepreneurship Research, 1997 Ed.* Retrieved August 2, 2005, from the Babson College Website: *www.babson.edu/entrer/fer/papers97/cooper/coop1.htm.*

Cope, Jason. "An Entrepreneurial-Directed Approach to Entrepreneurship Education: Mission Possible?" *Journal of Management Development, 25 (1),* 80–94.

————, and M. J. Naughton. "Integrating Entrepreneurship with the Liberal Arts: Theology for Entrepreneurship Students." Retrieved May 15, 2004, from *www.abe.villanova.edu/cornwall.pdf.*

Cornwall, J. R., D. O. Vang, and J. M. Hartman. *Entrepreneurial Financial Management: An Applied Approach.* Upper Saddle River, N.J.: Prentice Hall, 2004.

Coulter, Mary. *Entrepreneurship in Action (2nd Ed).* Upper Saddle River, N.J.: Prentice Hall, 2003.

Covey, Stephen. *The Seven Habits of Highly Effective People: Restoring the Character Ethic.* New York: Fireside, 1989.

Crainer, Stuart. *The Ultimate Book of Business Gurus: 110 Thinkers Who Really Made a Difference.* New York: America Management Association, 1998.

Crawford, Charles, Ed. *Montreal Entrepreneur's Guidebook.* Montreal: Youth Employment Services, 1997.

Cruikshank, Jeffrey. *Shaping the Waves: A History of Entrepreneurship at Harvard Business School.* Boston: Harvard University Press, 2005.

David, Fred. *Strategic Management: Concepts and Cases (10th Ed.).* Upper Saddle River, N.J.: Pearson, 2004.

Darling-Hammond, L., and J. Bransford, Eds. *Preparing Teachers for a Changing World: What Teachers Should Learn and Be Able to Do.* Toronto: John Wiley & Sons, 2005.

DeGeorge, Gail. *The Making of a Blockbuster: How Wayne Huizenga Built a Sports and Entertainment Empire From Trash, Grit, and Videotape.* New York: John Wiley & Sons, 1996.

Devlin, D., and P.B. Gray. "Heroes of Small Business." *Fortune Small Business,* October 23, 2000. Retrieved September 18, 2005 from *www.fortune.com/fortune/print/0,15935,360005,00.html.*

Dewey, John. *How We Think: A Restatement of Reflective Thinking to the Educative Process.* Boston, Mass: Heath, 1933.

Dollinger, Marc. *Entrepreneurship: Strategies and Resources (3rd Ed.).* Upper Saddle River, NJ.: Pearson, 2003.

"Don't Laugh at Gilded Butterflies." *The Economist,* April 22, 2004. Retrieved May 4, 2005, from *www.economist.com/PrinterFriendly.cfm?Story_ID=2610485.*

Dorsey, David. "The New Spirit of Work." *Fast Company, 16,* 124. Retrieved May 15, 2004 from *www.fastcompany.com/magazine/16/barrett.html.*

"Dr. Kevin Matthews, Oxonia." *Oxford Science Enterprise Centre Newsletter,* December 2004. Retrieved June 21, 2007 from *www.science-enterprise.ox.ac.uk/html/KevinMatthews.asp.*

Drucker, Peter. *The Executive in Action: Managing for Results, Innovation and Entrepreneurship, & The Effective Executive.* New York: HarperCollins, 1996.

————. *Management: Tasks, Responsibilities and Practices.* New York: Harper & Row, 1973.

————. *The New Realities: In Government and Politics/In Economics and Business/In Society and World View.* New York: Harper & Row, 1989.

Durham, Lynn. "Spirituality and Business—Can the Two Be Joined?" *Seacoastonline,* May 2002. Retrieved May 15, 2004, from *www.seacoastonline.com*

Dwek, Raymond. "Commercializing University Research—Threats and Opportunities: The Oxford University Model." Library of Congress document. Retrieved July 1, 2007, from *www.loc.gov/today/cyberlc/feature_wdesc*

"An Entrepreneurial Journey." HBS Bulletin Online, December 1996. Retrieved September 18, 2005, from *www.hbs.edu/bulletin/1996/december/entre.html.*

eBay Website: *www.ebay.com.* Viewed August 11, 2005.

Farrell, Larry. *The Entrepreneurial Age: Awakening the Spirit of Enterprise in People, Companies, and Countries.* New York: Allworth Press, 2000.

————. *Getting Entrepreneurial! Creating and Growing Your Own Business in the 21st Century.* Hoboken, N.J.: John Wiley & Sons, 2003.

————. "The Government's Most Important Job." *Across the Board,* January/February 2006, 65–6.

————. "Growing Pains." *Across the Board,* July/August 2004, 65–6.

"Entrepreneurship Program at Harvard Business School Wins Top Award." News Release. January 22, 2004. *www.hbs.edu.*

"The 50 Top Business Gurus (2003)." _Outlook, 1._ Retrieved May 1, 2004, from _www.accenture.com/outlook._

Fink, L. D. _Creating Significant Learning Experiences._ San Francisco, Calif: Jossey-Bass, 2003.

Fisher, R., and W. Ury. _Getting to Yes: Negotiating Agreement Without Giving In (2nd Ed.)._ New York: Penguin Books, 1991.

Flaherty, Julie. "Entrepreneurship Courses: It Pays to Pick the School." _New York Times,_ April 1, 2004. Retrieved May 10, 2005 from _www.nytimes.com/2004/04/01/business/01sbiz.html._

Flanigan, J., and P. Mulligan. "Drucker, Management Guru, Dies at 95." _Los Angeles Times,_ November 11, 2005. Retrieved November 11, 2005, from _www.latimes.com/news/local/la-111105drucker_lat,0,2724903.story?coll=la-home-headlines._

Foresight Nanotech Institute. Website _www.foresight.org/nano/whatisnano.html._

"Frank Batten: Thriving on Challenge." HBS Working Knowledge. [_hbswk.hbs.edu/pubitem.jhtml?id=2864&t=new-entrepreneurs._

Freeman, R. E., and S. Venkataraman, Eds. "Ethics and Entrepreneurship" The Ruffin Series, No. 3. Society for Business Ethics. Washington, D.C.: Georgetown University, 2002.

Fuerst, O., and U. Geiger. _From Concept to Wall Street: A Complete Guide to Entrepreneurship and Venture Capital._ Upper Saddle River, N.J.: Pearson, 2003.

Garrison, D. R. "Inquiry and Critical Thinking—Reflective Inquiry." Learning Commons: Communities of Inquiry. Retrieved March 20, 2006, from _www.commons.ucalgary.ca._

Genentech, Inc. Website: _www.gene.com._] Viewed August 1, 2005.

Gerber, Michael. _The E-Myth Revisited: Why Most Small Businesses Don't Work and What to Do About It._ New York: HarperCollins, 1995.

Gibb, Allan. "Designing Effective Programs for Encouraging the Business Start-Up Process: Lessons From UK Experience." _Journal of European Industrial Training, 11 (4),_ 24.

———. "Enterprise Culture—Its Meaning and Implications for Education and Training." _Journal of Industrial Training, 11 (2),_ 11–38.

———. "The Entrepreneur as the Core Competence of the Firm: Implications for Management Educators." _EntreNews, 2,_ 2.

———. "Entrepreneurship: Unique Solutions for Unique Environments— Is it Possible to Achieve This With the Existing Paradigm?" Background paper to the plenary presentation to the International Council for Small Business World Conference, Melbourne, Australia. June 18–21, 2006.

———. "In Pursuit of a New 'Enterprise' and 'Entrepreneurship' Paradigm for Learning: Creative Desconstruction, New Values, New Ways of Doing Things and New Combinations of Knowledge." _International Journal of Management Review, 4 (3),_ 213–31.

Gill, M., and S. Paterson. *Fired Up! The Proven Principles of Successful Entrepreneurs.* New York: Penguin, 1996.

Ginsberg, L., and B. McDougall. *The Complete Idiot's Guide to Being an Entrepreneur in Canada.* Toronto: Prentice Hall, 1996.

Good, Walter. *Building a Dream: A Canadian Guide to Starting Your Own Business (6th Ed.).* Toronto: McGraw-Hill Ryerson, 2005.

Goossen, Richard J., ed. (2007). *Entrepreneurial Leaders: Reflections on Faith at Work.* (Vancouver: Trinity Western University Publishing).

Gray, Douglas, and Diana Gray. *The Complete Canadian Small Business Guide (3rd Ed.).* Toronto: McGraw-Hill Ryerson, 2000.

Greenleaf, Robert. *Servant Leadership: A Journey Into the Nature of Legitimate Power and Greatness.* Ramsey, N.J.: Paulist Press, 1977.

H. Irving Grousbeck. Doctor of Humane Letters. Retrieved September 18, 2005, from *www.amherst.edu/commencement/2000/hondeg00.html#hig.*

———. "'eBay': Case E-74." Palo Alto, Calif.: Stanford. November 1, 2002. (Jamie Earle revised this case from the previous version prepared by Nathaniel Durant III, under the supervision of Professor H. Irving Grousbeck.)

———. "JetBlue: Executing the plan (A): Case E-182A." Palo Alto, Calif.: Stanford. May 1, 2005. (Alexander Tauber prepared this case under the supervision of Professors Joel C. Peterson and H. Irving Grousbeck.)

———. "You Gotta Have an Attitude." *Stanford Graduate Business School Magazine.* Retrieved October 15, 2005, from *www.gsb.stanford.edu/community/bmag/sbsm0397/attitude.html.*

Gumpert, D.E., and J. Timmons. *The Insider's Guide to Small Business Resources.* Garden City, N.Y.: Doubleday, 1982.

Handy, Charles. "The Search for Meaning: A Conversation With Charles Handy. *Leader To Leader Institute, 5.* Retrieved February 26, 2004, from *www.pdf.org/leaderbooks/t.2t/summary97/handy.html.*

Hannefey, Francis. "Entrepreneurship and Ethics: A Literature Review." *Journal of Business Ethics, 46 (2),* 99–110.

Harrell, Wilson. *For Entrepreneurs Only: Success Strategies for Anyone Starting & Growing a Business.* Franklin Lakes, N.J.: The Career Press, 1995.

Heinonen, J., and S. Poikkijoki. "An Entrepreneurial-Directed Approach to Entrepreneurship Education: Mission Impossible?" *Journal of Management Development, 25 (1),* 80–94.

Hill, Charles. *International Business: Competing in the Global Marketplace (4th Ed.).* New York: McGraw-Hill/Irwin, 2003.

Hilton, Conrad. *Be My Guest.* New York: Prentice Hall, 1957.

Hisrich, R. D., and M. P. Peters. *Entrepreneurship (5th Ed.).* New York: McGraw Hill/Irwin, 2002.

Hockaday, Tom. "Starting a Spin-out Company" [booklet] Oxford: Isis Innovation. 2005. Retrieved July 4, 2007, from _www.isis-innovation.com/ researchers/spin-out.pdf._

Hockaday, T., B. Blumberg, T. Cook, et. al. (2007, May 24). "Commercializing University Research—Threats and Opportunities: The Oxford University Model." Library of Congress Presentation. For further reference, view summary at _www.loc.gov/today/cyberlc/feature_wdesc.php?rec=4056._

Hollister, Bernard. "Reflective Thinking, John Dewey and PBL [Problem-Based Learning]." Retrieved March 1, 2006, from _www.imsa.edu/programs/ pbln/problems/bernie/dewey.html._

Honig, Benson. "Entrepreneurship Education: Toward a Model of Contingency-Based Business Planning." _Academy of Management Learning and Education, 3 (3)_, 258–73.

"How the Center Fits into the Graduate School of Business." Center for Entrepreneurial Studies, Stanford Graduate School of Business. Retrieved September 18, 2005, from _www.gsb.stanford.edu/ces._

Huitt, William, G. "Moral and Character Development." Retrieved June 8, 2004, from _chiron.valdosta.edu/whuitt/col/morchr/morchr.html._

Hynes, Briga. "Entrepreneurship Education and Training—Introducing Entrepreneurship into Non-Business Disciplines." _Journal of European Industrial Training, 20 (8)_, 10–7.

Iacocca, Lee. _Iacocca._ New York: Bantam Books, 1984.

International Masters Program in Practicing Management Website: _www.impm.org._ Viewed September 5, 2005.

"The Institute for Enterprise Education: Instilling the Spirit of Enterprise." Retrieved December 20, 2003, from _www.entreplexity.ca._

"Investment Group Buys Celtics." CNNMoney, September 27, 2002. Retrieved August 15, 2005, from _www.cnnmoney.printthis.clickability.com/pt/ cpt?action=cpt?action=cpt&title=Celtics+sold+to+Boston._

Isachsen, Olaf. _Joining the Entrepreneurial Elite: Four Styles to Business Success._ Palo Alto, CA: Davies-Black, 1996.

"Isis Innovation Annual Report." 2006. Retrieved June 21, 2007, from _www.isis-innovation.com/emailtemplates/E-NewsOct06.html._

Isis Innovation Ltd. Website: _www.isis-innovation.com._ Viewed June 21, 2007.

"Isis Innovation: Technology Transfer from the University of Oxford." PowerPoint presentation. Retrieved June 21, 2007, from _www.isis-innovation.com._

Jack, S. L., and A. R. Anderson. "Entrepreneurship Education Within the Enterprise Culture: Producing Reflective Practitioners." _International Journal of Entrepreneurial Behaviour and Research, 5 (3)_, 110–25.

JetBlue Airways Website: _www.jetblue.com._ Viewed September 10, 2005.

Jim Pattison Group Website: _www.jimpattison.com._ Viewed August 10, 2005.

Kanter, R. M., J. Kao, and F. Wiersma, F., Eds. *Innovation: Breakthrough Thinking at 3M, DuPont, GE, Pfizer and Rubbermaid.* New York: HarperCollins, 1997.

Kaplan, Jack. *Patterns of Entrepreneurship.* New York: John Wiley & Sons, 2003.

Katz, Jerome. "The Chronology and Intellectual Trajectory of American Entrepreneurship Education: 1876–1999." *Journal of Business Venturing, 18 (2),* 1, 283–300.

Kawasaki, Guy. *The Art of the Start: The Time-Tested, Battle-Hardened Guide for Anyone Starting Anything.* New York: Penguin Group, 2004.

Kim, W. C., and R. Mauborgne. *Blue Ocean Strategy: How to Create Uncontested Market Space and Make the Competition Irrelevant.* Boston, Mass.: Harvard Business School, 2005.

Kinder, Gary. *Ship of Gold in the Deep Blue Sea.* New York: Random House, 1998.

Kirby, David. *Entrepreneurship.* Maidenhead, Berkshire, UK: McGraw Hill Education (UK), 2003.

———. "Entrepreneurship Education: Can Business Schools Meet the Challenge?" *Education + Training, 46 (89),* 510–19.

———. "Management Education and Small Business Development: An Exploratory Study of Small Firms in the UK." *Journal of Small Business Management, 28.*

———. "In Search of Excellence Among Business School Professors: A Rejoinder." *European Journal of Marketing, 33 (9/10),* 824–6.

Kishel, Gregory, and Patricia Gunter Kishel. *Growing Your Own Business: Growth Strategies for Meeting New Challenges and Maximizing Success.* New York: Berkley, 1994.

Kolb, David. *Experiential Learning.* New York: Prentice-Hall, 1984.

Knowles, Ron. *Small Business: An Entrepreneur's Plan (4th Cdn. Ed.).* Toronto: Thomas Nelson, 2003.

Krass, Peter. *Carnegie.* Hoboken, N.J.: John Wiley & Sons, 2002.

Kroc, Ray. *Grinding it Out: The Making of McDonald's.* New York: Berkley, 1977.

Kuratko, Donald. "Entrepreneurship Education: Emerging Trends and Challenges for the 21st Century." 2003 Coleman Foundation White Paper Series, USASBE. 2003.

———. "Entrepreneurship Education in the 21st Century: From Legitimization to Leadership." Coleman Foundation White Paper Series, USASBE National Conference. January 16, 2004.

Lagace, M., S. Silverthorne, and W. Guild. "Does Spirituality Drive Success?" Harvard Business School Working Knowledge. Retrieved May 15, 2004, from *www.hbswk.hbs.edu.*

Lambing, P. A., and C. R. Kuehl. *Entrepreneurship (3rd Ed.).* Upper Saddle River, N.J.: Prentice Hall, 2003.

Leider, Richard. _The Power of Purpose: Creating Meaning in Your Life and Work._ San Francisco, Calif.: Berrett-Koehler, 1997.

"Less Glamour, More Profit." _The Economist,_ April 22, 2004. Retrieved May 4, 2005, from _www.economist.com/PrinterFriendly.cfm?Story_ID=2611017&ppv=1._

Lewis, Diane. "Networking Tips: Maintain Old Contacts, Establish New Ones." _The Boston Globe,_ September 7, 2003. Retrieved July 20, 2005, from _www.bostonworks.boston.com/globe/articles/090703_network.html._

Lobler, H., M. Maier, and D. Markgraf. "Evaluating the Constructivist Approach in Entrepreneurship Education." Department of Marketing, University of Leipzig, Germany. Retrieved August 1, 2006, from _www.marketing.uni-leipzig.de._

Loewenstein, R. _Buffett: The Making of an American Capitalist._ New York: Random House, 1995.

Longenecker, J.G., et al. _Small Business Management: An Entrepreneurial Emphasis (2nd Cdn. Ed.)._ Scarborough, Ont.: Thomas Nelson, 2003.

Lowery, Joseph. _Netpreneurs: The Dimensions of Transferring Your Business Model to the Internet._ Indianapolis, Ind.: Que, 1998.

Maciariello, Joseph, Ed. T_he Daily Drucker._ New York: HarperCollins, 2004.

MacMillan, I., and R. G. McGrath. _The Entrepreneurial Mindset: Strategies for Continuously Creating Opportunity in an Age of Uncertainty._ Boston: Harvard Business School, 2000.

———. _Market Busters: 40 Strategic Moves That Drive Exceptional Growth._ Boston: Harvard Business School, 2005.

Markoff, John. "And Not a Personal Computer in Sight. _The New York Times,_ October 6, 1991, 1, 6.

Matsushita Electrical Corporation of America. "Matsushita Management Philosophy." Secaucas, N.J.: Matsushita Electrical Corporation of America.

McCrimmon, Mitch. _Unleash the Entrepreneur Within: How to Make Everyone an Entrepreneur and Stay Efficient._ London: Pitman, 1995.

McGirt, Ellen. "Hacker. Dropout. CEO." _Fast Company,_ May 2007, 74–81,112.

Media One Website: _www1.iwon.com/home/careers/company_profile/0,15623,1197,00.html._ Viewed September 18, 2005.

Merriam Webster English Dictionary and Thesaurus, online edition: _www.merriamwebsteronline.com._ Viewed August 1, 2005.

Miner, John. _The 4 Routes to Entrepreneurial Success._ San Francisco: Berrett-Koehler, 1996.

Mintzberg, Henry. "Gopi's Farm." Retrieved August 12, 2005, from _www.henrymintzberg.com._

———. _Managers, Not MBAs: A hard Look at the Soft Practice of Managing and Management Development._ San Francisco: Berrett-Koehler, 2004.

————. *Mintzberg on Management: Inside Our Strange World of Organizations.* New York: Free Press, 1989.

————. *The Rise and Fall of Strategic Planning.* New York: Free Press, 1994.

Mintzberg, H., and J. Gosling. "The Education of Practicing Managers." Retrieved August 25, 2005, from *www.impm.org.*

————. et. al. *The Strategy Process: Concepts, Contexts, Cases (4th Ed.).* Upper Saddle River, N.J.: Prentice Hall, 2003.

Moore, Geoffrey. *Crossing the Chasm: Marketing and Selling Disruptive Products to Mainstream Customers.* New York: HarperCollins, 1991.

Mueller, S. L., and A. S. Thomas. "Case for Comparative Entrepreneurship: Assessing the Relevance of Culture." *Journal of International Business Studies, 2000,* 31.

Mungazi, D. A. *The Evolution of Educational Theory in the United States.* New York: Praeger, 1999.

Nash, L., and S. McLennan, S. *Church on Sunday, Work on Monday: The Challenge of Fusing Christian Values With Business Life.* San Francisco: Jossey-Bass, 2001.

Nash, L., and H. H. Stevenson. *Just Enough: Tools for Creating Success in Your Work and Life.* Hoboken, N.J.: John H. Wiley & Sons, 2004.

Newby, Peter. "Entrepreneurship Education: Effective Learning." PowerPoint Presentation. Middlesex University, London. December 7, 2005.

Newman, Peter. *The Canadian Establishment (Vol. 1).* Toronto: Bantam Seal, 1979.

————. *The Acquisitors: The Canadian Establishment (Vol. 2).* Toronto: Bantam Seal, 1981.

Norsworthy, Beverley. "An Intruder in My Own World: Critical Reflective Methodology." Paper presented at New Zealand Association for Research in Education. Auckland, New Zealand, November 29–December 3, 2003. Retrieved March 18, 2006, from *www.aare.edu.au/03pap/nor03084.pdf.*

————. "Revisiting Reflection." *Waikato Journal of Education, 8,* 101–14.

Novak, Michael. *Business as a Calling: Work and the Examined Life.* New York: Free Press, 1996.

Nusbaum, Marci Alboher. "Small Business: Learning Entrepreneurship the U.S. Way at M.I.T." *New York Times,* March 18, 2004. Retrieved May 2, 2005, from *www.query.nytimes.com/gst/abstract.html?res=F3061FFC39550C7B8DDDAA0894DC404482.*

Oster, M. J., and M. Hamel, M. *The Entrepreneur's Creed: The Principles & Passions of 20 Successful Entrepreneurs.* Nashville, Tenn.: Broadman & Holman, 2001.

O'Toole, Kathy. "Basketball Barons." Retrieved August 16, 2005, from *www.gsb.stanford.edu/news/headlines/grousbeck_celtics.html.*

Oxford Catalysts Group plc Website: *www.oxfordcatalysts.com*. Viewed July 4, 2007.

"Oxford Catalysts Group PLC Annual Report and Accounts." 2006. Retrieved June 21, 2007, from *www.oxfordcatalysts.com*.

Oxford University Press Website. *www.oup.com/about/history/*.

Oxonica Materials plc Website: *www.oxonica.com*. Viewed July 4, 2007.

Palmer, Parker. *The Courage to Teach: Exploring the Inner Landscape of a Teacher's Life*. San Francisco: Jossey-Bass, 1998.

———. *Let Your Life Speak: Listening for the Voice of Vocation*. San Francisco: Jossey-Bass, 2000.

Pattison, Jim. *Jimmy: An Autobiography*. New York: Bantam Seal, 1987.

"Peter F. Drucker Passes Away at Age 95." Claremont Graduate University Website, November 11, 2005. Retrieved November 12, 2005, from *www.cgu.edu/pages/357.asp?EventID=176*.

Pino, Lawrence. *Finding Your Niche: A Personal Guide for Entrepreneurs*. New York: Berkley, 1994.

Pittaway, Luke. "Entrepreneurship Education—A Systematic Review of the Evidence." Discussion Paper No. 2005.19, University of Sheffield Management School. November 2005. Retrieved from *www.sheffield.ac.uk*.

Porter, Michael. *Competitive Strategy: Techniques for Analyzing Industries and Competitors*. New York: Free Press, 1980.

Portsmouth, Ian. "The Trial of Ray Loewen." *Profit Magazine,* February/March 1996. Retrieved November 11, 2005, from *www.profitguide.com/magazine/article.jsp?content=29#*.

Pugh, D. S., and D. J. Hickson. *Writers on Organizations: An Invaluable Guide to the Ideas of Leading Authorities on Management (5th Ed.)*. London: Penguin, 1996.

Rae, David. "Entrepreneurial Learning: A Narrative-Based Conceptual Model." *Journal of Small Business and Enterprise Development, 12 (3)*, 323–35.

———. The Entrepreneurial Spirit: Learning to Unlock Value. Dublin: Blackhall, 1999.

———. "Mid-Career Entrepreneurial Learning." *Education + Training, 47 (8/9)*, 562–74.

———. "Practical Theories From Entrepreneurs' Stories: Discursive Approaches to Entrepreneurial Learning." *Journal of Small Business and Enterprise Development, 11 (2)*, 195–202.

———. "Understanding Entrepreneurial Learning: A Question of How?" *International Journal of Entrepreneurial Behaviour & Research, 6 (3)*, 145–59.

Rae, D., and M. Carswell. "Towards a Conceptual Understanding of Entrepreneurial Learning." *Journal of Small Business and Enterprise Development 8 (2)*, 150–58.

——. "Using a Life-Story Approach in Researching Entrepreneurial Learning: The Development of a Conceptual Model and its Implications in the Design of Learning Experiences. *Education + Training, 42 (4/5),* 220–8.

Rand Corporation. "Case Study Methodology." Retrieved March 18, 2006, from *www.rand.org/pubs/monograph_reports/MR969/MR969.appd.pdf.*

Redding, S. Gordon. *The Spirit of Chinese Capitalism.* Berlin: Walter de Gruyter, 1990.

Redekop, Calvin, et. al. *Mennonite Entrepreneurs.* Baltimore, Md.: Johns Hopkins, 1995.

"Registry: Who's Who in Small-Business Research." *Inc.* magazine. Retrieved August 13, 2007 from *www.inc.com/magazine/19950515/2690_pagen_7.html*

Reiss, Bob, with J. L. Cruikshank. *Low Risk, High Reward: Starting and Growing Your Business With Minimal Risk.* New York: Free Press, 2000.

Rodgers, William. *Think: A Biography of the Watsons and IBM.* New York: Stein & Day, 1969.

Rogers, D., M. Georghiou, and M. Williams. *GoVenture: Live the Life of an Entrepreneur.* Toronto: Pearson Prentice Hall, 2004.

Rogers, Jim. *Adventure Capitalist: The Ultimate Road Trip.* New York: Random House, 2003.

Rothchild, J. *Going for Broke: How Robert Campeau Bankrupted America's Retail Giants.* New York: Penguin, 1991.

Rumball, Donald. *The Entrepreneurial Edge: Canada's Top Entrepreneurs Reveal the Secrets of Their Success.* Toronto: Key Porter, 1989.

Schank, Roger. *Coloring Outside the Lines.* New York: HarperCollins, 2000.

Schevitz, Tanya. "Dot-Com Dreams Elude New MBAs, Mainstay Firms Back to Recruit at Stanford." *San Francisco Chronicle,* June 17, 2001. Retrieved September 18, 2005, from *www.sfgate.com/cgi-bin/article.cgi?file=c/a/2001/06/17/MNL72400.DTL&type.*

Schon, Donald. *Educating the Reflective Practitioner: Toward a New Design for Teaching and Learning in the Professions.* San Francisco: Jossey-Bass, 1987.

——. *The Reflective Practitioner: How Professionals Think in Action.* London: Temple Smith, 1983.

Schultz, Howard, with D. J. Yang. *Pour Your Heart Into It: How Starbucks Built a Company One Cup at a Time.* New York: Hyperion, 1997.

Schumpeter, Joseph A. *The Theory of Economic Development: An Inquiry Into Profits, Capital, Credit, Interest, and the Business Cycle.* Cambridge, Mass.: Harvard University Press, 1934.

Seventh Symposium on Spirituality and Business at Babson. March 18–19, 2004. Office of Spiritual Life and Volunteer Programs, Babson College. Retrieved January 5, 2004, from *babson.edu/Events/spiritualityandbusiness/EventOverview.cfm.* (Mission statement of the International Symposium on Spirituality and Business retrieved January 5, 2004, from *babson.edu/Events/spiritualityandbusiness/AboutUs.cfm.*)

Sexton, D. L., and R. W. Smilor, Eds. *Entrepreneurship 2000.* Chicago: Upstart, 1997.

Silverthorne, S., and W. Guild. "Does Spirituality Drive Success?" *Working Knowledge.* Retrieved May 21, 2004, from *www.hbswk.hbs.edu.*

Sirico, Robert. "A Worthy Calling." Acton Institute for the Study of Religion and Liberty, November 22, 1993. Retrieved January 5, 2004, from *www.acton.org/ppolicy/editorials/sirico/calling.html.*

————. "The Entrepreneurial Vocation." Acton Institute for the Study of Religion and Liberty. Retrieved January 5, 2004, from *www.action.org/ppolicy/business/entrepreneur.*

Skoll Foundation Website: *www.skollfoundation.org.* Viewed September 15, 2005.

Solomon, S. D., and J. Sloane. "Thinkers: The Top Ten Minds in Small Business." *Fortune Small Business,* February 4, 2005 Retrieved September 18, 2005, from *www.fortune.com/fortune/fsb/specials/thinkers/thinkers.html.*

"Special Collection: Enron & Ethics." Retrieved March 20, 2006, from *www.businessethics.ca/enron/.*

Spence, Rick. *Secrets of Success From Canada's Fastest-Growing Companies.* Toronto: John Wiley & Sons, 1997.

Stanislaw, J., and D. Yergin. *Commanding Heights* (1998; excerpt). Retrieved July 4, 2007, from *www.pbs.org/wgbh/commandingheights/shared/minitextlo/prof_margaretthatcher.html.*

Stanley, T.J., and W.D. Danko. *The Millionaire Next Door: The Surprising Secrets of America's Wealthy.* New York: Simon & Schuster, 2006.

Stemberg, Thomas. *Staples for Success: From Business Plan to Billion-Dollar Business in Just a Decade* Santa Monica, Calif.: Knowledge Exchange, 1996.

————. "Why Entrepreneurship Has Won!" Coleman White Paper, U.S. Association of Small Business & Entrepreneurship Plenary Address, San Antonio, TX. February 17, 2000.

————. with David Gumpert. "The Heart of Entrepreneurship." *Harvard Business Review, March/April 1985,* 85–94.

Stevenson, Howard, with Jose Carlos Jarrillo-Mossi. "Preserving Entrepreneurship as Companies Grow." *Journal of Business Strategy, 1,* 10–23.

Thermo Electron Corporation Website: *www.thermo.com.* Viewed July 5, 2005.

"Thinkers50—The Original Global Ranking of Business Thinkers." 2003. Retrieved July 10, 2005, from *www.thinkers50.com.*

Thornton, Patricia. "The Sociology of Entrepreneurship." *Annual Review of Sociology, 1999.*

————. *The Entrepreneurial Mind.* Amherst, Mass.: Brick House, 1989.

————. *Venture Capital at the Crossroads.* Boston: Harvard Business School, 1992.

Timmons, Jeffry, with Stephen Spinelli. *New Venture Creation: Entrepreneurship for the 21st Century (6th Ed.).* New York: McGraw Hill, 2003.

Trochim, William. "Non-Probability Sampling." January 16, 2005. Retrieved March 24, 2006, from *www.socialresearchmethods.net/kb/sampnon.htm.*

Trump, D., and T. Schwarz. *The Art of the Deal.* New York: Warner, 1987.

Turner, Colin. "The Spirit of Entrepreneurship #562." *Innovative Leader, 11, (10).* Retrieved May 16, 2004, from *www.winstonbrill.com/bril.001/html/article_index/articles/551-600/article562_body.html.*

Urlacher, Lavern. *Small Business Entrepreneurship: An Ethics and Human Relations Perspective.* Upper Saddle River, N.J.: Prentice Hall, 1999.

Vesper, Karl. "Maintaining Focus: Entrepreneurship Education, Research and Service." Rothman Institute of Entrepreneurial Studies, Fairleigh Dickinson University. Retrieved July 25, 2005, from *www.fdu.edu/academic/rothman/vesperessay.htm.*

———. *New Venture Experience: Cases, Text, Exercises (Revised Ed.).* Seattle: Vector, 1998.

———. *New Venture Strategies (Revised Ed.).* Englewood Cliffs, N.J.: Prentice Hall, 1990.

———. "Unfinished Business (Entrepreneurship) of the 20th Century. USABE Address, San Diego, California, January 1998. Retrieved July 27, 2005, from *www.publicforuminstitute.org/nde/sources.*

Vesper, K. H., and W. B. Gartner. "Measuring Progress in Entrepreneurship Education." *Journal of Business Venturing, 12 (5),* 403–21.

Vogl, A. J. "Managerial Correctness." *cross the Board,* July/August 2004. Retrieved July 15, 2005, from *www.conference-board.org/articles/atb_article.cfm?id=266.*

Watson, Thomas, Jr. *A Business and its Beliefs: The Ideas That Helped Build IBM.* New York: McGraw-Hill, 1963.

Weber, Max. *The Protestant Ethic and the Spirit of Capitalism.* (Trans. by Talcott Parsons, 1958). Mineola, N.Y.: Dover, 1996, 2003.

Welch, Jack, with John Byrne. *Jack: Straight From the Gut.* New York: Warner, 2001.

Wolff, Michael. "Lord in Vain." *New York Magazine,* January 12 2004. Retrieved March 20, 2006, from *newyorkmetro.com/nymetro/news/media/columns/medialife/n_9705/.*

"Women Entrepreneurs: Leading the Charge." *CIBC Small Business.* Toronto: CIBC World Markets, 2005.

Zimmer, T.W., and N.M. Scarborough. *Essentials of Entrepreneurship and Small Business management (4th Ed.).* Upper Saddle River, N.J.: Prentice Hall, 2005.

Zoghlin, Gilbert. *From Executive to Entrepreneur: Making the Transition.* New York: American Management Association, 1991.

Index

About the Author

Richard J. Goossen, Ph.D., is the CEO of M&A Capital Corporation, a consulting firm for high-growth ventures, as well as an Adjunct Professor of Entrepreneurship & Strategy at the Trinity Western University School of Business (Greater Vancouver, British Columbia, Canada). He directs the Entrepreneurship Program at the School of Business, and teaches at the undergraduate level as well as in the MBA program.

Rick has more than 20 years of experience as a strategy, finance, and growth consultant. He has been a director, officer, advisor, and shareholder of/for a number of companies in the following business sectors: financial services; pharmaceuticals; medical device technology; wireless internet; IT training and online education; online travel and loyalty programs; e-business systems integration; computer hardware distribution; application service providers; software development; resource and mining; property development; and management consulting.

Prior to his time at TWU, Rick worked in Hong Kong for five years at its largest national law firm (Johnson, Stokes & Master) and a leading merchant bank (Hambro Pacific). With respect to professional credentials, Rick was admitted as Barrister and Solicitor of the Province of British Columbia, Canada, in 1987, and voluntarily withdrew his membership in 1993 to focus entirely on entrepreneurial pursuits.

Rick's education includes the following: a Ph.D. from Middlesex University (London); a Master's of Law (LL.M.) from Columbia University (New York, New York); a Bachelor of Laws (LL.B.) (Hons.) from McGill University (Montreal); and a Bachelor of Arts (B.A.) (Hons.) (First Class) from Simon Fraser University (Vancouver).

In addition, Rick is a professional public speaker. He has had countless speaking engagements in Europe, North America, and

Asia. He has also written three books, edited three books, and written more than 120 articles for diverse publications throughout the world, from leading academic journals to trade magazines and newspapers.

Rick is a member of the Columbia Club of New York and a life member of the Simon Fraser University President's Club.

Richard J. Goossen's Entrepreneurship Works

Books

The Christian Entrepreneur: Insights from the marketplace (Vol. I). Langley, B.C.: Trinity Western UP, 2005.

The Practice of Entrepreneurial Thinking and Learning. Langley, BC: Trinity Western UP, 2006.

Articles/Chapters

"Bringing 'the entrepreneurial practices way' to big companies: An interview with Larry Farrell." *Journal of Business Strategy.* Retrieved from online article archives, January 2005. *www.journalofbusinessstrategy.com/articles/archive2.shtml.*

"Canadian business negotiations in post-Mao China: A progress report on the new foreign economic legislation." *McGill Law Journal, 31 (1),* 1–49. (December 1985).

"A clash of cultures: 'Thinking like a lawyer' and 'the entrepreneurial mind.'" *Journal of Business Strategy.* Retrieved from online article archives, July 2004. *www.journalofbusinessstrategy.com/articles/archive2.shtml.*

"The entrepreneur, from classroom to the field: An interview with Murray Low." *Journal of Business Strategy.* Retrieved from online article archives, January 2005. *www.journalofbusinessstrategy.com/articles.*

"Entrepreneurial death spiral: 10 ways to grow your company without killing it." *Journal of Business Strategy.* Retrieved from online article archives, September 2004. *www.journalofbusinessstrategy.com/articles.*

"Entrepreneurs and company growth." (Editorial.) Journal of Business Strategy. *Retrieved from online article archives, September 2004. www.journalofbusinessstrategy.com/articles.*

"Entrepreneurship—Education and success." (Editorial.) *Journal of Business Strategy* Retrieved from online article archives, January 2005. *www.journalofbusinessstrategy.com/articles.*

"Entrepreneurship and the meaning of life." *The Journal of Biblical Integration in Business, Fall 2004*: 21–74.

"Google, Inc.–2005." In F. R. David, *Strategic Management: Concepts and Cases, 11th Ed.* (pp. 34–49). Upper Saddle River, N.J.: Pearson, 2007.

"An interview with Laura Nash regarding *Just enough: Tools for Creating Success in Your Work and Life." Journal of Business Strategy.* Retrieved from online article archives, August 2004. *www.journalofbusiness strategy.com/articles.*

"Legal, business and cross-cultural aspects of offering property and immigration-linked investments in Hong Kong." *Pacific Region Forum on Business and Management Communication: Forum Reports 1991 to 1992.* Vancouver: David Lam Centre for International Communication. November 26, 1991.

"Metro Ministries – 2005." In F. R. David, *Strategic Management: Concepts and Cases, 11th Ed.* (pp. 312–21). Upper Saddle River, N.J.: Pearson, 2007.

"Saddleback Church–2005." In F. R. David, *Strategic Management: Concepts and Cases, 11th Ed.* (pp. 322–31). Upper Saddle River, N.J.: Pearson, 2007.

"Teaching students to become entrepreneurs: An interview with Jeff Timmons." *Journal of Business Strategy.* Retrieved from online article archives, January 2005. *www.journalofbusinessstrategy.com/articles.*

"What entrepreneurs and their lawyers should know about each other." *Minnesota Journal of Business Law and Entrepreneurship, 3 (1).* Retrieved from online archives, 2004. *www.kommerstad.org/journal.*

"What is enough?" (Editorial.) *Journal of Business Strategy.* Retrieved from online article archives, August 2004. www.journalofbusiness strategy.com/articles.

Interviews

Peter L. Bernstein [audio recording]. Telephone interview conducted by the author, Vancouver, B.C., August 17, 2005. Tape in author's possession.

Peter L. Bernstein [audio recording]. Telephone interview conducted by the author, Vancouver, B.C., September 21, 2005. Tape in author's possession.

Fred David, Florence Marion University [audio recording]. Conducted by the author, Vancouver, B.C., December 3, 2005. Tape in author's possession.

Larry C. Farrell, The Farrell Company [audio recording]. Telephone interview conducted by the author, Vancouver, B.C., December 9, 2004. Tape in author's possession.

Roger Fisher, Harvard Law School [audio recording]. Conducted by the author, Vancouver, B.C., June 17, 2005. Tape in author's possession.

H. Irving Grousbeck, Codirector, Center for Entrepreneurial Studies, Stanford Graduate School of Business [audio recording]. Telephone interview conducted by the author, Vancouver, B.C., August 5, 2005. Tape in author's possession.

Ray Loewen, founder and former CEO, Loewen Funeral Home Group [audio recording]. Conducted by the author, Burnaby, B.C., September 16, 2005. Tape in author's possession.

Murray Low, Director, Lang Center for Entrepreneurial Studies, Columbia Graduate School of Business [audio recording]. Telephone interview conducted by the author, Vancouver, B.C., December 2, 2004. Tape in author's possession.

Joseph Maciariello, Claremont Graduate University [audio recording]. Conducted by the author, Vancouver, B.C., June 3, 2005. Tape in author's possession.

Rita Gunther McGrath, Columbia Graduate School of Business [audio recording]. Telephone interview conducted by the author, Vancouver, B.C., March 29, 2005. Tape in author's possession.

Henry Mintzberg, McGill University [audio recording]. Telephone interview conducted by the author, September 27, 2004, Vancouver, B.C. Tape in author's possession.

Henry Mintzberg, McGill University: Mintzberg Interview #2 [audio recording]. Telephone interview conducted by the author, Vancouver, B.C., April 20, 2005. Tape in author's possession.

Kenneth P. Morse, Director, Center for Entrepreneurship, MIT [audio recording]. Telephone interview conducted by the author, Vancouver, B.C., August 12, 2005. Tape in author's possession.

Laura Nash, Senior Research Fellow, Harvard Business School [audio recording]. Conducted by the author, June 16, 2004, Vancouver, B.C.. Tape in author's possession.

Laura Nash, Senior Research Fellow, Harvard Business School: Nash Interview #2 [audio recording]. Conducted by the author, Boston, Mass., March 20, 2005. Tape in author's possession.

Jim Pattison, founder and CEO of Jim Pattison Group [audio recording]. Telephone interview conducted by the author, Vancouver, B.C., October 6, 2005. Tape in author's possession.

G. S. Redding, INSEAD [audio recording]. Telephone interview conducted by the author, Vancouver, B.C., February 16, 2005. Tape in author's possession.

Roger Schank, Head, Institute for the Learning Sciences, Northwestern University [audio recording]. Telephone interview conducted by the author, May 15, 2003, Vancouver, B.C. Tape in author's possession.

Stephen Spinelli, Director, The Arthur M. Blank Center for Entrepreneurship, Babson College [audio recording]. Conducted by the author, Wellesley, Mass., March 22, 2005. Tape in author's possession.

H. H. Stevenson, Harvard Business School [audio recording]. Telephone interview conducted by the author, Vancouver, B.C., August 8, 2005. Tape in author's possession.

Jeffry Timmons, Olin Distinguished Professor of Entrepreneurship, Babson College [audio recording]. Telephone interview conducted by the author, November 17, 2004, Vancouver, B.C. Tape in author's possession.

K. H. Vesper, University of Washington: Vesper Interview #1 [audio recording]. Telephone interview conducted by the author, Vancouver, B.C., August 8, 2005. Tape in author's possession.

K. H. Vesper, University of Washington [audio recording]. Telephone interview conducted by the author, Vancouver, B.C., August 17, 2005. Tape in author's possession.